Praise for *Agile Strategy*

'This is the new frontier of strategy – a timely and practical guide to succeeding in the fast-changing environments in which we now operate'.

Kevin Keaney, CEO, The Works

'In our world of fast and permanent transformation, agility is a hotly contested business topic and one of the most important success factors of any organisation. *Agile Strategy* cuts through the noise to offer clear, practical guidance on how even the largest of companies can become more responsive and adaptable.'

Denis Terrien, Chairman, Vivarte Group

'This is a deeply practical guide to the tools, culture and mindset required for agile strategies.'

David Robinson OBE, CEO, Le Chameau

'Business has always continued to evolve and change, but there feels like a much more significant shift going on at the present time; one that requires a different way of thinking and a quicker and more agile response. This book is both thought-provoking and challenging whilst the methodology is based on solid principles relevant to today's volatility, uncertainty, complexity and ambiguity (VUCAno). For those who want to challenge themselves, their business and their teams, this book provides a more contemporary framework to understand what is going on and how best to develop a relevant strategy that overcomes many of the legacy issues faced by businesses today.'

Peter Taylor, Brand CEO

'The last thing the world needs is another heavy tome on strategic management! But hold on a minute, this RADAR approach actually offers me practical advice that I can dip into as I run my business. It is a VUCA world, so the concept of shorter-term Horizon management grabbed me.'

Andrew Shand, CEO Europe and MEA, Helinox

D1189171

RADAR
Focus on the horizon

Agile Strategy

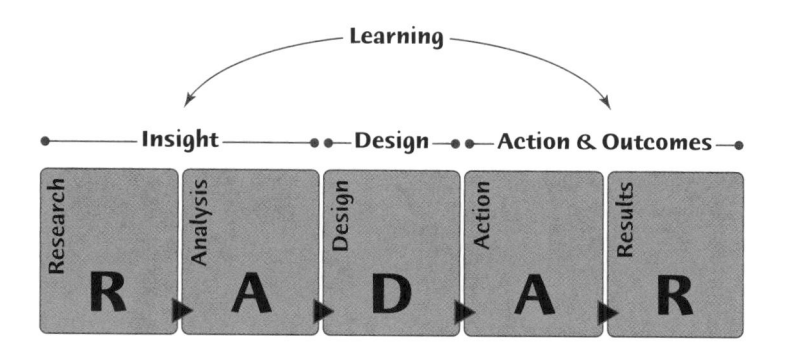

Pearson

At Pearson, we have a simple mission: to help people make more of their lives through learning.

We combine innovative learning technology with trusted content and educational expertise to provide engaging and effective learning experiences that serve people wherever and whenever they are learning.

From classroom to boardroom, our curriculum materials, digital learning tools and testing programmes help to educate millions of people worldwide – more than any other private enterprise.

Every day our work helps learning flourish, and wherever learning flourishes, so do people.

To learn more, please visit us at **www.pearson.com/uk**

[RALPH FERNANDO]

Agile Strategy

How to create a strategy ready for anything

Pearson

Harlow, England • London • New York • Boston • San Francisco • Toronto • Sydney • Dubai • Singapore • Hong Kong
Tokyo • Seoul • Taipei • New Delhi • Cape Town • São Paulo • Mexico City • Madrid • Amsterdam • Munich • Paris • Milan

PEARSON EDUCATION LIMITED
KAO Two
KAO Park
Harlow
CM17 9SR
United Kingdom
Tel: +44 (0)1279 623623
Web: www.pearson.com/uk

First edition published 2019 (print and electronic)

© Pearson Education Limited 2019 (print and electronic)

ISBN: 978-1-292-26298-7 (print)
        978-1-292-26299-4 (PDF)
        978-1-292-26300-7 (ePub)

British Library Cataloguing-in-Publication Data
A catalogue record for the print edition is available from the British Library

Library of Congress Cataloging-in-Publication Data
A catalog record for the print edition is available from the Library of Congress

10 9 8 7 6 5 4 3 2 1
23 22 21 20 19

Cover design by Two Associates
Cover image: © Bortonia/DigitalVision Vectors/Gettyimages
Print edition typeset in 9.75/12 pt Helvetica Neue LT W1G by Pearson CSC
Printed by Ashford Colour Press Ltd, Gosport

NOTE THAT ANY PAGE CROSS REFERENCES REFER TO THE PRINT EDITION

To Marielle, Lucas and Aaron
  Thank you for the love, support and patience that made this possible.

  'Travel, change, interest, excitement! The whole world before you, and a Horizon that's always changing!'

  Toad speaking in *The Wind in the Willows* by Kenneth Grahame (1908)

Contents

About the author

Ralph Fernando is a business leader, consultant and writer. He draws together strategy, operations and technology experience earned on an international stage, where he focuses on value creation in private, public and voluntary organisations.

Ralph recognises that the boundaries between functional disciplines are far blurrier in real life than many would have you believe, and that true agility lies in how they interact. He is driven by the need to make this agility a practical, commercial reality within organisations, after ten years of hearing leading thinkers and executives talk a good game about it.

A Cambridge graduate and Warwick Business School MBA, Ralph enjoys spending his spare time with his wife, Marielle, and their two boys Lucas and Aaron, as well as writing and recording songs at his home studio.

He can be reached at www.AgileStrategyHub.com and on twitter@radarstrategy.

Publisher's acknowledgements

2 Simon & Schuster: Toad speaking in The Wind in the Willows by Kenneth Grahame (1908) **6 Steve Wright:** Steven Wright **19 David S. Rose:** David Rose, Keynote speech "The Future of Financial Markets" **39 Voltaire:** Voltaire **45 Cable News Network:** http://money.cnn.com/magazines/business2/business2_archive/2007/05/01/8405654/index.htm **52 Macmillan Publishers:** Goethe, JW (1906) The Maxims and Reflections of Goethe. Translated from the German by Thomas Bailey. London: Macmillan and Company p130 **72 Bertrand Russell:** Bertrand Russell **72 Cosmo Learning:** Sagan, C. E. (1980) Cosmos: A Personal Voyage, Episode 2: One Voice in the Cosmic Fugue [Television series episode]. In Adrian Malone (Producer), Arlington, VA: Public Broadcasting Service. **75 Taylor & Francis:** McDonald, M. and Payne, A. (2012) Marketing Plans for Service Businesses: A Complete Guide. Abingdon: Routledge **78 Harvard Business Publishing:** Kim, W. C. and Mauborgne, R. (2005) Blue ocean strategy: How to create uncontested market space and make the competition irrelevant Boston, Mass.: Harvard Business School Press **83 International Air Transport Association:** Pearce, B. (2013) Profitability and the air transport value chain, IATA Economics Briefing No. 10 **87 Asian Online Journal Publishing Group:** Porter, M.E. (1980) Competitive Strategy: Techniques for Analyzing Industries and Competitors New York: The Free Press **88 Bloomberg L.P.:** Steve Jobs interview with Business Week in 1998 **90 Walmart Inc:** Corporate.walmart.com [Accessed on 10/09/17] **93 Ziferblat:** Ziferblat **114 Open court Publishing Company:** David Hume **130 Mahatma Gandhi:** Mahatma Gandhi **131 Chartered Institute of Marketing:** The Chartered Institute of Marketing's official definition of marketing **132 Oxford University Press:** Kujala, S. et al (2014) UX Curve: A method for evaluating long-term user experience. Interacting with Computers (23) pp.473–483 **133 HarperCollins Publishers:** Brown, T. (2009) Change by Design. New York: Harper Collins **135 C4Media:** Matts, C. and Maassen, O. (2007) "Real Options" Underlie Agile Practices https://www.infoq.com/articles/real-options-enhance-agility **139 Steve Jobs:** Steve Jobs **150 HarperCollins Publishers:** Christensen, C.M., Allworth, J. and Dillon, K., 2012. How will you measure your life? London: Harper Collins Publishers **152 World Economic Forum:** WORLD ECONOMIC FORUM, 2018. Operating Models for the Future of Consumption [viewed 01 May 2018]. Available from: https://www.weforum.org/reports/operating-models-for-the-future-of-consumption **153 McKinsey & Company:** MCKINSEY QUARTERLY PODCAST, April 2018. Microsoft's next act [viewed 01 May 2018]. Available from https://www.mckinsey.com/industries/high-tech/our-insights/microsofts-next-act **156 Harvard Business Publishing:** Kirby, J. and Stewart, T.A. The Institutional Yes Harvard Business Review October 2007 **160 Pablo Picasso:** Pablo Picasso **171 Lamb publishing:** Oscar Wilde, His life, with a critical estimate of his writings, Lamb, 1909. **179 FoodBev**

Media: https://www.foodbev.com/news/mars-announces-1bn-plan-tackle-urgent-global-issues/ [Accessed 16 May 2018] **187 The Body Shop International plc:** https://www.thebodyshop.com/en-gb/about-us [Accessed on 20 May 2018] **191 Winston Churchill:** Winston Churchill **192 Penguin Random House:** CATMULL, E. AND WALLACE, A. (2014) Creativity Inc.: Overcoming the Unseen Forces That Stand in the Way of True Inspiration London: Bantam Press **193 MIT Press:** Chandler, A.D. Jr. (1962). Strategy and Structure: Chapters in the History of the American Industrial Enterprise. Cambridge, MA: MIT Press **194 Harvard Business Publishing:** Campbell, A., Goold, M and Alexander, M. (1995) Corporate Strategy: The Quest for Parenting Advantage. Harvard Business Review, Mar/Apr95, Vol. 73 Issue 2, pp120–132 **201 Stephen Covey:** Stephen Covey **22 ADP:** ADP, LLC.

Author photo image courtesy of Mike Godliman.

Introduction

Getting past the buzzwords to become agile

'Change is inevitable, except from vending machines.'

Steven Wright

In this introduction we do the following:

- Define business agility and the levers for shaping it.
- Define the four objectives of strategy.
- Introduce RADAR, how it differs from traditional strategy development and its key benefits.
- Introduce the structure of this book.

Let me start with a confession. Despite writing an entire book on the topic, I do not like the term 'agile'. Alongside others such as innovation, customer-centric and value-add, it is a word that has been exhausted by casual overuse. Consequently, many have consigned it to the box labelled 'fad'. Yet, as with those other terms, its practical, central tenet – the ability to adapt quickly – is critical to businesses operating in increasingly dynamic and uncertain markets.

The VUCAno erupts

First expounded by the US Army War College in the early 1990s, the term VUCA (an acronym for volatility, uncertainty, complexity and ambiguity) has finally found its time. Political and economic turbulence, terrorism, fluctuating currency exchange rates and volatile consumer demand are choppy waters through which businesses must now steer a path. Consider the price of West Texas Intermediate over the past 30 years – a grade of crude oil used as a benchmark in oil pricing.

Broken into three equal-sized decade tranches, we see that the price is over seven times more volatile in the past decade (as measured by standard deviation) than it was in the first. Whilst this analysis is crude in more than one sense, it makes a point that is echoed in a wide range of domains from the half-life of consumer trends to the spread of economists' growth projections.

Figure 1 WTI spot price

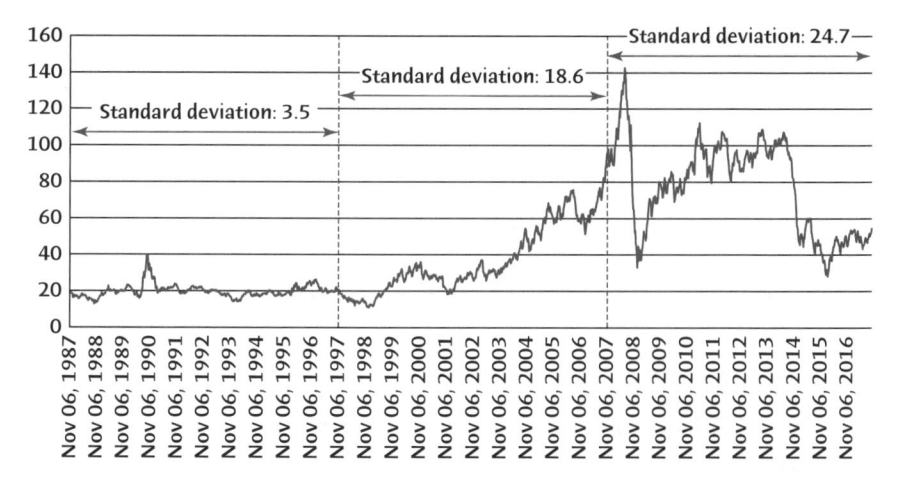

Markets are changing at increasing speeds, driven by technology, data and socio-cultural shifts. Lines are blurring between corporate and entrepreneurial, online and offline, physical product and personal experience. The result is increased volatility, uncertainty, complexity and ambiguity. With apologies to Ricky Martin fans, we are finally living la vida VUCA.

How to achieve agility

Proposing agility as the answer has been the common, and obvious, response. However, when faced by rapid change, concluding that you must adapt quickly hardly qualifies as insight, and the recommendations of many experts around agility, with a few notable exceptions, feel too theoretical. To make agility a practical goal, we must do two things: first, define it and then second, understand the levers for managing it.

Accepting the simple definition of agility as 'the ability to respond quickly', an organisation's agility can be judged against three criteria: responsiveness, adaptability and control (RAC). The RAC rating of your organisation (discussed in Chapter 4) is an important indicator of its agility and ability to respond to changes both inside and outside the business.

Figure 2 The RAC criteria of agility

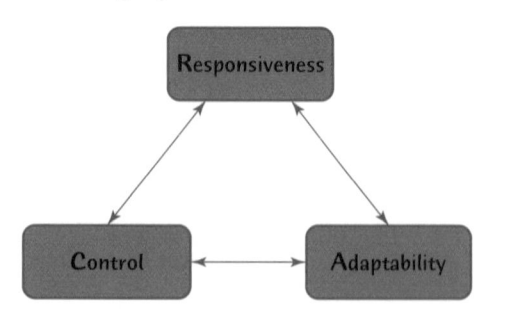

Table 1 The RAC criteria of agility

Criterion	Description
Responsiveness	When discussing agility, the first thing most people think about is speed or, more specifically, responsiveness: the speed with which one reacts to organisational or market stimuli. Responsiveness can be improved in two ways: 1 Anticipating change more effectively. 2 Reacting more quickly to changes when they happen.
Adaptability	Responsiveness has two scenarios: in the first, the organisation is already set up to respond to a specific stimulus and does so; in the second, it must first change (e.g. processes, structures, systems and people) to be able to respond. The effectiveness with which an organisation can do the latter is the measure of its adaptability. Adaptability requires an organisation to determine in a timely fashion what and how it must change.
Control	Responsiveness and adaptability require control to maintain consistency and ensure that the organisation does not simply lurch from one stimulus to the next. Control requires both direction and the appropriate measures to keep the organisation on course.

How to control agility: a world in 4D

If responsiveness, adaptability and control are the key criteria against which to evaluate agility, then how do organisations fulfil them? Unlike the two-dimensional caricature of agility portrayed by some, practical agility is experienced in 4D: direction, data, design and delivery. Collectively, these are the mechanisms through which to drive your RAC rating.

Figure 3 Agility in 4D

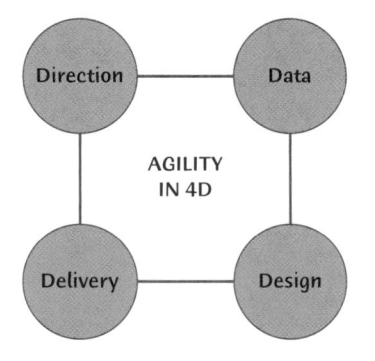

Table 2 The 4Ds of strategic agility

Criterion	Description	RAC relevance
Direction	Having a clear organisational purpose, governance structure and leadership ensures that you are consistent in how you adapt.	Determines what and how to adapt (adaptability), and parameterises how those changes are made (control).
Data	Agility is data hungry – it demands systematic organisational (internal) and market (external) intelligence to understand when and how to adapt. This does not necessarily mean more voluminous data, but it does mean more relevant data, and bringing together the right insight and decision-makers, irrespective of levels, functions and organisational boundaries. It also requires a different rhythm to organisational performance management and strategic decision-making.	Drives all three – anticipating, identifying and informing changes (responsiveness and adaptability) and expressing the potential and actual impact of such changes (control).
Design	There is no agility without operational flexibility, and it requires this flexibility to be designed into the operating model and very culture of the organisation.	Determines the extent to which an organisation can respond quickly (responsiveness) and adapt to change (adaptability). We discuss the concept of 'Dynamism by Design', the method by which agility is designed into the organisation in Chapter 7.
Delivery	In an increasingly VUCA world, the traditional impermeable barrier between strategy and operations needs to open up to a new managerial osmosis, as agility feeds off action: testing, learning and iterating.	Delivery is a dialogue between you and your customers, suppliers and other key stakeholders, and between your strategy and your operational reality. The learning this provides will drive your responsiveness and adaptability through your governance (control).

Those of you familiar with discussions around agile thinking may feel that other structural or procedural elements deserve discussion here, such as iteration, structural flexibility or decomposition, role integration, culture, a learning focus, innovation and creative destruction, continuous improvement or innovative budgeting models. These can all play a role – and we address several of them in this book – but they are essentially supporting cast members in a production with four lead actors – direction, data, design and delivery.

Furthermore, agility cannot be a simple overlay in an organisation. It must be infused through it. Yet whilst it is gaining ground in some areas – most notably in software development, from where it originated, and in some start-ups – we are a long way from seeing it successfully and consistently implemented across entire established businesses.

Strategy at the speed of life

Strategy is the ideal mechanism through which to create agility, given its Janus-faced role of both facing out towards the market and in towards the organisation. Yet two recent reports reveal that more than one in four (28 per cent) of all strategic initiatives fail to meet their original goals and business intent,[1] with insufficient agility identified as one of the top three barriers to successful strategy implementation.[2] Blame for failure is typically attributed to poor strategic choices and implementation. My experience, gained through working with a wide range of businesses and investors over the past 20 years, is that these are, in many cases, symptoms – the real issue lies in the very way in which strategy is set and managed.

Put simply, our approach to strategy has calcified. The rote journey through visions, missions and values – and inevitable 'blue sky' thinking – all too often results in 'flavour-of-the-month' ideas, grand plans and 'implementation problems'. How many organisations do you know that conclude they need to be 'customer-focused, innovative leaders' in their markets, yet remain unclear how they will achieve it?

Figure 4 The traditional strategy development process

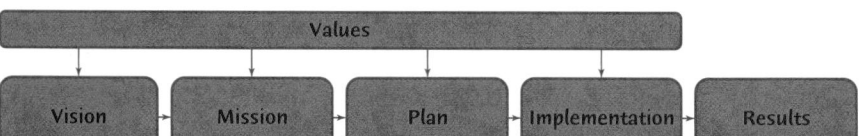

[1] Project Management Institute (2017) Pulse of the profession, available at https://www.pmi.org/-/media/pmi/documents/public/pdf/learning/thought-leadership/pulse/pulse-of-the-profession-2017.pdf [accessed 21 January 2019].

[2] The Economist Intelligence Unit (2017) Closing the Gap: Designing and Delivering a Strategy that Works, available at https://www.brightline.org/resources/eiu-report/ [accessed 21 January 2019].

To continue to operate in the same way that we have done for the past 50 years – albeit with a social media overlay here, or an innovation programme there – is not the answer. Our fundamental approach to strategy must change.

This book shows you how to offer a fresh approach to addressing your organisation's key strategic questions and transforming its commercial performance. It is the first practical strategy guide designed for today's dynamic business environments. Whilst grounded in the latest research and thinking from the fields of strategy, operations, entrepreneurship, finance, technology and economics, it wears this knowledge lightly. It is designed to provide you – someone charged with leading the strategic development of your organisation – with the frameworks, tools and techniques required to succeed in 'the new normal' of increasingly dynamic environments. In short, it is a practical handbook to achieve strategy at the speed of life.

The four objectives of strategy

Academics and leading management thinkers have spent decades debating the definition and goal of strategy. For our purposes, we can define strategy as serving four main objectives.

Table 3 The four objectives of strategy development

	Objective	Description
1	**Set direction**	Strategy lifts the organisation's collective head to focus on its longer-term future, beyond its near-term tactical and operational imperatives. This requires understanding and insight – both of the organisation and of the markets in which it operates.
		This consideration of the future has one driving purpose: to set the organisation's direction. This is sometimes misinterpreted as creating a purely aspirational future for the organisation. We will focus on how to extend your current organisation into future opportunities – creating the bridge from the here and now to the there and then.
		I often describe good strategy as being evidence-based and experience-led – combining the 'science' of research and analysis with the 'art' of individual and group experience. It invariably requires a deep understanding of customers and the competitive environment, as well as a willingness to challenge deep-seated assumptions. The approach outlined in this book redefines what it means to set strategic direction, regularly re-evaluating and adjusting it through a process known as 'Horizon Management' (described in Chapters 1 and 8).

	Objective	Description
2	**Create meaning**	Setting direction is, in itself, not enough. Strategy is no different to any other group endeavour – it requires purpose and context to engage, inspire and enable people to make the right choices consistently.

This binding purpose, often accompanied by a compelling story for the organisation, creates meaning for stakeholders both within and outside the organisation, answering their key questions.

STAKEHOLDER	EXAMPLE QUESTIONS
Employees	1. Why should I work for you? 2. Will I be content or even proud to be associated with the organisation? 3. How does what I am doing fit into the bigger picture? 4. Why does what I do matter?
Customers	5. Why should I buy from you? 6. Do your values, principles and self-image match mine?
Investors	7. Why should I invest in you? 8. Does your risk profile match my risk appetite? 9. Does this organisation have long-term value-generating potential?
Suppliers	10. Why should I supply you? 11. Why would I treat you better than other companies I supply?

We will explore how a Unifying Purpose informs both direction and meaning – unifying aspiration and action (see Chapters 1 and 7).

	Objective	Description
3	**Determine choices and actions**	The consequences of setting direction and creating meaning find their ultimate expression in the choices and actions of individuals and teams across your organisation. All strategy is ultimately about choices – choosing both what to do and what not to do. This has important implications for your organisation:

- Choosing what *not* to do is often ignored. As an exercise, list all the significant things your organisation has *actively* chosen *not* to do (e.g. customer segments not targeted, product categories not produced, markets not served). If you cannot list them with conviction, you probably do not have a clear strategy.

- Key choices are not the exclusive domain of the senior executive team. Increasingly, they happen at lower levels of the organisation.

Table 3 The four objectives of strategy development (*continued*)

	Objective	Description
		● Having made key choices, an organisation needs to commit to them. This requires time and resources (human, physical and financial). It also requires processes, structures and governance mechanisms which can communicate changes quickly and effectively.
4	**Create value**	All the above are simply means to strategy's ultimate end: the creation of value, which is typically achieved in one of seven ways:

WHERE YOU PLAY

1. **Market selection/creation:** operating in attractive markets (i.e. geographic locations, end-markets)
2. **Value chain:** determining which part of the market's value chain you serve
3. **Channel selection:** participating in the right channels
4. **Customer selection:** targeting the right customers

HOW YOU WIN

5. **Positioning:** positioning the offer and execution in the mind of the customer to create appeal and demand pull
6. **Proposition:** an offer that outshines the competition (e.g. quality, innovation)
7. **Performance:** superior execution through operational advantages (e.g. a more responsive supply chain, better routes to market)

If this feels reductive, it is intentionally so. Strategy is often made to feel rarefied and aloof, when in fact it is gritty and the fundamental driving force of the business. As well as being commercially astute, strategy must be financially and operationally literate – considering the implications of key choices for the overall organisation.

Hippeas and the power of meaning

Green Park Holdings are the makers of organic chick pea puffs, sold under the brand Hippeas. Unlike many consumer-packaged goods, where the focus is typically first and foremost on the product, in the case of Hippeas the focus was initially on the brand story and creating a positioning in the market that customers could believe in. By targeting the millennial and Gen

Z 'modern hippie' with a playful and healthy snack brand, the business's strategy:

- Set direction (attracting the modern hippie with healthy snacks)
- Determined choices (e.g. using chickpea flour as a hero ingredient in its product, reinforcing its hippie credentials through its messaging and packaging)
- Created meaning. As Livio Bisterzo, the founder and CEO, explains: 'That allowed us to launch in 18,000 points of sale in the first year. Because we had something that connected with retailers, with consumers, with anybody that touched that brand.'[3]

Introducing RADAR

Perhaps because the four objectives of strategy have remained a constant over the past 50 years, the classic template for strategy development has remained equally unchanging. It comprises the strategic trinity of vision, mission and values, accompanied by a set of financial goals and an operational plan or roadmap, and typically runs on an annual basis with a three- or five-year outlook.

Yet rapidly changing markets are paying no heed to companies' slow-set rhythms. The cautionary tales of giants slayed – from Blockbuster to Kodak, Tower Records to Woolworths – are increasingly seen as portents of an emerging new world order. Strategy's objectives may have remained the same, but its methods must now change.

This book defines those new methods, encapsulating them in an approach I call RADAR, with each letter corresponding to one of its facets (research, analysis, design, action, results). It contrasts in several key areas with the traditional strategy model.

Table 4 Contrasting characteristics of traditional and RADAR approaches to strategy

	Traditional strategy	*RADAR*
Starting point	Blue sky discussions	The Horizon (see Chapter 1)
When is it done?	Typically annually	Typically monthly
Who does it?	Executive function (with selective support)	Multi-disciplinary team cutting across levels, functions and organisational boundaries

(continued)

[3] See http://awesomeoffice.org/blog/hippeas-ceo-livio-bisterzo [accessed 21 January 2019].

Table 4 Contrasting characteristics of traditional and RADAR approaches to strategy (*continued*)

	Traditional strategy	*RADAR*
What does it look like?	A grand plan for implementation	Coordinated activities, investments and resources, reviewed and managed regularly
Time spent	Long cycle times, most of the time is spent up-front and at the end of each cycle	Rapid initial development, time invested on an ongoing basis
Measures of success	Lagging indicators – find out at the end whether you have succeeded	Lagging, leading and anticipatory indicators tailored to your strategic choices – find out earlier whether your strategy is working, and redirect if it is not

These contrasting characteristics have a significant impact on *how* strategy is managed in the organisation. The most notable differences are:

- **Approach:** strategy development becomes a management system, not a process. It acts as an integral and regular part of business as usual rather than a periodic, parallel executive process.

- **Focus:** the strategic focus shifts from a static set of objectives to a dynamic Horizon, the place where market opportunities meet organisational capabilities.

- **Pace and responsiveness:** given the dynamic nature of this Horizon, the organisation's strategic pulse beats monthly rather than annually or bi-annually, driving greater responsiveness.

- **Control and results:** greater responsiveness is enabled by RADAR's unique results framework, designed to increase agility in dynamic markets. Rather than just track lagging indicators, or even traditional leading ones, it goes further, creating the earliest possible anticipatory indicators based on the Horizon's underlying ARC (assumptions, risks and choices or consequences).

- **Team:** strategy steps out of the boardroom to be guided by a multi-disciplinary team cutting across levels, functions and organisational boundaries'.

You will be introduced to the key elements of RADAR that underpin these differences, as well as outlining the overall approach (see Chapter 1). Please note that I am not sacrificing all that has come before at the altar of the new. Rather, consider RADAR an evolution, a Darwinian adaptation to modern business environments – the survival of the strategist.

The benefits of RADAR

No introduction to a new approach would be complete without an explanation of *why* you should adopt it. Being different without being useful is the role of novelty. To be innovative requires compelling benefits, and RADAR offers four of them.

Table 5 Benefits of RADAR

1. MEASURABLE RESULTS

RADAR places benefits realisation at the core of strategy. It offers a complete results framework that uses short- and medium-term observable changes to link strategy to its long-term financial and non-financial benefits.

2. INCREASED LIKELIHOOD OF SUCCESS

RADAR increases the likelihood of success through:

- **Focus:** it defines the organisation's Horizon – the place where market opportunity meets organisational capability. This provides both a governing focus for the present and a destination for the future.

- **Engagement:** it cuts across levels, functions and organisational boundaries, tapping into the expertise and motivations of relevant stakeholders.

3. ENHANCED COMPETITIVE POSITION

RADAR aligns the organisation through the five key questions (see Chapter 1), enabling better organisational development choices and a clearer and more compelling competitive position.

4. REDUCED RISK

Through its approaches to direction-setting, performance management and the creation of operational flexibility, RADAR instils the 4Ds of agility (direction, data, design, delivery) in the organisation. This ability to adapt quickly to internal and external changes reduces the overall risk profile of the organisation.

Outline of this book

The remainder of this guide provides the framework, tools and techniques required to deliver RADAR's benefits in your business. It is organised around the five components that form its acronym.

Figure 5 High-level summary of RADAR approach

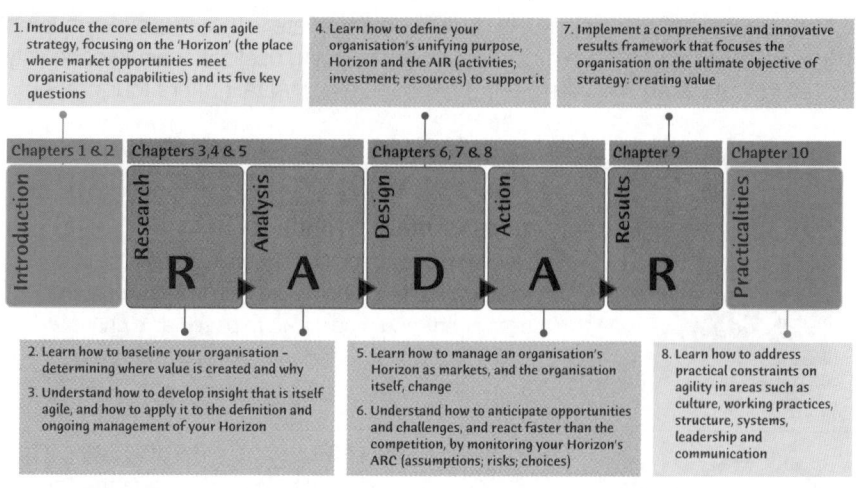

The table below provides a more detailed outline of what can be found in each chapter.

Table 6 Outline of book structure

PART 1: GETTING STARTED

Chapter 1: What you need to design an agile strategy	We begin by outlining the RADAR approach, and introducing its key elements:

1 **Unifying purpose:** an organisation's unifying purpose (UP) is a set of principles that shape its two overarching Horizon decisions (i.e. which opportunities to pursue and how to design and execute its competitive position).

2 **The Horizon and its five key questions:** the whole RADAR approach focuses on the Horizon, the place where market opportunity meets organisational capability. These questions identify and define that Horizon.

3 **AIR:** an organisation's ability to serve its Horizon is determined by three elements: activities, investments and resources (AIR).

4 **Results framework:** RADAR offers a comprehensive model, which aligns strategic intent with lagging, leading and anticipatory measures that evaluate its performance and validity.

5 **Horizon management:** this technique chunks long-term strategic change into shorter-term Horizon adjustments or shifts, tracking external and internal changes to determine whether, and how, to pivot the organisation to remain successful.

6 **Strategic intelligence system (SIS):** a SIS is the combined processes, systems and data through which RADAR's data and insight requirements are managed and met.

PART 1: GETTING STARTED

Chapter 2: Get some perspective – how to ask the right questions	An agile strategy does not begin by answering questions but begins by asking them. This chapter describes techniques for framing your strategic issues and defining the killer questions to drive the design of your Horizon.

PART 2: RESEARCH AND ANALYSIS

Chapter 3: How to gain insight in a VUCA world	This chapter introduces the role of research and analysis within RADAR, exploring the key principles of insight and how the five key questions direct it. We also consider insight's evolution, and the factors and mechanisms which make insight itself agile.
Chapter 4: VUCAnomics – learn where and why you make money	Context and baselining are about understanding where you are, starting with two simple questions: Where is value created? And why? This necessitates analysis of market attractiveness, competitive position and current performance through RADAR's results framework. I also introduce a framework for identifying new potential market opportunities, and an approach to evaluating the agility of your own organisation.
Chapter 5: Use your intelligence – how to track market and organisational intelligence	Where Chapter 4 explored taking stock of an organisation at a point in time, this chapter explores how to analyse and track its onward path. Strategic intelligence is RADAR's approach to agile insight as introduced in Chapter 3.

PART 3: DESIGN AND ACTION

Chapter 6: How to foster agility in your organisation	This chapter is about grounding the design and action tools and techniques described in Chapters 7 and 8 in the foundational concepts and context which underpin them. It elaborates on how three areas of thought and practice influence RADAR's approach: the test-and-learn approach of entrepreneurial thinking, the principles of design thinking and real options.
Chapter 7: How to develop strategic intent and operational flexibility	In strategy, the failures attributed to implementation are often failures of design. In this chapter, I explore the practicalities of defining UP (unifying purpose), outline key considerations when designing your organisation's Horizon, discuss the role of 'Beyond the Horizon' and introduce dynamism by design, the core of RADAR's design ethos and the method by which agility is designed into the organisation.

(continued)

Table 6 Outline of book structure (*continued*)

Chapter 8: **How to** **execute agile** **strategies**	I have described the strategy's fourth objective, and ultimate end, as the creation of value. The action part of RADAR is where that value is realised. In this chapter, I describe how to perform Horizon management in practice, covering Horizon tracking, planning and gateways.
PART 4: RESULTS	
Chapter 9: **How to** **measure** **success**	RADAR translates strategy into a series of measurable benefits through its results framework. This chapter describes its three key elements – SCORE, ERAs and ARC – covering lagging, leading and anticipatory indicators respectively.
Chapter 10: **How to** **hurdle the** **barriers to** **success**	This final chapter provides advice and direction on how to introduce the approach successfully into your organisation, exploring eight potential barriers to success: culture, working practices, organisational structures, governance, systems and technologies, leadership, communication and change fatigue.

At the end of each chapter, we also do the following:

- Explore the key themes raised through a case story, with each chapter building on those preceding it. The subject of the story is a multi-national apparel and accessories brand (a composite of real businesses and case studies, anonymised).
- Raise questions and set tasks to support you in applying RADAR in your own organisation.

But that is enough of introductions. In the first chapter we explore the full scope of RADAR and the core concepts that underpin it.

Summary

- We are operating in a VUCA world (volatile, uncertain, complex, ambiguous), and traditional strategy practices are no longer keeping pace.
- However, the four core objectives of strategy have not changed: to set direction, create meaning, determine choices and actions, and create value.
- Agility, defined as 'the ability to respond quickly', expresses itself in three ways: responsiveness, adaptability and control (RAC), and is enabled through the 4Ds of direction, data, design and delivery.

- RADAR is the framework defined in this book to support you in creating practical, agile strategies. It differs from traditional strategy in several dimensions:
  - It is a management system rather than a discrete process.
  - It focuses on the Horizon, the place where market opportunities meet organisational capabilities.
  - It is faster paced.
  - It incorporates a unique results framework, which anticipates and manages change systematically.
  - It uses a multi-disciplinary team, which cuts across levels, functions and organisational boundaries.
- RADAR increases the likelihood of success, decreases risk and enhances your competitive position.

[PART ONE]

Getting started

What you need to design an agile strategy

1

'**Any company designed for success in the 20th century is doomed to failure in the 21st.**'
  David Rose, keynote speech at 'The Future of Financial Markets'

In this chapter we do the following:

- Outline the idea of a 'Unifying Purpose'.
- Explore the 'Horizon' at the heart of RADAR, and the five key questions that define it.
- Introduce the three elements that drive your response to market opportunities: activities, investments and resources (AIR).
- Describe the RADAR results framework.
- Introduce 'Horizon management', the technique that enables organisations to adapt quickly to internal and external changes.

RADAR is a structured approach to agile strategy, a set of tools and techniques and an attitude: a way of seeing and managing your organisation's place in the world. There are six core elements that drive it, shown in Table 1.1, and this chapter introduces each of them in turn. The purpose here is to give you a top-level view of what they are and how they relate to the 4Ds of practical agility mentioned in the introduction. Each is revisited and examined in more detail in later chapters.

Table 1.1 Key RADAR elements

Element	Description	AGILITY DIMENSION (4Ds)			
		Direction	Design	Data	Delivery
Unifying Purpose (UP)	UP is a set of principles that shapes all your strategic choices, and therefore your positioning within, and proposition to, your chosen markets.	✓			
The Horizon and its five key questions (5KQs)	At the heart of the RADAR approach is the 'Horizon', the place where market opportunity meets organisational capability, and the five key questions that define it. All strategic thinking in the organisation ultimately returns to this.	✓	✓		
AIR	Your organisation's AIR (activities, investments and resources) defines its ability to respond to opportunities. To answer the 5KQs requires a full and consistent understanding of these elements across your organisation.	✓	✓		
Results framework	Success is ultimately judged by results, both financial and otherwise. RADAR provides a comprehensive results framework, linking together lagging, leading and anticipatory measures.		✓	✓	✓
Horizon management	This technique chunks long-term strategic change into shorter-term 'Horizon adjustments or shifts', tracking external and internal changes to determine how to maintain the organisation's relevance and success.		✓	✓	✓
Strategic intelligence system (SIS)	A SIS is the combined processes, systems and data through which RADAR's ongoing data and insight requirements are managed and met.		✓	✓	✓

Defining 'Unifying Purpose'

Moving on from mission and vision statements

The use of mission and vision statements remains common across many organisations. A mission statement defines what an organisation does and for whom (i.e. what it is), whereas a vision statement defines its ideal end state (i.e. what it hopes ultimately to become). Both must combine being specific (and therefore having practical meaning, but at the risk of limiting the organisation) with being all-encompassing (but consequently being vague and unhelpful in guiding thinking).

Whilst these tools have value – e.g. creating a spur to achieve – too often this value is buried beneath vagaries and bluster. When this happens, these statements typically fall into one of three categories:

1 **Be the best:** there are plenty of these types of statements, which are status- or position-based and focus on being number one in our markets. At best, these are goals. At worst, fantasies.

2 **Be everything, mean nothing:** these shopping list statements contain every desirable trait or outcome, and in doing so manage to both detach themselves from reality and sound like everyone else. Be prepared to read about being innovative, customer-focused, a great place to work, etc.

3 **Please everyone, mean nothing:** like the previous category, but this time focused on key stakeholder groups, these statements list the satisfaction the organisation will bring to customers, employees, suppliers, shareholders, wider society, and so on without acknowledging any of the inherent conflicts or trade-offs that exist.

Criticising bad examples of mission and vision statements does not invalidate their well-executed counterparts. However, even when more effectively articulated, the inherent limitations of mission and vision statements can be seen. Consider the following examples.

Table 1.2 Example mission and vision statements

Company	Vision statement	Mission statement
Volvo	To be the most desired and successful transport solution provider in the world	To drive prosperity through transport solutions
ADP	Be the world's authority on helping organisations focus on what matters.	Power organisations with insightful solutions that drive business success.
Google	Provide access to the world's information in one click	To organise the world's information and make it universally accessible and useful

Across these three companies, some of the limitations of such statements are visible:

- **A disparity between the statements and strategic reality:** where hyperbole gets in the way of genuine direction-setting, gaps form. In the case of Volvo, the idea of 'driving prosperity through transport solutions' sounds more like PR than strategy.
- **A lack of inspiration and meaning:** One role of these statements is to inspire and engage employees, investors and suppliers. ADP's high-level statements about 'focus on what matters' and 'insightful solutions' are too generic to do so.
- **Insufficient guide to action:** In examples such as Volvo's and ADP's vision statements, it is unclear what trade-offs and choices, if any, are implied by them. The statements do not guide meaningful decision-making.
- **Falling out of sync:** the pace of change can often outstrip the statements that are supposed to guide the responses to it. For example, Google's vision and mission statements fit its development around search activities, including its extension into Google Home. However, they only tenuously, if at all, reflect large swathes of its other commercial activities from mobile operating systems to venture capital funds, and cannot be said to be driving these aspects of its strategic thinking. Google clearly acknowledged this when it pulled 'companies that are pretty far afield of our main internet products' out of the core Google entity and placed them under the new parent company Alphabet.[4]

The primary purpose of outlining these limitations is not to say that these statements are wrong, but rather that the nature of mission and vision statements themselves is unsuitable for agile strategy and guiding Horizon thinking. Instead, we will use an alternative tool, which provides both the benefits of traditional (and well-written) vision and mission statements and adds to them. I call this tool 'Unifying Purpose', and its application 'defining UP'.

What is a Unifying Purpose?

A Unifying Purpose comprises a set of principles, which:

1 Define the why and guide the how of the organisation – unifying aspiration and action.
2 Provide a directional imperative for all Horizon choices.
3 Provide criteria by which to assess all strategic choices (i.e. how to respond to the 5KQs in areas such as positioning, proposition and AIR choices).

A Unifying Purpose is shaped by the following ABCD factors.

[4] Source: https://abc.xyz [Accessed on 06/01/19].

Figure 1.1 Influencing factors when defining UP

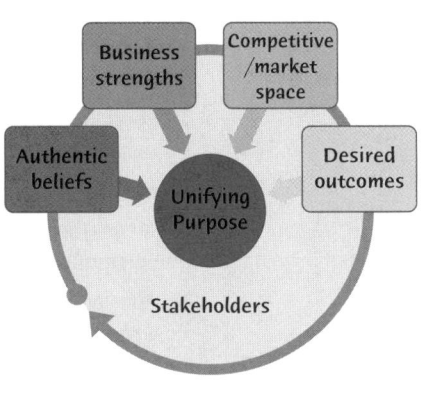

Table 1.3 ABCD factors

	Influence	Description
A	**Authentic beliefs**	Genuine, consistent beliefs that do not change unless the bases for them do
B	**Business strengths**	Resources or capabilities that differentiate your organisation from the competition
C	**Competitive/market space**	Untapped, emerging or under-served 'meta-needs' in the market (e.g. poor service, uninspired product designs)
D	**Desired outcomes**	What you want the organisation to achieve beyond simple financial success

A well-written Unifying Purpose is specific, concise and necessitates choices. It typically comprises three to seven principles or statements, and as such is longer than a typical mission or vision statement, which has trended in recent years to being of slogan length. The long-form nature of a Unifying Purpose may surprise, trouble or horrify some individuals, depending on the extent to which they embrace the post-modern paradox of combining inadequate depth with broad-brush overstatement. My counter is that the foundations of an organisation's purpose can rarely be fully and meaningfully captured in a single phrase. However, once defined, the aspects of the Unifying Purpose and messaging most relevant to each stakeholder group can and should be communicated succinctly, with the confidence that the overall messaging will be consistent and anchored in the fuller description.

This is an important distinction: mission and vision statements are often quoted in full on external marketing and communication materials; by contrast, a Unifying Purpose in its 'full form' is decoupled from such communication. Once UP has been defined, formulating the messaging for key stakeholder groups

Table 1.4 New Burger King Unifying Purpose

The brand's US website emphasises its reputation for high-quality, great-tasting and affordable food and its commitment to premium ingredients, signature recipes, and family-friendly dining experiences	**Unifying Purpose** 1 A 'premium economy' offer 2 Food that is tastier and distinct from mass-market competitors 3 Fuel for every day, for every daypart 4 An environment designed to be comfortably quick 5 An international face with a local voice

such as customers, staff, suppliers or investors is then the role of those with the appropriate responsibilities within the organisation (e.g. marketing, sales and customer-service staff in the case of customers).

As an example, contrast the following statements for Burger King:

- With the exception of the word 'affordable', the Burger King description could be describing a gourmet burger positioning. But this is not what Burger King is targeting. By contrast, the Unifying Purpose describes the food offer as 'premium economy' (a genuine market positioning – see figure opposite) and looks to edge tastiness and distinctiveness a notch above its mass-market branded international chain competition. This provides a focus for differentiating from McDonalds, whilst not attempting to add a lot of complexity (and cost) into the supply chain by adopting the higher quality ingredients and levels of personalisation associated with the gourmet burger chains. It also capitalises on its capabilities and resources – flame grilling giving a different flavour to the burgers.

- The next principle - 'Fuel for every day, for every daypart' – raises several points: it is a mass market and frequent purchase; it typically serves a refuelling mission for its customers, it must offer menu breadth to support the needs of different dietary and socio-demographic segments and visit frequency, it needs a strong offering across dayparts (breakfast, mid-morning, lunch, mid-afternoon, dinner, late night).

- There is a tension between the menu-breadth and mass-market 'premium economy' affordability points made above. These tensions are not uncommon when defining UP, and it is the trade-offs between them that are important for an organisation to understand and debate. For example, in the case of quick service restaurants, direct competition comes not only from other players in the burger market and other QSR concepts (e.g. burritos, chicken) but also from fast casual dining (such as Nandos, which sits between QSR and full-service dining both in terms of service and price). The combination of tastiness, distinctiveness, menu breadth and affordability therefore needs to be seen in this context, and decisions taken accordingly to ensure that the Horizon the organisation pursues is the right one. The subsequent two principles, 'an environment designed to be comfortably quick' and 'an international face with a local voice', are examples of how this might be achieved.

Figure 1.2 'Premium economy' positioning in the UK burger market

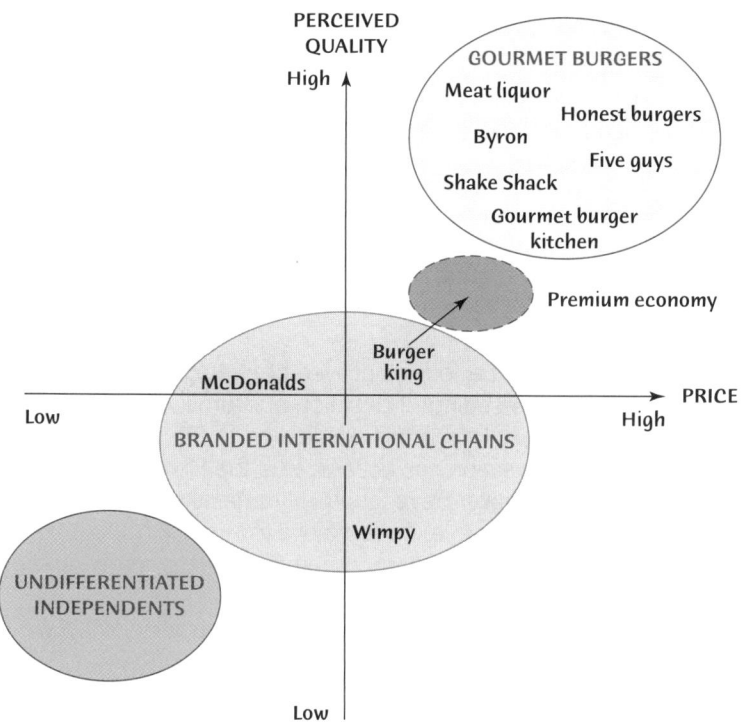

You may disagree whether this is the right Unifying Purpose for Burger King, but that is not the point of this example. What I hope it shows is that defining UP fulfils the three roles required to drive your Horizon thinking, in that it provides:

- Guidance on defining the 'why' of an organisation (e.g. providing 'tasty, distinctive…fuel for every day') and the 'how' (e.g. a 'premium economy food offer' and a 'comfortably quick environment' with local adaptations that go beyond just the menu items to the way in which it engages with local communities – providing an 'international face and local voice').

- A directional imperative (e.g. menu, operational delivery – comfort is typically underplayed in a QSR environment, marketing and communications).

- Criteria by which to assess all strategic choices (e.g. AIR choices, where menu development will need to manage a limited number of ingredients to optimise cost and minimise wastage whilst still offering a broad range of customer end products).

A Unifying Purpose colours and shapes your responses to the 5KQs, defining the edge of your organisation's spotlight: what lies beyond it in the darkness is actively rejected (but potentially still monitored through your strategic intelligence system and results framework). We will explore how to define UP in more detail in Chapter 7.

The 5KQs model

Defining the Horizon

In the introduction, I wrote that the concept of the Horizon is the core of RADAR. But what do I mean when I talk about the 'Horizon'? I define it as follows:

> **Horizon**
>
> 1 The place where market opportunity meets organisational capability.
> 2 A governing focus for the present and a destination for the future.

Considered in terms of the four objectives of strategy, the Horizon offers a destination – enabling the setting of direction and providing a determinant for action – whilst meaningfully linking this destination to the resources and capabilities to which the organisation has access. Like the Horizon in the real world, the strategic Horizon can never be reached – it remains a line in the distance, a vanishing point that draws the eye. As you move towards it, new elements come into view and you respond accordingly, changing course as needed either to avoid obstacles or to approach newly discovered areas of interest.

If this all sounds a little abstract, let me make it practical. In any business, the Horizon is defined by five key questions.

These five questions are interdependent and inseparable.

Figure 1.3 The 5KQ model

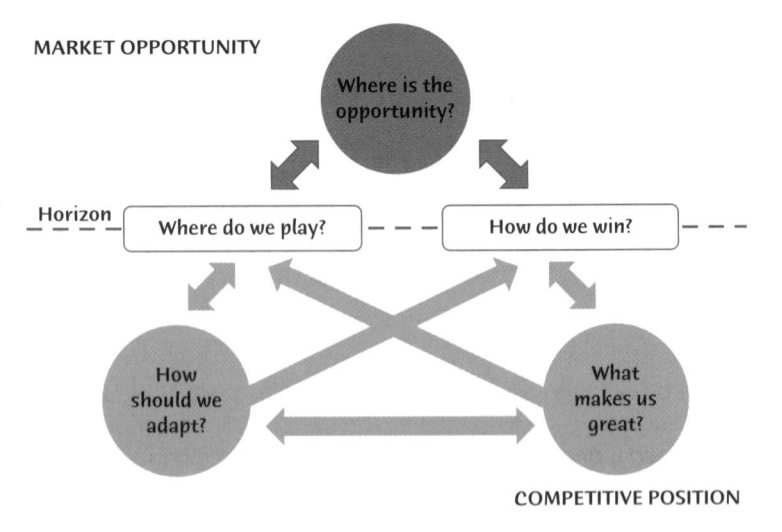

Table 1.5 The five key questions (5KQs) model

	Question	Description
1	**Where is the opportunity?**	To succeed you need opportunity – an emerging, unmet or under-served need that you can satisfy more effectively or efficiently than others in the market.
2	**What makes us great?**	To answer this requires a response to three related questions: 1 Where do we make most of our money? 2 What differentiates us? 3 What activities, investments or resources (AIR) underpin this differentiation? Answering these will point you towards your core market appeal and the organisational elements that enable it.
3	**How should we adapt?**	To understand how to adapt, ask the five related ADAPT questions:

A	**Aim**	Are we targeting the right markets and customers?
D	**Drivers and trends**	Looking to the future, which drivers and trends necessitate significant changes to how we operate?
A	**AIR**	Where do our activities, investments and resources fall short of what is required to address identified opportunities?
P	**Position- ing and proposition**	Given target market needs, drivers, trends and competitive threats, is our positioning and proposition right?
T	**Technology**	How can we capitalise on emerging technologies?

4	**Where do we play?**	Determining where to play is a function of: 1 **Attractiveness:** the opportunity's size, growth, accessibility and other factors will affect its overall attractiveness. 2 **Feasibility:** your organisation's ability to serve the opportunity (e.g. capability, resources). 3 **Viability:** your ability to make the required financial returns.
5	**How do we win?**	Just participating is not enough: you must be clear how you will win, linking to what makes you great and how you will adapt. This in turn will influence your choices on where to play.

These questions should feel familiar. Answering them, informed by rich organisational and market data, is where traditional strategy work often ends. For RADAR, they signal the start. Horizon management – described below – continues the journey, using data to evaluate the performance and validity of the current Horizon on a regular basis, and to determine whether and how to adapt. The 5KQs become a mantra in the organisation, and the Horizon its guiding light.

Strategy: nothing but AIR

Strategy, when defined poorly, is often criticised for being nothing but hot air – a set of buzzwords and platitudes too far removed from the reality of the organisation. Yet, when defined well, AIR (activities, investments and resources) is precisely what strategy should determine – the observable and tangible choices made by an organisation in order to deliver its Horizon.

Figure 1.4 AIR elements

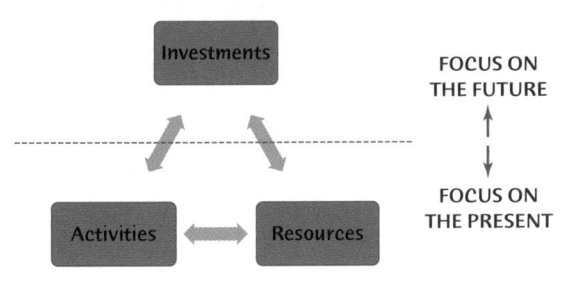

Table 1.6 AIR definitions

	Element	Description
1	**Activities**	Key activities to deliver your Horizon, which fall under three categories:
		• *Core:* contribute directly to the value delivered to the customer and are essential in realising the organisation's goals (e.g. product development, manufacturing)
		• *Support:* enable the core activities by providing resources and infrastructure, but do not directly deliver value (e.g. accounting, IT services)
		• *Management:* used to plan, measure, monitor and control business activities (e.g. strategy, planning and budgeting, compliance)
2	**Investments**	Investment in activities and resources to ensure future success (targeting both existing and new opportunities, as well as key considerations beyond the Horizon – see below)

Table 1.6 AIR definitions (*continued*)

	Element	Description
3	**Resources**	The physical (e.g. buildings, machines), human (i.e. capabilities) and intangible (e.g. brands, intellectual property, reputation) resources that enable you to:
		● Target desired customers and markets
		● Realise your target positioning
		● Fulfil the promise of your proposition
		● Achieve the performance targets required by your desired competitive position

In the AIR model, activities and resources relate to the *current* state of the organisation and how it serves its existing customers and markets. Investment relates to the choices about *future* activities and resources. It is the interaction between activities and resources, and the investment supporting their development over time, which ensures an organisation's continued success. Indeed, if you want to get a fix on the priorities (and constraints) of an organisation, look at where it plans to spend its CapEx and OpEx.

But what should inform AIR choices? There are three main considerations:

1 *Strategic intent:* I refer throughout the book to the notion of 'strategic intent'. This has a very specific meaning within RADAR, and comprises the following four elements:

Figure 1.5 The components of strategic intent

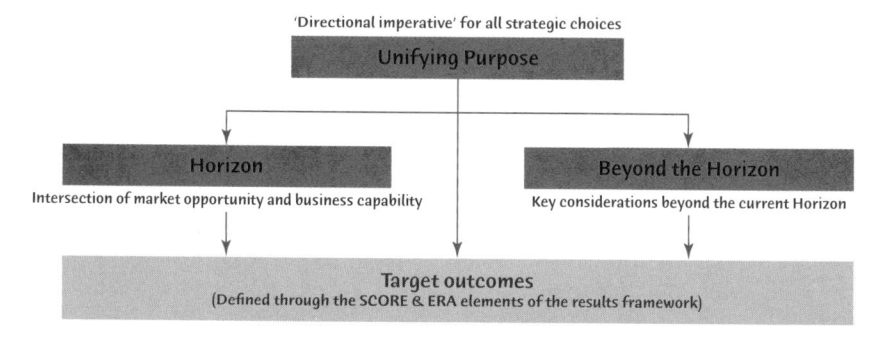

- *Unifying Purpose:* as we saw earlier, UP provides a directional imperative for all strategic choices.
- *Horizon:* defined by the 5KQs, the Horizon determines where to play and how to win.

- *Beyond the Horizon:* whilst RADAR focuses on the Horizon, it must also look selectively beyond it for three reasons: first, to manage longer lead times associated with certain changes; second, to manage emerging market developments; and third, to enable broader organisational changes that are only indirectly related to the Horizon.
- *Target outcomes:* these are expressed through the SCORE and ERA elements of the RADAR results framework, described next in this chapter.

I cover strategic intent, and these topics, in more detail in Chapters 5 and 7.

2 *Existing resources and capabilities:* these are the starting point for exploiting or creating an opportunity, and for consideration of 'How should we adapt?'

3 *Performance:* significant under- or over-performance relative to the market that will necessitate AIR choices.

All of this, of course, is true of strategy immemorial. The challenge for an agile strategy is to make these AIR choices adaptable and responsive, and for that we require what I call 'Dynamism by Design': the embedding of flexibility and adaptability in the design of the Horizon itself. In the context of AIR, this means investing in ways that enable your organisation to anticipate change and adapt to it quickly. We address these topics in the Design and action and Results sections of this book.

Results framework

Having defined UP and your Horizon, and made the associated AIR choices, the natural next step is to track the results of these decisions. This is an area where strategy has been slow to change. Determining a strategy's impact has historically been the almost exclusive domain of 'lagging', predominantly financial, metrics. RADAR includes a fuller results framework by which to evaluate a strategy. This framework takes your strategic intent and links it to three levels of results tracking.

1 Lagging indicators: keeping SCORE

Ultimately, there are five sets of measures against which any strategy should be evaluated. These are the classic lagging indicators of performance, which can be measured through a SCOREcard.

2 Leading indicators: experienced RADAR achievements (ERAs)

The challenge with keeping SCORE is that success or failure is only visible after the event. An agile strategy needs to anticipate and act earlier, and RADAR addresses this by managing two types of leading indicator. The first of these are ERAs.

Table 1.7 The elements of a SCOREcard

	Element	Description
S	Social	Measures the effect of your organisation on its stakeholders, starting within the organisation but extending out to communities and wider society (e.g. equity and welfare, ethical trading).
C	Commercial	Covers both the organisation's performance in financial and market terms (e.g. sales growth, market share) and the effectiveness and efficiency of the sales, marketing, business development and R&D activity that drives it.
O	Operational	Addresses all operational aspects of the organisation across activities, resources, data, suppliers, structure and governance, from the percentage of on-time, in-full deliveries through to the number of reported incidents.
R	Reputational	Evaluates the perceptions of key stakeholder groups, including customers, employees and suppliers (e.g. net promoter scores, employee satisfaction).
E	Environmental	Assesses the organisation's impact on natural resources (e.g. energy consumption, waste footprint).

An ERA is the impact you can see, hear, touch, taste, smell or feel that ultimately feeds your SCORE. It is some observable outward expression of the strategy you have developed. It could be the opening of the first store in Prague, the first product batch from the new range coming off the production line or the thousandth customer experiencing the revised service.

3 Anticipatory indicators: measuring the ARC of the possible

If ERAs are the early shoots of your strategy, then the ARC (assumptions, risks and choices or consequences) is the soil that feeds them:

- Assumptions are the silent shapers of choice.
- Risks are their acknowledged cousins, reflecting areas which could potentially change.
- Finally, choices are the positive decisions you take to make a change, with consequences their passive counterparts.

By systematically documenting and evaluating the ongoing validity of your Horizon's ARC, you can anticipate the likelihood of the Horizon's success and make any required changes. This is the crux of Horizon management. Figure 1.6 illustrates how your Unifying Purpose, AIR, ARC, ERAs and SCORE link together to form a comprehensive results framework.

Figure 1.6 The RADAR results framework

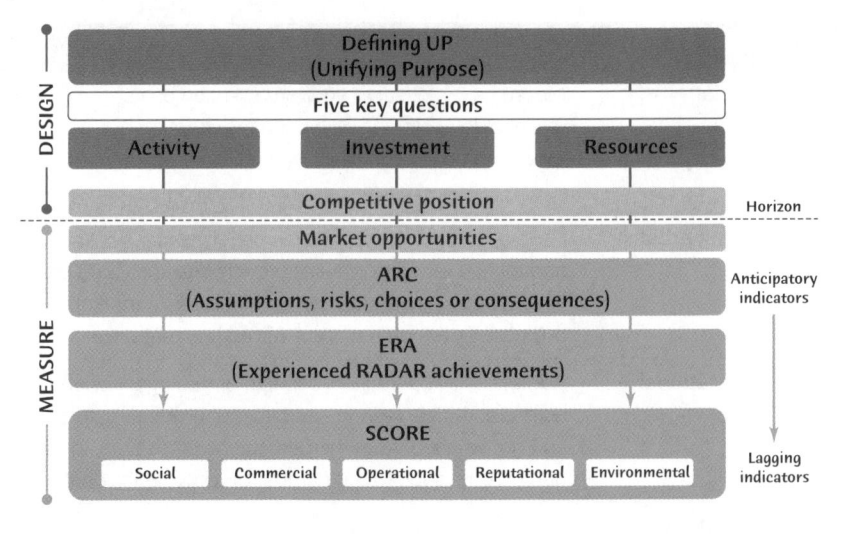

We explore the use of this framework, with examples, in Chapter 9.

Horizon management

Having defined all of the above, you must still be able to adapt when circumstances change. The technique for doing so – Horizon Management – chunks long-term strategic change into shorter-term 'Horizon adjustments or shifts',

Figure 1.7 Horizon management

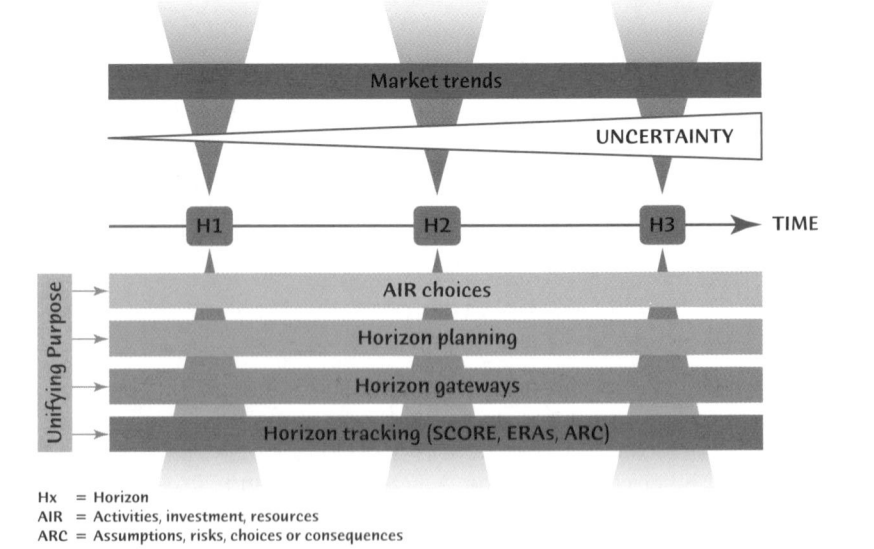

Hx = Horizon
AIR = Activities, investment, resources
ARC = Assumptions, risks, choices or consequences

Table 1.8 Key elements of Horizon management

	Element	Description
1	**Horizon tracking**	This is the process by which you evaluate the performance and validity of your current Horizon using the results framework and additional strategic intelligence (see below).
2	**Horizon planning**	The consequence of Horizon tracking is one of three Horizon decisions, depending on market, competitive and organisational circumstances: <ul><li>Stay on the selected course.</li><li>Make modest Horizon adjustments.</li><li>Undertake a full-scale 'Horizon Shift', either by redirecting the organisation towards different opportunities or developing its capability to address the current ones with sufficient depth and distinction.</li></ul> This is done with a rhythm and pace that is far smoother and quicker than that of traditional strategy, avoiding the debilitating launching, lurching and reneging of many strategic initiatives that accompany annual processes and three- or five-yearly cycles.
3	**Horizon gateways**	These are the meetings in which the Horizon tracking is reviewed, and Horizon planning decisions taken. These decisions may necessitate changes to both AIR choices and the associated target outcomes, and the Horizon gateways ensure that these are managed effectively by: <ul><li>Taking place regularly (typically monthly), maintaining a swift tempo of strategic decision-making.</li><li>Involving a multi-disciplinary team, which cuts across levels, functions and organisational boundaries (e.g. involving customers or suppliers), ensuring the understanding and authority required to make decisions is 'in the room'.</li></ul> Horizon gateways can be integrated into existing governance structures.

enabling your organisation to navigate and capitalise on, rather than merely react to, market changes and organisational developments in a controlled manner. It is driven by three mechanisms.

Horizon Management is the practical face of agility, and I cover it in Chapter 8.

Strategic Intelligence System (SIS)

The SIS is RADAR's data backbone: the combined processes, systems and data through which RADAR's ongoing data and insight requirements, known as the minimum enterprise data set (MEDS), are managed and met. The MEDS is determined by three elements:

1 The full range of data sources relating to market and organisational dynamics, available for anticipating, diagnosing and prescribing required action.

2 The organisation's strategic intent.

3 The four objectives that drive the SIS:

- Anticipation of future market and organisational changes.
- Control and governance.
- Improvement of current performance.
- Communication of information to stakeholders.

The SIS manages all of RADAR's data requirements, with the organisation's strategic intent and SIS objectives determining which market and organisational data should be used. Furthermore, the SIS itself is agile, adapting as the organisation adjusts or shifts its Horizon.

I dedicate the whole of Chapter 5 to exploring this crucial topic.

Figure 1.8 Determinants of a Minimum Enterprise Data Set (MEDS)

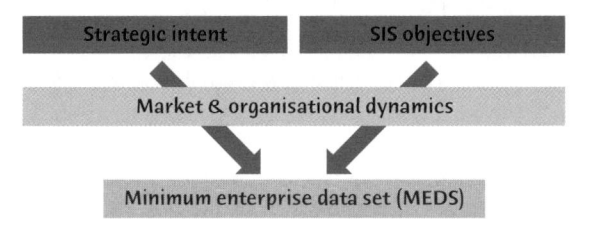

Bringing an agile strategy and the RADAR approach together

This chapter has provided brief introductions to several new concepts and acronyms. The intention has been to create an initial awareness of them. It is the most condensed and therefore most challenging part of the entire book – so thank you for bearing with me.

The remaining chapters decant these ideas and let them breathe, exploring each in more detail, showing how they fit within the overall RADAR approach and offering guidance on how to apply them in real-world situations. In addition, through the 'In your organisation' sections at the end of each chapter, you will have the chance to apply them. By the end of the book, the use of a Unifying Purpose, the 5KQs, the results framework, Horizon management and the strategic intelligence system will become second nature, and self-evident.

The figure below outlines the full RADAR approach, which draws the key elements together and forms the broad structure of the rest of this book. The next chapter begins this journey with an important truism of strategy development: we could all use some perspective.

Figure 1.9 Outline of the RADAR approach

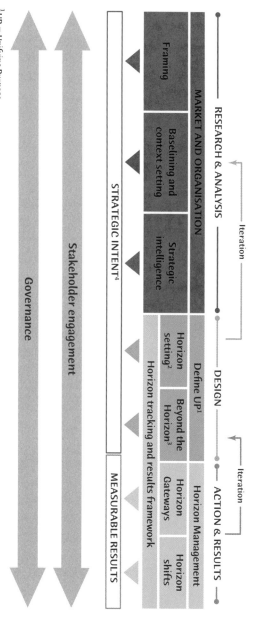

[1] UP = Unifying Purpose
[2] Comprises identification and prioritisation of opportunities and definition and design of competitive position
[3] Areas beyond the current Horizon, monitored and managed due to required lead times, emerging market developments or broader organisational change needs
[4] Strategic intent comprises the Unifying Purpose, Horizon, key considerations beyond the Horizon and target outcomes (SCORE and ERAS)

Summary

- Agility is managed through the 4Ds of direction, design, data and delivery.

- RADAR is a structured approach to doing this, and is driven by six core elements: a Unifying Purpose, the Horizon and the five key questions (5KQs) which determine it, AIR (activities, investments and resources), the results framework, Horizon Management and a Strategic Intelligence System (SIS).

- A Unifying Purpose comprises simple but substantive statements that provide a directional imperative for all strategic choices. It defines the why and the how of the organisation – unifying aspiration and action.

- At the heart of RADAR is the Horizon – the place where market opportunity meets organisational capability. It is defined by the 5KQs and the approach continually returns to them.

- Your organisation's AIR defines its ability to respond to opportunities. Having defined your Horizon, AIR is your means to serve it.

- RADAR's results framework links together three types of performance measurement: lagging SCORE (social, commercial, operational, reputational and environmental outcomes), leading ERAs (experienced RADAR achievements) and the Horizon's anticipatory ARC (assumptions, risks, choices or consequences).

- Horizon management is a core technique that chunks long-term strategic change into shorter-term Horizon adjustments or shifts, tracking external and internal changes in order to determine if, and how, to pivot the organisation to remain relevant and successful.

- The Strategic Intelligence System (SIS) is RADAR's data backbone. It comprises processes and systems used to manage an integrated set of strategically critical quantitative and qualitative data and insight known as the minimum enterprise data set (MEDS).

Case story: Introducing Leisurious

As Emma sat in her office, she considered her options. As the co-founder and Chief Executive of Leisurious, the British women's fashion brand bringing style, comfort and a hint of luxury to women's leisurewear, she had overseen rapid growth in the 19 years since it was first launched with her friend, co-founder and Chief Designer Sam. Now in eight countries across Europe and distributed through a range of channels including own stores, online (their own transactional website and third-party marketplaces), wholesale and concessions, growth was suddenly slowing and margins being squeezed. Something had to change.

When Sam and Emma had first started the business, they had been spurred on by two things: a desire to create the kind of clothing they wanted and just couldn't find in the shops, and sheer force of will. At the time, the women's leisurewear market seemed to fall into one of two categories: 'daily dull' (the standard items you saw in every department store) and 'branded bluster' (labelled items with big aspirations and prices to match). Where were the comfortable, refined and stylish items, made from durable and attractive fabrics, which bridged the divide between going out and going to the shops? This was the gap they sought to fill.

It was clearly a gap other people felt existed too. From its market stall beginnings in Oxford, via early wholesale arrangements, concessions in key department stores, a strong e-commerce offering and a smattering of own stores, the company had grown into a £100m revenue business. At this scale, they had attracted significant attention, and no shortage of competitors trying to emulate their style and positioning. They had moved from being young pretenders to challengers and now style leaders. Where should they go next?

Emma invited Sam to go out for a morning coffee, and as they sat down, she began talking:

Emma: I have been thinking about the changes we are seeing in the market right now.

Sam: Me too. It looks as if the market is starting to move away from us. People are feeling the pressure in their disposable income, consumer confidence is wavering, and belts are tightening.

Emma: Exactly. I have heard the same from some of our direct competitors too. We rode out the last recession, but I agree with you that this feels different - more like a shift than a dip.

Sam: If it is a structural change, we need to respond.

Emma: Let's go back to basics and consider our five key questions. Where do we see the opportunity?

Sam: I still think the desire for our style of product remains strong. We are keeping on top of trends – and continue to set some of them – and customers still love us for it. But there is a lot more competition in our categories now.

Emma: I agree. Several pure play, specialist and fast-fashion players are all pushing hard into our space and Amazon has really upped its

▶

game in fashion. That suggests three things to me. First, we need to understand the future market opportunity, and how attractive it is. Second, we need to sharpen our competitiveness in existing markets for our current categories. And third, we need to look at potential adjacent categories into which we can expand.

Sam: Exactly. My gut feel is that the market opportunity is still there, but just more hotly contested. Style, fit and durability are still the defining characteristics of Leisurious, but others have closed some of the gap and, with our steadily rising prices, the value for money equation is starting to look less appealing given current economic conditions. With our scale and focus, we could be best in class in cost at this quality point, but we have never really focused on getting our costs right. Now is the time to do so.

Emma: That's true. But we must not forget what makes us great: we should maximise our strengths as well as address our weak-nesses. I want to make us even more untouchable in our core area of style. Some high-profile collaborations with designers and key influencers would go a long way to doing that, reinforc-ing our casual chic reputation.

Sam: So what do we need to change? Let's take a long, hard look at our sourcing, as we should be able to make a difference there. And it is not just about cost – I think there is an opportunity for buying in footwear and strengthening our accessories range.

Emma: That sounds good. Our twentieth anniversary next year also offers a great opportunity to get some high-profile people on board to celebrate our history – how many 20-year-old compa-nies do you know that can claim to have set the bar in women's fashion so consistently for so long?

Sam: So, we continue to focus on our core market of women's leisure-wear, but, depending on our views on the market, we may well need to expand into a greater footwear and accessories range. I think there may also be opportunity for us in homeware.

Emma: Possibly. We need to be careful to not spread ourselves too thinly. We should set up a separate session to define UP for us going forward – I don't think we will solve everything over one cup of coffee. I mean, we are good, but. . .

> **Sam:** Ha, ha! Fair enough, let's set aside a half-day to think that through more thoroughly. It will be a useful test as well for our international footprint – where we play going forward may require some tough decisions about certain markets. But in terms of how we win, I think reinforcing our style credentials, leveraging our position to reduce costs, extending our offer to natural adjacencies and upping our marketing game with some high-profile collaborations for our twentieth anniversary all sound sensible. We need to think about what insight would give us confidence those are the right levers to pull.
>
> **Emma:** Let's get the ball rolling – I can think of few things as important right now as getting our thoughts clear on this.
>
> And with that, Emma and Sam left the café and headed back to their respective desks. Change was in the air.

In your organisation

Exercise 1: Five key questions

Form a small team of five to eight people, known for all future exercises as the 'core group', to discuss the 5KQs for your organisation. In choosing the participants, consider the mix of:

- functions (customer-facing and support services);
- seniority levels;
- specialist expertise.

Before the session, collate, analyse, synthesise and circulate information that could shed light on future market opportunities and what makes your organisation great:

- Macro-economic data.
- Market data and reports.
- Competitor intelligence.
- Customer, partner and supplier feedback.
- Commercial performance data.
- Feedback from market-facing staff (e.g. sales, customer service).
- Information on current key initiatives, and those undertaken in the past two or three years, that focus on changing the organisation to support improved competitiveness.

In the session itself, consider the following questions as a group:

1 What does this insight suggest about each of the 5KQs?

2 Consider the following questions to spur debate:

2.1 Where is the opportunity?

- What has driven the dynamics of the market over the past five years?
- Are these drivers set to continue or are new ones becoming more prominent?
- Which are the most attractive opportunities?
- Which ones are you best placed to serve?

2.2 What makes us great?

- Where has your organisation experienced historical success?
- What has driven this success?

2.3 How should we adapt?

- What do you need to change (consider your AIR of current activities, investments and resources)?
- What are competitors doing?
- What is happening in adjacent sectors?
- What is happening in your sector in other countries?
- What broader technology developments could affect your sector over the next five years?

3 Based on the discussion, collate ideas on the following three areas:

- Which opportunities the organisation should prioritise.
- The organisation's strengths.
- What needs to change.

4 Determine what further data and actions are required to validate these lists and the discussion. Create a list of next steps to address them.

Get some perspective! How to ask the right questions

2

'Judge a man by his questions, rather than by his answers.'

Voltaire

In this chapter we do the following:

- Describe the 'name, tame and frame' technique that helps focus the organisation on the right questions.
- Examine a series of useful tools that you can use to support the development of these questions.

An agile strategy does not begin by answering questions, it begins by asking them. Answering the wrong question brilliantly is far less helpful than answering the right one adequately, yet organisations often leap into developing their strategy with only the haziest notion of which questions they must ask. But how should one go about defining the right questions?

In RADAR, the governing focus is the Horizon and the 5KQs that define it. But these questions are, in themselves, not enough. They require *framing* – a context that informs the way in which you interpret, interrogate and respond to them. For example, consider 'Where is the opportunity?' Our response will depend on several factors including:

- the definition of your 'addressable market' (the market in which you seek opportunities);
- the eyes through which you look at the opportunity (e.g. shareholder, customer, employee);
- the criteria by which you determine the opportunity attractive;

- the timeframe (e.g. short-term vs. long-term);
- your appetite for risk.

In practice, framing is about adopting multiple perspectives to ensure you explore the topic thoroughly, and then settling on the elements most relevant to the issue(s) you are trying to resolve. Framing not only brings clarity to thinking; it also leads to more creative solutions.

What makes framing challenging in the context of an increasingly VUCA world is that the frame is itself subject to change as the markets in which you operate, and your organisation, evolve at pace. Agile strategy therefore requires you not only to frame your strategic questions carefully, but also to challenge the validity of that frame on an ongoing basis. How to do this is the subject of the rest of this chapter.

Name, frame and tame

Strategy development is an exemplar of complex, high-stakes problem-solving. Requirements are often fuzzy, insight partial, stakeholders numerous, dependencies complex and consequences significant. The challenge is to simplify without becoming overly reductive – a goal that can be achieved through the three-step 'name, frame and tame' process.

Step 1: Name

This first step involves giving a name to the key issue(s) or topic(s) requiring action. This may sound trivial, but distillation of the many issues and considerations into succinct topics or domains is the basic starting point of strategy development. A key method for doing so is 'root purpose analysis' (described in the tools section below). Prioritisation and timing are critical, for example, international expansion may be the wrong topic if your current proposition is failing in existing markets.

Step 2: Frame

Having identified the focus topic(s), this next step interrogates the topic(s) from multiple angles, giving it context and uncovering the salient aspects to be addressed. The objective is to identify the key factors or drivers affecting the root purpose. To paraphrase personal injury lawyers, 'Where there's frame, there's blame'.

Step 3: Tame

Having identified these key factors or drivers, we can then outline the changes that need to be made to tame and manage them and then create plans to do so.

These three steps, and the tools that support them, are summarised in the table below.

Table 2.1 The name, frame and tame framework

	Step	Key question(s)	Useful tools
DEFINE	**1. Name** *Distil and define*	● What objectives must our strategy fulfil? ● What are the core issues and topics we must address? (e.g. growth, cost, flexibility)	1 Root purpose analysis 2 Zoom-out/Zoom-in 3 Perspective connectives 4 Restate of mind 5 Absolutely! 6 Attribute listing 7 SCAMPER
	2. Frame *Contextualise and analyse*	● In what different ways could you look at it? ● What is common to all these ways of looking at it? ● What key factors are influencing this issue?	
SOLVE	**3. Tame** *Design solution*	● What factors contribute to a solution? ● How should they be prioritised and organised?	

Useful tools and techniques

The remainder of this chapter describes the tools listed above, and how they contribute to the name, frame and tame process. These tools come predominantly from the fields of creative and critical thinking, reflecting the twin disciplines required at the framing stage of RADAR.

Root purpose analysis

You may already be familiar with root cause analysis and the 'Five Whys' technique, which was invented by Sakichi Toyoda, founder of Toyota Industries, in the 1930s. Used to determine the underlying reasons for problems, the technique involves repeatedly asking why until the root cause is uncovered.

The table below gives a simple example, applying the technique to the problem of a car breaking down.

Table 2.2 Traditional root cause analysis example

	Question	Answer
1	Why did the car breakdown?	Because it ran out of petrol
2	Why did it run out of petrol?	Because I forgot to fill it before I left
3	Why did you forget to fill it?	Because I was late, stressed and rushing to leave
4	Why were you rushing?	Because I agreed to meet Jane at 7 pm, but I rarely get home before 6.45 pm and it is a 30-minute drive
5	Why did you agree to meet at 7 pm?	There was no real reason – we could have agreed 7.30 pm. Dinner was booked for 8 pm
ROOT CAUSE:		Work commitments and travel times prevent me from making appointments that start before 7.30 pm
SOLUTION:		Do not arrange to meet before 7.30 pm on a work day

This technique, whilst useful in the field of operational improvement and quality management, may appear to have more limited application in the field of strategy. As we saw in the Introduction, the four objectives of strategy primarily concern purpose (i.e. direction, meaning, value creation) rather than causality. Nevertheless, the Five whys still apply, but the nature of the why changes. Rather than asking 'Why did it happen?' (seeking the cause), we ask 'Why does it *matter*?' (seeking the *purpose*). I call this 'root purpose analysis', and it helps to identify the key objective(s) the strategy must address. See below the same problem of a car breaking down, with root purpose analysis applied to it.

The facts of the event have not changed, but the two analyses, focused on root causes and root purpose respectively, frame these facts very differently. The former focuses on solving the shorter-term operational problem, whilst the latter focuses on the longer-term strategic purpose.

Table 2.3 Strategic root purpose analysis example

	Question	Answer
1	Why did it matter that the car broke down?	Because it meant I was late meeting Jane
2	Why did it matter that you were late meeting Jane?	Because I wanted her to be in a good mood when I arrived, and not frustrated at my continual lateness
3	Why did it matter that she was in a good mood?	Because I wanted the evening to be perfect
4	Why did it matter that the evening was perfect?	Because I wanted to propose
	ROOT PURPOSE:	Make my engagement to Jane perfect
	SOLUTION:	Schedule it for the weekend or when we are on holiday

Granted, this example is playful and trivial (although not for our suitor and Jane), but consider these two more commercial cases:

- Manufacturers of cardiac rhythm management devices (i.e. pacemakers and cardioverter defibrillators), including Medtronic, Biotronik, Philips and St. Jude Medical, focused for a long time on incremental functional enhancements when what the health system and patients really wanted was basic reliability and better value for money (a health system's overarching root purpose is value for money in achieving good health outcomes).
- Blockbuster saw its role as a provider of video and DVD rentals through a global network of stores (c. 9,000 at its peak). This led to a focus on store access and stock availability as the key (operational) levers for growth. It did not realise quickly enough that its root purpose was providing entertainment to consumers on their terms, regardless of channel and devoid of late fees (which, at peak, comprised 16 per cent of its revenues). The last of its US stores closed in 2013.

Zoom-out/Zoom-in

When trying to identify core issues, it often helps to zoom in and zoom out on the problem to see it at various levels of abstraction. For example, consider a management team wrestling with flattening sales in its US subsidiary.

Figure 2.1 Example of zooming in and out of a problem

ZOOM OUT	Level 3	**IN THE INDUSTRY:** • Are sales flattening for the affected product category/categories outside the US?
	Level 2	**IN THE MARKET:** *Supply* • Are competitors experiencing similar issues? • Has something changed in supply (e.g. new competitors; substitutes)? *Demand* • Have key demand drivers changed?
	Level 1	**IN THE ORGANISATION:** • Financial performance: What other measures are declining? • Non-financial performance: What other measures are declining?
ISSUE		**US SUBSIDIARY SALES ARE FLATTENING**
ZOOM IN	Level 1	**IN THE US MARKET:** • Is it across all states, or focused in certain areas?
	Level 2	**IN THE LOCAL STATE MARKETS:** • Have local market conditions changed (e.g. new state regulation)?
	Level 3	**IN THE ORGANISATION:** • Have particular products/categories stalled? • Have particular stores/points of sale/offices stalled?

The example in the table above is clearly not exhaustive, but it does illustrate how zooming out (from the organisation to the US market to the global market) and zooming in (from the US market to the local state-level markets and then to the organisation) forces questions to be asked at each level and different lines of thinking to be explored.

Perspective connectives

This technique encourages the examination of an issue through the eyes of a range of different stakeholders, before drawing together a single view of the essential elements. It comprises two stages.

Stage 1: Adopt different perspectives: First, explore the topics and issues from a range of perspectives including your own and at least two other stake-holder groups who are involved, or close to, the topic (e.g. when looking at the development of new children's toys, a manufacturer might consider the per-spectives of the child herself, parents, older and younger siblings, retailers, gov-ernment regulators, etc.). Also consider other role archetypes (e.g. a journalist, judge, psychologist).

Stage 2: Synthesise the different perspectives: Identify the elements that are common to the different perspectives (the perspective connectives), as well as the differences (the perspective disconnectives) and synthesise them into a viewpoint that covers the essential elements of the problem.

Restate of mind

The choice of words used to express an idea can fundamentally affect people's responses to it. Daniel Kahneman's work on the psychology of judgement and decision making shines the light on, for example, loss aversion, where the opportunity to do something where there is a 10 per cent chance of losing is considered less attractive than something that has a 90% chance of success. If language can change your state of mind with regard to risk, then restating problems in a different language can shine a light on alternative considerations and choices.

For example, consider the phrase 'How can you make your job easier?' Here are a few simple ways in which you could explore this statement by changing words within it:

1 Substitute key words, e.g.

   - How can **I/the company/the government** make your job easier?
   - How **do others** make **their** job easier?
   - **Where** can you make your job easier (i.e. in which areas)?
   - How can you make your **life** easier?

2 Explore the opposite 'How can you make your job **harder**?'

3 Reduce it to one word (e.g. easier) and explore what that word means to you or how it is defined by others. Does this evoke thoughts on other words that might more appropriately encapsulate the spirit of the original question you had (e.g. efficient, satisfying)?

Absolutely!

Another way to push yourself into new perspectives is to explore extremes using absolutes. For example:

1 How could you become the *fastest* growing company in the world?

2 What would you do if money were *unlimited*?

3 What would your business look like if customers did *everything* themselves?

4 What would you need to do to eliminate *all* competition?

In this technique, do not be concerned about whether something is possible or acceptable – the idea is to surface a wide range of unfiltered possibilities, and in doing so show the issue you are exploring in a new light.

Attribute listing

Attribute listing, originally devised by Robert Platt Crawford, is a way of exploring the many attributes of a root purpose, topic or issue, generating innovative ideas and opportunities for varying them. The process comprises three steps:

Step 1: List the key attributes of the root purpose, topic or issue
Identify the main attributes (dimensions, characteristics, qualities or parts) of the root purpose, topic or issue under discussion. Try to keep this to a manageable number (ideally five to seven key ones).

Step 2: List potential modifications or alternative options for each attribute
For each attribute, ask yourself the question 'How might we change, vary or improve it?' Approach this systematically using an attribute listing matrix (ALM). An extract from an ALM used at a small bakery is shown below.

Table 2.4 Attribute listing matrix (ALM) example for a local bakery

Feature	Attribute	Change, vary or improve ideas
Product offer	12 core bread types, 3 guest bread types each week, traditional English cakes, soft drinks cabinet by door	Breads/cakes of the world, 'Upper Crust' premium range, health range (lower GI, lower sodium/sugar), specialist (e.g. gluten free), sandwich bar, artisan confectionery, special occasion cake service, specialist blend coffees, teas and milkshakes, premium juices
Retail experience	Limited seating (c.12), all items behind counter	Bistro seating, veranda, visual merchandising, e.g. 'Table Wares', artisan baking lessons
Channels (points of sale)	Three shops	Online (with home delivery), local supermarkets, local restaurants, vans at train stations

Step 3: Review the listed modifications, consider combinations and note the most interesting
The most promising individual ideas and combinations (e.g. artisan confectionery range sold through supermarkets) are then selected for further exploration and validation.

SCAMPER

SCAMPER is an acronym introduced by Bob Eberle in 1971, building on ideas from Alex Osborn nearly two decades earlier. Actually a collation of several different idea-generating techniques, it acts as a useful stimulus for divergent thinking and solution finding. Within RADAR, its value lies in taking an identified root purpose, topic or issue and interrogating each aspect of it to test for potential solutions or beneficial actions.

The table below outlines the seven areas of SCAMPER, with examples of questions used under each.

Table 2.5 SCAMPER example questions

	Area	Explanation	Example questions
S	Substitute	Replace some part of the thing/idea with something else	What or who could I replace with something/ someone else?
C	Combine	Combine the thing/idea with one or more other things/ideas	What could I add to this to create something new?
A	Adapt	Adapt some other thing/ idea for your needs/ purposes	Is there a solution I can take from somewhere else?
M	Modify/magnify	Change/emphasise some aspect of the current thing/idea	What could I change, emphasise or highlight?
P	Put to other uses	Apply the thing/idea in a new way or to a new end	Where else could we apply this?
E	Eliminate/ 'minify'	Remove/reduce some aspect of the current thing/idea	How could we simplify/ streamline the thing/ idea?
R	Reverse/ rearrange	Reverse or reorder ele- ments of the thing/idea	What could I rearrange to improve the thing/ idea?

SCAMPER is most effective when applied with specificity:

- If looking at a broad topic (e.g. revenue growth), first break down the topic into more manageable areas (e.g. by country, channel, product category, customer segment) and then apply the SCAMPER thinking to each.
- Similarly, if looking, for example, at what makes your organisation great, break down key processes into their constituent parts (e.g. a returns process may comprise communication, authorisation, documentation, packing, collection/deposit and reimbursement). SCAMPER could be applied to each step of this process, as well as the overall idea of a return.

Nintendo reframes the game[5]

Back in 2006, Nintendo was experiencing rapid decline in its gaming division as consumers migrated to Sony's PlayStation and Microsoft's Xbox, which focused on the latest technologies, most powerful processors and market-leading graphics. Rather than answer the question 'How do we create a next-generation console with even more powerful technologies?', Nintendo took a different tack. Through its launch of the Nintendo DS handheld game system and games such as Nintendogs (where users could nurture and raise virtual puppies) and Brain Age (a puzzle game for older players), it validated its hypothesis that there was latent demand for gaming that was easy to access and play for short bursts (what we now call casual gaming). Moreover, such games opened up parts of the market (e.g. women, older age groups) that were under-served by existing platforms.

The original question was reframed as 'How do we create a console that appeals to a broader audience beyond the traditional gamer?', leading to an entirely new type of game system – the Wii. It did not use the latest technology. The Wii was built around a chip similar to that used on its earlier GameCube in stark contrast to the high-powered chips used by Sony and Microsoft. Instead, it focused on new gaming experiences and interactions driven by its motion controller. The Wii marked the turnaround of Nintendo's gaming division and the reinvigoration of the wider company.

Over a decade later, it would adopt a similar approach with the Nintendo Switch, once again turning around its fortunes through a different take on the future of gaming, even offering the low-tech add-on of the Nintendo Labo (a cardboard construction toy that can be brought to life by the Nintendo Switch) that sets it apart from its competitors and captures the imagination of a new generation.

How to reconcile framing with agility

Conceptually, there is an inherent tension between framing and agility: the former fixes a context; the latter anticipates that this context is continuously changing. Like politicians and straight answers, are these concepts simply irreconcilable? Given that I have just taken you through a whole chapter on the topic of framing,

[5] See https://money.cnn.com/magazines/fortune/fortune_archive/2007/06/11/100083454/ [accessed 21 January 2019].

you will be unsurprised to hear that my answer is no. Agility cannot be endlessly untethered – we need context and to be anchored into something to act.[6]

As with design, framing works with the acknowledgement of the assumptions, risks and choices or consequences that underpin it. By systematically capturing these in your ARC tracker at the point of framing, and adding to them as you define your Horizon (see Chapters 6 and 7), you can then refer back to and adjust them as part of the governance of your strategy (see Horizon gateways in Chapter 8). If your ARC ceases to be valid, the framing and the Horizon may need to change.

Conclusions on framing

The name, frame, tame framework described in this chapter, and the tools and techniques that underpin it, are simply ways of ensuring that the analysis of your market opportunities and organisation, as prompted by the five key questions, is thorough. For example, if the marketing director says that the Netherlands is a big opportunity for a division, exploring this through techniques such as root purpose analysis (i.e. why does that matter?), perspective connectives (e.g. seeing it through the eyes of a Dutch consumer or the head of the national trade body) or Absolutely! (e.g. how would you execute the fastest ever entry into the Dutch market?) will raise questions, reveal data requirements and encourage debate. These techniques are not substitutes for research and analysis, but rather routes to them. And it is to these topics that we now turn.

Summary

- In RADAR, the starting point is the five key questions. However, these questions need context to inform the way in which you interpret, interrogate and respond to them. The act of creating this context is called framing.
- Framing typically involves the adoption of multiple perspectives to ensure you explore the topic thoroughly, and then settling on the elements most relevant to the issue(s) you are trying to resolve.

▶

---

[6] This agility paradox, which demands that agility also requires stability, is described in the article, Agility: it rhymes with stability, available at https://www.mckinsey.com/business-functions/organization/our-insights/agility-it-rhymes-with-stability [accessed on 12 April 2018].

- The name, frame and tame approach can support you in simplifying the many issues associated with answering the five key questions without being overly reductive. The role of each of the three phases is:

  - Name   Give a name to the key issue(s) or topic(s) requiring action.
  - Frame   Interrogate the topic(s) from multiple angles, giving it context and uncovering its salient aspects, with the objective of identifying the key factors on which to focus.
  - Tame   Outline the changes that need to be made to manage these factors.

- There are a range of techniques that can be adopted to support this process, from root purpose analysis to help identify key objectives through to attribute listing, which supports their realisation.
- Framing is still an important activity, even in a VUCA environment. You need to be anchored into something to make decisions. By systematically capturing the ARC (assumptions, risks, choices or consequences) that underpin your framing, you can monitor and manage it as your markets and organisation evolve.
- Time and resources spent framing the questions at the earliest stages of RADAR offer significant returns when moving into the latter stages of design and action, and ultimately lead to better results.

Case story: Framing the beast of slow growth

Sam sat at her desk with three words at the top of an otherwise blank page: Name, Frame and Tame. 'Sounds like a bad Saturday night game show,' she thought to herself and gave a wry smile. Considered extremely capable by all who knew her, Sam was a rare mix of the creative and the commercial, a paradox of openness and cynicism, and she always adopted a healthy scepticism towards management frameworks. Nevertheless, Emma's words that there were 'few things as important right now as getting our thoughts clear on this' rang in her ears. She grabbed the piece of paper and headed to the meeting room to see her.

Three hours later, the two friends looked at each other and let out time-for-a-break sighs. It had been a productive session. They had spent over three-quarters of the time just exploring their original thoughts about the four areas of focus: style leadership, cost reductions, market expansion and a 20th anniversary marketing campaign. Through root purpose analysis, zooming in and out, perspective connectives and attribute listing they had come to the following conclusions:

- The style topic was actually a subset of the broader need to revise the 'proposition appeal' – from an improved range through to greater store theatre and a true omnichannel experience (linking online and offline brand engagement much more effectively).
- Whilst sourcing was the right place to start with cost reduction, a root purpose analysis highlighted that the purpose of cost management was to offer a compelling consumer value proposition (quality and price) whilst maintaining or improving cash margin. Adopting the perspectives of a consumer and a store manager had led to heated discussions on cost-to-serve by channel and to an outlet 'perspective connective', and the way in which that channel might be a profitable source of special make-up products at a different price point, as well as a managed clearance channel for end-of-season stock. This could further confirm the proposition appeal, but they would have to be careful about managing those channels to ensure it did not devalue the core proposition.
- The root purpose analysis had also clarified their thoughts on market expansion – it had to be incremental, de-risking the current portfolio and offering alternative channels for growth, and it should not be instead of, or disproportionately distract from, strengthening the competitiveness and appeal of Leisurious' existing business and 'growing the core'. In this context, building up the accessories range made sense – both Emma and Sam knew from previous consumer insight work that these categories were assumed to be part of the Leisurious core offering, and that the complementarity would strengthen sales of the core range. However, given the limited capacity of the management team, and the other requirements on their time, they both felt footwear and homeware development should be deprioritised for the forthcoming year, and revisited next year.
- An attribute listing exercise about their marketing focus had also raised some interesting considerations. The '20 Years of Leisure' campaign idea

▶

was still considered a good one but was also recognised as being purely tactical. The exercise had thrown light on a more strategic marketing need – building customer engagement, loyalty and advocacy. This would be a cornerstone of defending their position in the market, and the brand had some way to go in delivering a convincing plan to achieve it.

Emma summarised their thinking: 'There appear to be three interrelated elements here: first, refining and reinforcing the core appeal of our proposition, including strengthening accessories, whilst focusing on cost optimisation opportunities; second, channel optimisation, including a rethink of our digital and store experience, and the extension into outlets; third, a strategic approach to customer engagement.'

'Project ChIC!' laughed Sam, 'Channels, innovating our proposition and customer engagement!'

Emma laughed. She felt the name and frame session had been useful not only in defining what had to be done, but also in challenging each other and building a deeper common understanding of some of the dynamics at play. The challenge now was to tame those dynamics, and for that they would need insight.

In your organisation

Exercise 2: Name, frame, tame

1   Gather together the core group and, taking the list of opportunities raised in your 5KQ session from Chapter 1, apply at least two of the following tools to each entry in it (or to as many as you can complete in the time available to you):
   ● Root purpose analysis
   ● Zoom-out/Zoom-in
   ● Perspective connectives
   ● Restate of mind
   ● Absolutely!
   ● Attribute listing
   ● SCAMPER.

2 As you do so, capture the key assumptions, risks and choice or consequences emerging from the discussion in your ARC tracker (see Chapter 9 for an example of one).

3 Once you have completed the exercise, discuss as a group the following questions:

- How have your views of the original list of opportunities changed?
- What other opportunities has the discussion raised?
- What would you need to know or do to prioritise and address them?

4 Create a list of next steps.

[PART TWO]

Research and analysis

How to gain insight in a VUCA world

3

'There is nothing so terrible as activity without insight.'

Johann Wolfgang von Goethe[7]

In this chapter we do the following:

- Define the three fundamental questions that all insight seeks to answer.
- Explore seven key principles of insight.
- Show how the five key questions direct insight within RADAR.
- Consider the four stages of insight evolution.
- Introduce the five factors that define 'agile insight'.
- Consider the mechanisms through which agile insight is generated and applied.

Without insight to point the way, strategy is lost. Moreover, in a dynamic VUCA environment this insight needs to be regularly and consistently maintained – a constant stream used to irrigate the organisation's understanding and development, rather than an occasional oasis between barren periods of operational activity.

This is the role of research and analysis within RADAR, which sets out to be evidence-based *and* experience-led, combining the science of research and analysis with the art and know-how of experienced individuals and teams. If the previous chapter framed the questions to ask of ourselves and our markets, the next three chapters seek the insight to answer them.

---

[7] Goethe, J.W. (1906) *The Maxims and Reflections of Goethe*, translated from the German by Thomas Bailey. London: Macmillan and Company, p 130.

The three fundamental questions of insight

At its simplest, the pursuit of insight is a response to three fundamental questions:

Q1: What question(s) do I want to answer?
Being clear about the question(s) you want answered may sound obvious, but it is the main reason why insight work fails to deliver on its promise. The more specific you can be in formulating your question, the more effective and efficient the insight work will be. RADAR's starting point is the 5KQs, and they ultimately drive all strategy-related research and analysis. However, as we saw in the previous chapter, each of the 5KQs must be broken down and made more specific, reflecting the objectives, resources and current organisational situation of your business.

Amazon

Consider how the question 'Where is the opportunity?' has changed for Amazon over its history. Starting with the opportunity it saw as an online book retailer back in 1995, it initially responded to the classic question 'What other categories can I sell?', expanding into CDs and DVDs in 1998 and toys and electronics in 1999.

It then recognised the differentiating nature of its platform and its growing customer database and answered the question: 'How else can we exploit our market position?', resulting in the launch of its third-party marketplace in 2000. As it built up the server base to drive its online offering, it then changed the question again to ask: 'How can I maximise the return on our investment in this technology?', subsequently launching Amazon Web Services in 2002, which has been the profit engine for the business as it has continued to expand.

As the customer base continued to grow, the opportunity switched to 'How can I make this customer base more loyal?', resulting in the launch of Amazon Prime in the US in 2005 and the UK in 2007, extending into Kindle hardware to drive readers to Amazon ebooks in 2007 and original TV content to emphasise further the value of Prime membership through the launch of Amazon Studios in 2010.

Its acquisition of Whole Foods in 2017 was primarily a consequence of two complementary questions at the heart of Amazon's recent developments: 'How do we strengthen our offer in groceries?', which began with the launch of Amazon Fresh in Seattle in 2006, and 'How do we strengthen our offline network?' (e.g. stores, customers and data).

Clearly, the reality was neither as linear nor as neat as this retrospective summary might suggest. Yet, notwithstanding the convenient clarity of hindsight, it does illustrate the shifting nature of both framing the opportunity (as we saw in the last chapter), and asking the right question to drive clear research, insight and action.

Q2: What data do we need to answer it, and how should it be sourced?

Having determined the right question(s), identifying and sourcing the data required is the next step, with consideration given to the level of certainty needed and any constraints on cost, speed and accessibility. In my first consulting role, I once spent two days transferring paper-based operational data for a plastics company into a spreadsheet in order to analyse key elements of its operational performance. This provided insight into an area where the cost of poor quality was material to the financial performance and reputation of the business, yet the data had never been collated or analysed in that way.

Q3: How should we interpret the resultant data?

This broad question is the crux of insight, and involves preparing the captured data (e.g. cleansing and normalising it for analysis), interrogating the data (i.e. seeking the proofs or rejections of hypotheses), deploying statistical techniques (e.g. to determine the level of confidence we have in the answers we uncover) and visualising the output (i.e. creating easy-to-understand charts and visual representations of the output that enable confident, evidence-based decision making).

Stick to your principles

When responding to the three insight questions above, there are seven principles that should shape your approach.

1 The curious nature of insight

I cannot emphasise enough that the primary tool of organisational and market insight – or indeed insight of any kind – is curiosity. Some argue this cannot be taught, but it can undoubtedly be provoked. The fields of pedagogy and instructional design have long championed asking learners questions before, during and after they engage in a learning activity to support enhanced comprehension and critical thinking. In the field of strategy, asking yourself questions such as 'What do I have to believe for this to be successful?' or 'What information would enable me to respond to this issue?' will engage your curiosity and help you to actively interrogate the strategic challenges you face.

2 Question the objective, and then objectively question

The first of the three fundamental insight questions focuses on the objective driving the insight. In practice, this usually involves consulting relevant stakeholders across the business, and outside it. This aligns neatly with the RADAR approach, which engages widely and deeply with stakeholders to drive a common understanding of the five key questions, thereby enabling a quicker response when circumstances change. Questioning the objective is also about envisioning the end goal – being clear about the organisational change or value to which the insight will contribute. Once clear on the objective, it is important to maintain an unbiased approach to fulfilling it (i.e. objectively question), not allowing ingrained assumptions or bias to replace objective evidence.

3 Hypothetically speaking

Hypothesis-driven thinking, or the 'scientific method' as it is often labelled, has long been the mainstay of strategic thinking. The practice of using intuition, experience and partial data to hypothesise what you believe the answer to be, and then identifying the analysis and data required to confirm or refute it, is a skill that yields significant dividends by focusing the cost and time invested in insight.

4 Adopt a 'segmentality'

An important aspect of research and analysis is breaking a problem, idea or group down into its constituent parts, something referred to in computer science as 'problem decomposition', but which I prefer to call adopting a segmentality. This is common practice in market analysis, from segmenting a customer base to dividing competitors into strategic groups, but it also applies more broadly to a range of situations such as financial analysis (e.g. the breakdown of return on equity into its constituent measures) or the use of decision trees in operational decision-making.

5 Be systematic and creative (the HAD approach)

Robust insight requires a systematic approach. However, this is not enough. As we saw in the previous chapter, which provided tools to stimulate ideas through shifting perspective, creativity is an equally important element of strategic insight.

This combination of structure and creativity can be seen in the approach by which good insight is created. Having hypothesised the answer to the question(s) to be addressed, and adopted a segmentality to break it down into its constituent elements, you then need to identify which analysis to undertake and the data required for this analysis. An example of this HAD approach (hypothesis, analysis, data) is shown in the table below, which represents an extract from a fuller set of hypotheses.

Table 3.1 Example of the HAD approach

QUESTION: Why are our revenues falling?

Hypothesis	Analysis	Data and sources
Our product lacks appeal (vs. that of competitors)	● Consumer feedback on product appeal (blind test to mitigate against brand perceptions) ● Product FAB comparison (features, advantages, benefits)	● Consumer feedback (focus groups, survey, accompanied shops, customer service contacts, digital) ● Comparator product set data (websites, store visits, mystery shopping, catalogues)
Our prices are too high/ we offer poor value for money	● Competitor price benchmarking ● Consumer utility comparisons ● Consumer willingness to pay ● Consumer trade-offs (multivariate analysis)	● Competitor prices (websites, store visits, catalogues) ● Consumer survey (e.g. conjoint analysis, Van Westendorp and Gabor Granger approaches) ● Other stakeholder feedback (e.g. retailers, wholesalers)
We are no longer available in the right channels	● Company sales by channel by region, over the past 5 years ● Total market expenditure by channel over the past 5 years	● Transactional data ● Customer feedback (focus groups) ● Customer feedback (survey) ● Market data (e.g. from market reports, built up from supply base)

When using the HAD approach, you will inevitably find certain data sets are unavailable or inaccessible, whereupon one or more of three options are typically used:

1 Collect primary data.

2 Use proxy data sets.

3 Generate the required data through some form of business modelling.

6 Triangulate

Triangulation (using multiple sources to validate an output) is a vital element of research and analysis, particularly in cases where the authority of any one data set is questionable. Do not hesitate to draw on a broad range of quantitative and qualitative sources, if required, to come to a consensus conclusion, and be sure to explore and explain any significant differences between sources to give you all more confidence in the final data.

7 Good enough is good enough

Get to the depth and level of rigour required for the choices you must make, and no more. There is no benefit to spending further time and money on getting more accurate data, if all you really need is broad confirmation that the current assumptions were correct.

The evolution of insight

Although bound by these principles, insight is in fact a broad church ranging from basic performance evaluation through to full-blown market intelligence. As insight has increasingly become a source of competitive advantage (e.g. customer relationship management), or even simply a requirement to stay competitive (e.g. price-matching in grocery), organisations have been set on a path to 'insight maturity' which comprises four stages.

Figure 3.1 The evolution of insight

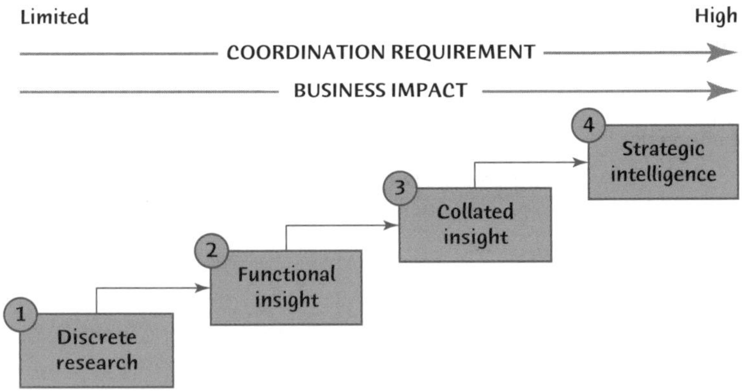

These different stages represent increasing business impact, in line with a requirement for greater coordination. They also serve different purposes, and reaching the stage of strategic intelligence does not mean that the other stages are not required, as there will always be the need for one-off areas of insight, or for functional insight that is of use primarily to drive that function's effectiveness (e.g. overall equipment effectiveness on a manufacturing floor). The characteristics, purpose and considerations for these different stages are summarised in the table below.

The strategic intelligence system (SIS), the processes and systems used to manage strategic intelligence within RADAR, is the engine room of Horizon

Table 3.2 The four stages of insight maturity

	Characteristics	Typical purpose and use	Considerations
Discrete research	• Addresses a one-off set of objectives • Responsive (answers the question) • Fixed timeline	• Baseline performance • Support strategic initiatives • Answer one-off questions	• Insight 'half-life' (i.e. how long the insight remains relevant)
Functional insight	• Deep and narrow scope (addresses a mix of one-off and ongoing intelligence) • Function first (e.g. marketing, operations)	• Drive functional effectiveness and efficiency • Often linked to functional KPIs or budget	• Validation of conclusions (through insight from other functions) • Alignment and buy-in across functions
Collated insight	• Collates data, information and insight from across the organisation • Scope determined by data availability	• Organisational diagnosis • Strategic planning • Budgeting	• The original objectives for the data collection • Prioritisation • Coordination • Consensus
Strategic intelligence	• Scope determined by strategic choices • Scope evolves in line with the strategy • Explorative (seeks change) • Periodic	• Horizon management • 'Pulse checking' (organisation and market) • Opportunities, risks and issues spotting	• Minimum enterprise data set (see Chapter 5) • Cost • Frequency • Ongoing relevance

management (see Chapter 5 which is dedicated to it). However, common to all these stages of insight maturity is one universal challenge: when there is so much you could capture and analyse, what do you prioritise? To answer that, we return to the 5KQs.

Insight and the 5KQs

Within RADAR, it is the Horizon and its associated outcomes that drive the organisation's insight requirements, whether to baseline its current position (Chapter 4), or dynamically track developments over time (Chapter 5). The Horizon, and the 5KQs that define it, represent the interface between two domains: the market and the organisation. We cannot answer either of the Horizon questions – 'Where do we play?' and 'How do we win?' – without considering all five of the 5KQs. Your most appropriate Horizon is the one that optimises your choices based on two criteria:

- The attractiveness of the market opportunities.
- The ability of your organisation to exploit these opportunities in the face of the competition.

Let us consider each of the 5KQs in turn.

Where is the opportunity?

Markets are constellations of opportunities and threats. The goal of this first question – 'Where is the opportunity?' – is to evaluate these constellations.

Figure 3.2 Where is the opportunity?

This requires research and analysis in six areas:

Table 3.3 Market insight framework components

#	Area	Description	Key analysis areas
1	**Customer** *Demand*	An individual person or entity that buys, or could buy, the products and services your organisation offers	• Need identification, e.g. − Customer insight and analytics − Field staff interviews − Stakeholder interviews − Customer journey mapping − Customer observation − Competition analysis − Understanding failures − Trade press • Customer segmentation • Customer value: cost to serve, lifetime value and profitability
2	**Market(s)** *Demand*	There are three levels of market defini- tion, relating to the *group(s)* of customers who: • Want/need your product/service (total addressable market) • Are reachable with your product/service (serviceable addressable market) • Are targeted by you (target market)	• Market definition • Market attractiveness − Size − Growth − Profitability − Macro-economic factors − Market forces and trends − Risk
3	**Channel(s)** *Demand and supply*	The mechanisms through which con- sumers can access, purchase and return products	• Channel effectiveness (e.g. revenue, share of channel) • Channel efficiency (e.g. cost to serve, profitability)

(continued)

Table 3.3 Market insight framework components (*continued*)

#	Area	Description	Key analysis areas
4	**Associated markets and industries** *Demand and supply*	Group(s) of customers and businesses, outside your current market(s) or industry, that contribute to creating, influencing or servicing them	• Interdependencies • Substitutes • Suppliers • Buyers
5	**Competition** *Supply*	There are two broad types of competitor: • *Direct:* offer products/services essentially the same as yours • *Indirect:* satisfy the same customer need through other means In some cases, further 'competitive' risks are that customers do nothing or satisfy the needs themselves (e.g. in B2B services)	• Strategic groups • Strategy and objectives • Competitive position • Investments
6	**Value propositions** *Supply*	The total offer to the customer, comprising: • Product/service functionality • Any brand (emotional) associations • Benefits • Price	• Products and services • Pricing and promotion

A considered exploration of these areas is key to baselining your Horizon. As important, however, is the ongoing tracking of trends, 'inflection points' and potential to 'bend the market in your direction', all of which can lead to new opportunities and which we discuss in Chapter 5. These six areas and how they interact are summarised in Figure 3.3.

Figure 3.3 Areas for consideration

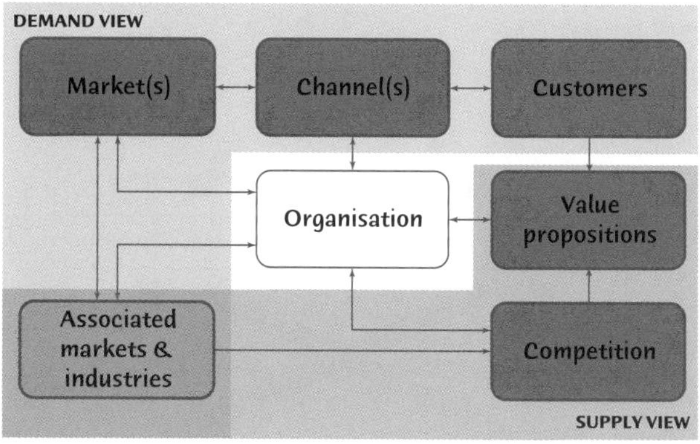

What makes us great?

To prioritise and capitalise on the opportunities identified in the previous question, you must understand your ability to do so. This begins with 'What makes us great?', and asking its three related questions:

1 **Where do we make most of our money?** This question is primarily about where value is created. As we see in the next chapter, this can be answered by looking at capital employed, and the return on that capital, for different cuts of the organisation (e.g. business segments, strategic business units, customers, products, channels). The contribution of indirect value generators that enable value creation elsewhere within the organisation must also be understood (e.g. physical retail showrooms that support online sales conversion). Tracking this over time can show where historical areas of strength are losing their relevance or new ones are emerging.

2 **What differentiates us?** Two factors drive business performance: market attractiveness and competitive position. In those segments where you make the most money, you must understand the extent to which differentiation allows you to outperform the market. Sources of this intelligence include competitor benchmarking, stakeholder feedback (e.g. customers, suppliers, channel partners) and observation.

3 **What AIR underpins this differentiation?** This question is perhaps the most challenging, as it requires you to map your competitive position to the AIR factors that drive it, i.e. linking the effect (success through differentiation) to its operational causes (activities, investment, resources). This requires an unbiased, honest and systematic approach to identifying and

evaluating organisational strengths. I discuss this topic – and the related concept of 'AIR cover' – in Chapters 4 and 7.

Figure 3.4 What makes us great

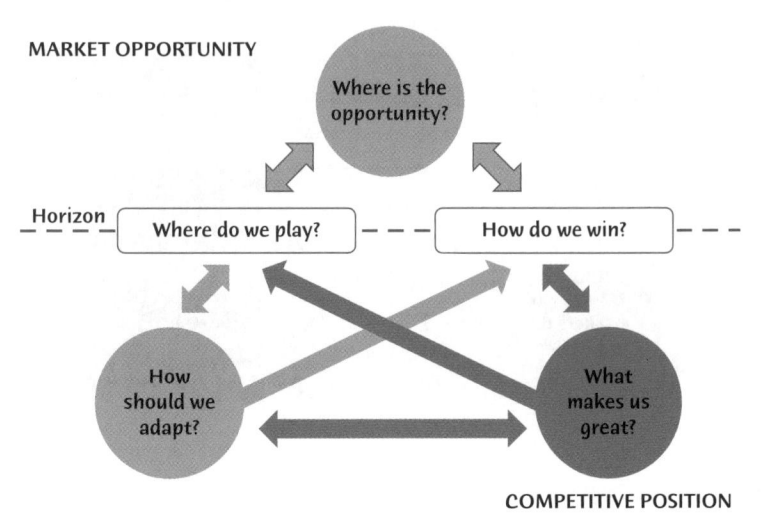

Answering these three related questions on an ongoing basis will keep you current on your core market appeal and the organisational elements that enable it. This is necessary, as these advantages are increasingly transient;[8] changes in the market (e.g. new competitors or technologies, regulation) or in the organisation itself (e.g. acquisitions, loss of key staff) can result in areas of 'greatness' suddenly becoming distinctly normal or obsolete, whilst new areas of distinction can suddenly burst into life (as is the case, for example, when a pharmaceutical company gets regulatory approval for an innovative and effective drug in an under-served area).

Kodak
Back in the early 1990s Kodak was the leading light in colour film manufacturing, a capability underpinned by nearly a century of cumulative expertise and a well-developed ecosystem of retail partners. At that time, only Fujifilm and Agfa-Gevaert had the credible scale and capability to challenge them.

---

[8] See Rita McGrath's argument that the pursuit of sustainable competitive advantage must be replaced by that of transient competitive advantage, exploiting short-lived opportunities, in McGrath, R.G. (2013). *The End of Competitive Advantage*, Boston, MA: Harvard Business Review Press.

> However, as digital photography started to expand, Kodak's resources and specialist activities no longer matched the requirements for its core B2C photography market, which was now shifting to be centred around semiconductors. Furthermore, as the transition to digital picked up pace, declines in volumes for traditional film led to challenges on batch sizes (film has a finite shelf-life) and retail distribution density (as retailers reassigned shelf space to alternative, growing categories). Many of the core elements that had made Kodak great – film manufacturing expertise, a large retail distribution network, a strong brand name – rapidly lost their value as the market moved towards digital.

How should we adapt?

Having understood where the opportunities are, and what makes your organisation great, the logical next question is 'How should we adapt?'

Figure 3.5 How should we adapt?

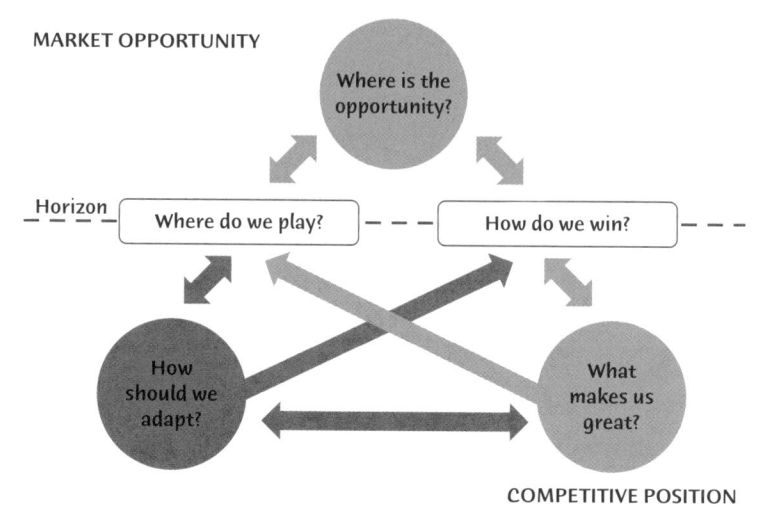

The responses may range from continuing as you are through to fundamental changes such as entering or withdrawing from markets or making acquisitions. When answering this question, consider the following five areas (Table 3.4) – memorable by the mnemonic ADAPT.

As we saw in our introduction to AIR (Chapter 1), what you adapt, and how, will be determined by your:

- strategic intent
- existing resources and capabilities (capability and capacity)
- current performance relative to the market.

Table 3.4 Key questions for 'How should we adapt?'

	Area	Key questions
A	Aim	• Are your Horizon statements still valid?
		• How does your unifying purpose relate to existing and emerging market opportunities?
D	Drivers and trends	• Will current drivers and trends significantly change the market opportunities or necessitate major changes to how we operate?
		• How can we exploit drivers and trends to further strengthen our competitive position?
A	AIR	• What are the critical AIR elements that are underpinning our competitive position and which we must protect?
		• Where does our AIR fall short of what is required to address identified opportunities or changes in the markets we serve?
		• Are the organisational mechanisms through which AIR is managed in the organisation driving the right behaviours and decisions?
P	Position-ing and proposition	• Does our current positioning still resonate in the markets in which we operate?
		• Is our proposition compelling and differentiated?
		• What new or changing competitive threats are at play?
		• How should we respond to them?
T	Technology	• How is technology affecting the behaviours of our customers, markets and competitors?
		• To what extent is our current technology differentiating or constraining us?
		• How can we capitalise on emerging technologies?

The Horizon: Where do we play and how do we win?

The research and analysis required to answer the first three of the 5KQs ultimately serve one purpose – to define, manage and validate the organisation's Horizon. Consequently, answering the two Horizon questions – 'Where do we play?' and 'How do we win?' – comprises primarily two ongoing activities:

1 The analysis and synthesis of responses to the earlier questions.
2 The tracking of the Horizon's performance and validity (using RADAR's Strategic Intelligence System and results framework).

Figure 3.6 Where do we play and how do we win?

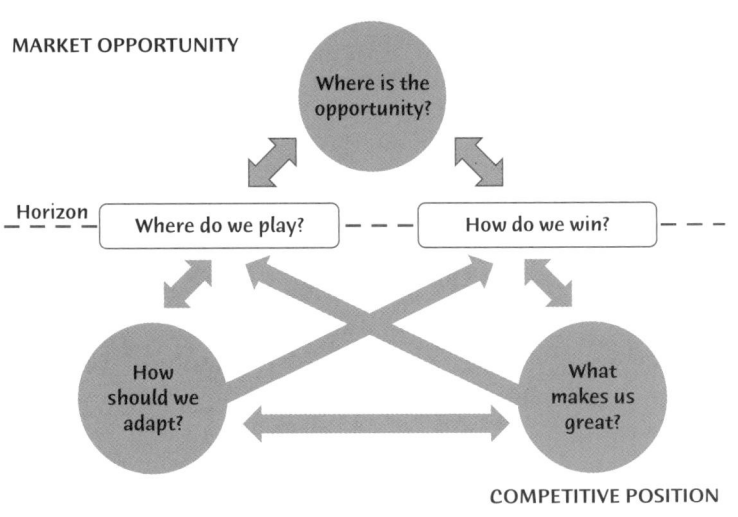

These activities require the following:

- **Adoption of multiple perspectives:** the analysis requires multiple perspectives to ensure that the full range of opportunities, constraints and risks are identified and considered. It is an integral part of the Horizon gateways (see Chapter 8).

- **Iteration:** the analysis iterates on a regular basis, continuously evaluating whether the Horizon's ARC is still valid.

- **Recognition of interdependencies:** there are strong interdependencies between 'where to play' and 'how to win', between opportunity and competitive position. An organisation's strategic assets (activities and resources that bestow an advantage) can create opportunities as well as offering a mechanism to respond to them. Consider the combination of Apple's technology, design capabilities and brand appeal used to create a market for tablets (after Microsoft had failed to do so a decade earlier).

- **Clarity on your competitive position:** Treacy and Wiersema[9] argue that an organisation determines its competitive position, and therefore how to win, through one of three broad approaches: operational excellence, customer intimacy or product leadership. More recent thinking argues that these are no longer necessarily discrete choices or positions, with data offering the opportunity to excel at all three. Academic theories and debate aside, being honest and evidence-based in your

[9] Treacy, M. and Wiersema, F. (1993) Customer intimacy and other value disciplines, *Harvard Business Review*, 71(1), pp 84–93.

evaluation of your competitive position is critical. I have seen a lot of organisations convince themselves they are strong in specific areas, with little evidence that this was truly the case.

- **Leveraging existing capabilities and resources:** this is a classic way of entering into new markets. Consider breakfast cereal companies such as Kellogg's, General Mills and Quaker, many of which have expanded into the snack bar market by leveraging their brands (an intangible strategic asset) and production capabilities.

I cover these topics in Chapters 4, 7 and 8.

Summary

The table below summarises how the 5KQs drive RADAR's research and analysis.

Whilst this summary may appear long, once the baselining has been established (see next chapter), the organisation can focus on only those elements that would necessitate a Horizon adjustment or shift if they changed (addressed in Chapter 5).

Table 3.5 Summary of how the five key questions inform research and analysis within RADAR

Key question	Core elements	Prompts for discussion
Where is the opportunity?	● Market ● Customer ● Channel ● Associated markets ● Competition ● Value proposition	● What key trends are shaping our market(s)? ● What role does or could technology play in this? ● Which markets/customer segments/product categories/ channels have seen the greatest growth? ● Which parts of the value chain are the most profitable? ● What else do our existing customers need? ● To which other customer segments would our proposition appeal? ● How could our activities and resources be applied to service other customer needs? ● How can any competitive advantage be maximised?

Table 3.5 Summary of how the five key questions inform research and analysis within RADAR (*continued*)

Key question	Core elements	Prompts for discussion
What makes us great?	• Value creation • Differentiation • AIR	• Which parts of the business generate the highest returns? • What drives these returns: our market selection, our competitive position, or both? • Why do our existing customers value us? • Where do we SCORE highest? • Which metrics on our SCOREcard have shown the greatest improvement? • Which activities and resources assets set us apart from competitors? • How well do we manage these?
How should we adapt?	• Aim • Drivers and trends • AIR • Positioning and proposition • Technology	• Which attractive opportunities are we currently unable to serve? • Where is our competitive position weak, and why? • Should we address this weakness? If so, how? e.g. through building (in-house development), borrowing (partnering) or buying (acquisition)? • Where do we SCORE lowest? • Which metrics on our SCOREcard have shown the greatest decline? • Is our Horizon's ARC still valid? • How can we further develop our strengths to become even more unassailable?

Table 3.5 Summary of how the five key questions inform research and analysis within RADAR (*continued*)

Key question	Core elements	Prompts for discussion
Horizon (Where do we play? How do we win?)	• Synthesis of responses to earlier questions • Horizon's SCORE, ERAs and ARC	• Where do we want to position ourselves in our market(s)? • Which aspects of our current strategy are successful? • How could we better or further serve our existing customers? • Which market opportunities are we better placed than the competition to serve? • How do we maximise the benefits we extract from existing resources and activities? • Where does our SCORE significantly exceed that of competitors? Why?

How does the need for agility affect research and analysis?

Focusing on what is changing amidst a small number of Horizon-related data points reduces complexity and increases responsiveness. This is an example of how an organisation's research and analysis practices can contribute to agility. The practical implications are that RADAR's research and analysis components reflect the RAC criteria of agility (responsiveness, adaptability, control). Indeed, five factors distinguish insight as agile.

1 Frequency

If your business environment is changing rapidly, then the frequency with which you capture and analyse data to understand those changes must reflect that. To prevent this being overwhelming, however, requires judicious selection of the key metrics that matter based on your Horizon and the results framework that underpins it.

2 Timeliness

Linked to this principle of frequency is the fact that perfection takes time, but an 80 per cent 'directional' solution, delivered sooner, will often be more valuable to the organisation. Decisions that require significant investment, are difficult to

Figure 3.7 Agile insight factors

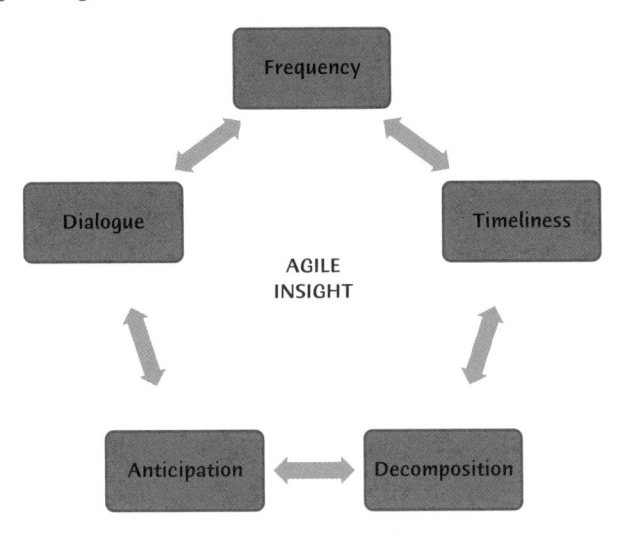

reverse, or which could have a large impact (positive or negative) require the most robust insight to support them. However, many decisions for which insight is required do not fit that profile and could therefore be addressed more simply and quickly through 'timely imperfection'.

3 Decomposition

Breaking down an area (e.g. opportunity, organisational performance domain) into its constituent parts allows insight to be provided in smaller, more manageable chunks. For example, statistical analysis of monthly footfall trends provides one indicator of UK high street market attractiveness, to be read alongside others (e.g. conversion rates, average transaction value, consumer confidence) to provide a fuller picture.

4 Anticipation

Agility implies responsiveness, and this in turn is greatly aided by an ability to anticipate the potential changes required. Identifying and evaluating emerging market and organisational performance trends, through tracking mechanisms and the leading and anticipatory insight offered by the RADAR results framework, are key elements of agile strategy.

5 Dialogue

One of the ways in which agile practices drive rapid development and improvement is through a test and learn approach (see Chapter 6). I find it helpful to picture this as a dialogue between your organisation and the world, an active process of exchange through which insight is formed, in contrast to the traditional passive view of gathering data for analysis and drawing conclusions. These dialogues can take two forms:

- *Pull:* the organisation actively engages with the market (e.g. customers) to draw out their requirements and changing behaviours. Examples include engaging groups through social media and traditional consumer research techniques such as focus groups.

- *Push:* the organisation creates experiments to evaluate the impact of changes. Examples include A/B testing of new propositions or geofenced marketing campaigns.

These factors are expressed through the continuous insight cycle of anticipating, analysing, acting and adapting, which serves three roles:

1 To understand and govern performance (descriptive and diagnostic).
2 To plan and anticipate change (predictive).
3 To determine action (prescriptive).

Figure 3.8 The mechanics of agile insight

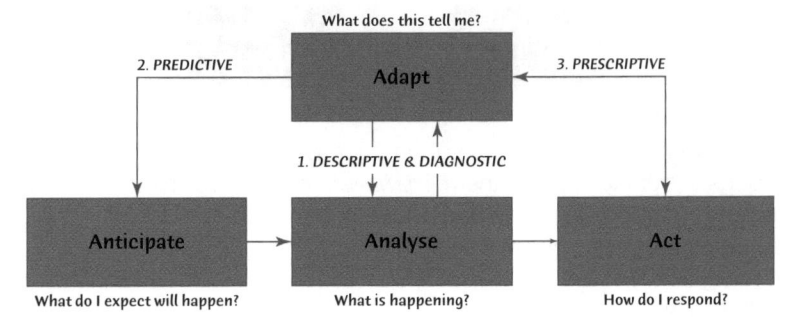

As a system, the four parts of this cycle act as an engine to deliver the strategic intelligence described earlier (see Chapter 5). However, for an organisation to design and implement strategic intelligence, it must first understand its market and organisational context in greater depth, and it is to that topic that we turn in the next chapter.

Summary

- All insight work must ultimately answer three questions:
  - What question(s) do we want to answer?
  - What data do we need to answer it, and how should it be captured?
  - How should we interpret the resultant data?

- Good practice in insight development typically adheres to the following principles:
  - Approach with curiosity.
  - Challenge the objective by consulting relevant stakeholders and envisioning the end goal.

- Use hypotheses to drive thinking.
- Adopt a 'segmentality', breaking problems down into their constituent elements.
- Be systematic and creative.
- Triangulate different sources to ensure robustness of results.
- Get to the depth and level of rigour required for the choice you must make, and no more.

There is a path to insight maturity that covers four stages:

Discrete research	A response to one-off requirements or questions, for example in support of a strategic initiative or to baseline performance.
Functional insight	Deep insight into one functional area (e.g. marketing, financial performance), often in isolation of the wider business.
Collated insight	Gathers together and synthesises functional insight to drive organisation-wide insight and conclusions.
Strategic intelligence	A holistic approach to addressing an organisation's strategic insight needs, for example to support Horizon management.

Reaching the stage of strategic intelligence does not mean that the other stages are not required.

- It is the Horizon, representing the interface between two domains of market and organisation, and its associated outcomes that drive the organisation's insight requirements, whether to baseline its current position or dynamically track developments over time.
- For an organisation to be agile, its research and analysis practices must themselves be agile. This agility is determined by five factors: frequency, timeliness, decomposition, anticipation and dialogue.
- We can consider the mechanisms through which agile insight is generated and applied as a continuous cycle of anticipating, analysing, acting and adapting. Insight therefore serves three roles: governing and guiding performance (descriptive and diagnostic), planning and anticipating change (predictive), and determining action (prescriptive).

Case story: Back to Base-ChIC

Having reflected on the scope of Project ChIC, Emma recognised that there was a lot to cover. Both she and Sam had been guilty in the past of trying to do too much at once, resulting in long hours, frustration and insufficient time dedicated to the core business. She did not want to go down that path again.

'What are the key questions that we need to answer?' Emma asked Sam later that morning, but really it was rhetorical, and she continued without pausing for breath. 'The channel element is ultimately about how we deliver a true omnichannel experience, whilst being cuter on costs. For proposition, we need to determine how to maintain relevance, increase appeal and sharpen value, and for customer engagement, it is about getting closer to the customer and driving greater share of pocket.'

Sam let Emma's words hang in the air for a moment, before dispersing them with her own. If Project ChIC was going to be something more than a playful name and a shopping list of traditional retail improvements, they would need to be creative and systematic in their approach. The thought reminded her of the HAD approach she had recently read about, and they set to work writing out their main hypotheses against each of Project ChIC's three workstreams.

Table 3.6 Application of the HAD approach

Hypothesis	Analysis required	Data and sources
CHANNEL		
1 Cost to serve can be reduced without adversely affecting service	Cost to serve analysis, customer service requirements	Trading data, activity-based costing analysis, expert interviews, customer survey, benchmarks
2 Channel investment is not optimised for the contribution that each channel makes, the role each channel plays in the customer journey, and the interaction between channels	Return on investment by channel, strategic role of each channel, channel dependencies, customer journey mapping	Trading data, investment data, customer data on channel usage, customer survey
3 Outlets offer an attractive opportunity for Leisurious, and can be exploited without damaging the brand and its full-price business	Business modelling of outlet opportunity	Trading data, outlet market data (e.g. performance, costs), catchment and cannibalisation modelling

Table 3.6 Application of the HAD approach (*continued*)

Hypothesis	Analysis required	Data and sources
INNOVATION OF THE PROPOSITION		
4 Price and cost of goods sold (COGS) are out of line with other retailers	Pricing and COGS analysis and benchmarking	Trading data, benchmarking (pricing, COGS)
5 Strengthening the accessories range will drive improved financial performance	Accessories review and financial modelling	Trading data, accessories market data, customer survey
6 Improvements in customer experience (Cx) will drive improved financial performance	Cx audit and benchmarking, Cx prototyping and customer testing	Customer journey mapping, customer testing data
CUSTOMER ENGAGEMENT		
7 Leisurious is not maximising the long-term value realisable from its existing customer base	Customer segmentation, market penetration, customer analysis, share of wallet, customer lifetime value	Customer database, market survey, sentiment analysis (social media), transaction data, customer complaints, competitor data/ financials
8 Leisurious is underpenetrated in certain key customer segments	Market segmentation, customer segmentation, customer analysis	Market survey, customer database, transaction data
9 Leisurious' key customer segments would value an appropriate loyalty scheme, which would translate to improved financial performance	Customer segmentation, customer shopping behaviours and attitudes, Cx analysis	Customer focus groups, customer database survey, sentiment analysis (social media), competitor loyalty scheme benchmarking

In addition to the Project ChIC workstreams, the pair also acknowledged there was some analysis to be done on Leisurious' core markets.

▶

Table 3.7 The HAD approach applied to core markets

Hypothesis	Analysis required	Data and sources
CORE MARKETS		
10 Growth in the core European markets has slowed	Market growth analysis, market modelling (assumption-driven)	Market reports, competitor financials, data releases and announcements, trade bodies, market interviews
11 Competition has significantly increased in core business segments	Trading data analysis by market, product category and customer type, market segment analysis	Leisurious trading data, market reports, competitor financials, data releases and announcements, trade bodies, market interviews
12 Leisurious has lost its differentiated position in some segments, although it remains differentiated in others	Consumer insight (e.g. brand perceptions), proposition benchmarking	Consumer research, store visits, competitor intelligence, digital review

Emma and Sam knew these hypotheses needed further work and refinement, but felt they were a useful start. Several thoughts struck them as they reviewed the list:

- They would need proper segmentation to underpin it all. Emma had a niggling suspicion that some core segments of their customer base were under-served by Leisurious' current proposition. However, with their reporting currently split only by country and category, it was difficult to see the customer beneath.
- The attractiveness of the different segments, and Leisurious' relative competitive position in each, would require some honest, objective scrutiny. Both felt there was opportunity to redirect limited funds more effectively across customers, markets, propositions and channels to gain a greater return.
- Triangulation of several sources would also be critical – Emma had seen too many innovation and loyalty schemes respond slavishly to customer feedback only to find that the resultant changes had very little import and impact.

Scanning the 'Analysis required' and 'Data and sources' columns, Emma realised there was a lot of work to be done. We will need to be pragmatic about this, she thought to herself. And that begins with understanding what data we already have.

In your organisation

Exercise 3: Data state

To what extent are the data and insight requirements of your organisation met? Launch a short project within your organisation, under the stewardship of a senior leader and with the support of a small project team, to undertake the following analysis.

Determine needs

Interview the executive team, divisional heads, heads of departments and selected stakeholders from across the business to understand the key questions for which they need data and insight to answer. These interviews should cover the following topics:

1　The 5KQs and the data they consider necessary to answer them.
2　The different types of data and insight, e.g.
　　2.1 Market
- Market performance data
- Market trends
- Regulatory requirements and changes
- Customer needs and behaviours insight
- Competitor intelligence

　　2.2 Organisation
- Competitive positioning
- Proposition
- Performance
- Resources and capabilities
- Compliance (regulatory, contractual)

　　2.3 One-off and regular or periodic requirements
- Qualitative and quantitative
- Online and offline
- Functional and central

Consider also the requirements to integrate these different data types.

Analyse current provision

3　Map out the key systems and databases used by the organisation.
4　Identify and review current data and insight used to manage and govern the organisation on a regular basis (e.g. monthly divisional reports, daily manufacturing performance sheets).

- Map these back to the organisation's systems and databases, where relevant.
- Note that not all of these will necessarily be digitised or even on paper (e.g. Kanban Boards used on factory sites).

5 Identify key one-off data and insight work commissioned across the organisation during the year (including the objective of the work, and what questions it was intended to answer).

- Why were these needs not met through the regular organisational insight and data?
- Are these genuine one-offs, or examples of regular requirements not currently being met?

Conclusions

6 Based on the analysis undertaken, consider the following questions:

- Where are there clear gaps in the organisation's data and insight?
- What is driving these gaps (e.g. people, processes, systems, priorities, funding)?
- Where is data being generated but not used?
- Which changes should be prioritised?
- Are there simple solutions available to close some of the gaps quickly and cost-effectively?

VUCAnomics – learn where and why you make money

'In all affairs it's a healthy thing now and then to hang a question mark on the things you have long taken for granted.'

Bertrand Russell

In this chapter we do the following:

- Consider the two key business context questions: where is value created, and why?
- Explore how to evaluate market attractiveness.
- Understand the key components of competitive position and how to assess them.
- Outline the use of the RADAR results framework for context and baselining.
- Provide a framework for exploring new opportunities.
- Explain how to evaluate the agility of your organisation using the RADAR RAC rating.

Whether you are running a traditional strategy process or adopting RADAR – to determine how to get to your destination, you first need to know where you are.

This chapter focuses on gaining that understanding, and it begins with what I described in the introduction as the ultimate goal of strategy – value creation – and two deceptively simple questions:

1 Where is it created?
2 Why is it created?

Where is value created?

'Value creation' is a phrase that is widely, but often loosely, used. In purely financial terms, it can be defined as earning a return on the money you invest (return on invested capital or ROIC) that exceeds what it costs you to secure that investment through a mixture of debt and equity, having accounted for risk (expressed as the weighted average cost of capital or WACC).[10] We will assume this financial definition for our purposes, although I would add that there are wider, non-financial aspects of value creation (e.g. social benefit, environmental impact) that broaden this definition and indeed constitute the governing purpose of many organisations (e.g. charities, government bodies).

Determining where, and to what extent, value is created is more complicated than it might at first appear. Looking at a business purely through the prism of standard organisational units of measure (e.g. strategic business unit, division, product, channel) rarely provides the insight needed, as hidden beneath these groupings are often wildly different levels of performance which, if not identified, will result in the limited resources of the organisation being deployed inefficiently. To address this, we must adopt the segmentality described earlier and understand the distinct business segments that the organisation serves. This typically involves a four-step process:

Step 1: Define your market

At the risk of sounding like Dr Seuss, if you want to determine where value is created, you first need to define what is where (i.e. define the market in which you operate). Your unifying purpose, and the ABCD factors (authentic beliefs, business strengths, competitive/market space, desired outcomes) that shape it (see Chapters 1 and 7), are the starting point. Beyond that, the four most important lenses through which to view and define your market are:

1 Product

At its most narrowly defined, this can be the specific, core product category that you currently offer (e.g. in the case of Domino's Pizza, quick-serve takeaway pizza). However, it could also be expressed in terms of the broader product market, including substitutes and indirect competitors. In that case,

---

[10] For a thorough review of value and valuation, I can recommend Koller, T., Goedhart, M. and Wessels, D. (2015) *Valuation: Measuring and managing the valuation of companies*, New Jersey: John Wiley and Sons.

Domino's might be compared to all quick-serve foods (e.g. hamburgers, fish and chips), all restaurant food (e.g. casual dining, fine dining), all convenience foods (e.g. supermarket ready-meals) or even all food eaten at lunch or dinner time (whether home-made or bought, and whether eaten on the move or at home or work).

2 Customer

If product is a supply-side definition of the market, then customers and customer segments are its demand-side equivalent. Again, definitions can range in their breadth, and should reflect your own customers, those of relevant competitors (including substitutes) and non-customers who are potentially addressable given their needs, wants, attitudes and behaviours. When defining your market through a customer lens, consider:

- What problems are you solving, or needs are you satisfying, for your target customer?
- For who else are these problems or needs relevant?
- What are the commonalities across your current customers (e.g. characteristics, needs)?
- Who are your competitors targeting?
- Are they targeting anyone you are not? Why?
- How might one segment the total customer pool into discrete groups with distinct needs?

Consider again Domino's Pizza. You could define the market in terms of home delivery customers or segment by consumer type (e.g. students, families, young professionals) or usage (e.g. social gathering, mid-week refuel, guilty pleasure) or attitude to food (e.g. convenience junkies, health-conscious grazers, comfort foodies).

3 Geographic area

Defining the geographic scope of the market can be complicated for businesses serving global niches (as many tech-based companies do), where the balance must be struck between targeting a larger number of geographies to ensure sufficient scale and managing the resultant complexity and cost to serve.

4 Business scope

A market can also be defined in terms of the business scope or parts of the value chain that it addresses. For example, by acquiring Booker, Tesco extended its retail footprint into wholesale.

In practice, the market definition will typically be determined by:

- a combination of these perspectives;
- the underlying goals or ambition of the organisation (e.g. consolidating and strengthening your existing position or diversifying to find new growth areas);
- the period under consideration (e.g. a one-year view, a ten-year span).

It takes discipline to ensure the availability of data does not skew one's thinking (e.g. market data is often not in the format you want, either partially covering areas or including elements you do not want) and to resist either defining a market too narrowly (and therefore constrain thinking around opportunities), or defining it too broadly (wasting time on reviewing areas that are inappropriate for the organisation).

Considering the four factors above, you can define the perimeter of the market – the borderline within which lies the total addressable market (TAM). Within this TAM, there are several increasingly smaller markets defined by their accessibility, each set within the previous one like Matryoshka dolls:

- **Total addressable market (TAM):** those in the population with needs that could be addressed by your product or service.
- **Serviceable addressable market (SAM):** the segment of your TAM that you can access right now, for example, in specific locations or through specific channels.
- **Target market:** the prioritised segments within your SAM that you are targeting (e.g. for reasons of higher profitability, ease of access, likelihood of success, etc).
- **Penetrated market:** those in the target market who have purchased your product or service.

Figure 4.1 The Matryoshka market model

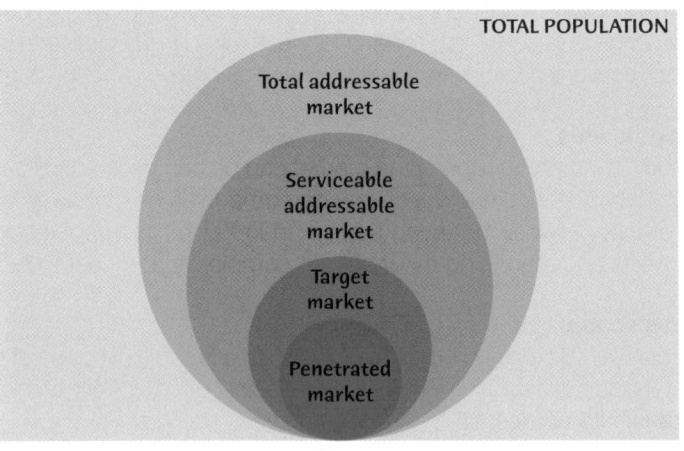

These different sub-markets are themselves dynamic. For example, technology might reduce the cost of purchase and this increased affordability will therefore increase the TAM (as has been the case with everything from flat-screen televisions to DNA testing).

Step 2: Define the business segments

Having defined your target market, you need to determine the business segments within it. A business segment is defined as a distinct proposition provided to a customer segment:

- *Customer segments:* groups of individuals in your market who 'share a similar level of interest in the same, or comparable, set of needs satisfied by a distinct marketing proposition.'[11] Put more simply, it is a group which wants broadly the same things, and will access them in broadly the same way.

- *Distinct propositions:* a good, service or some combination thereof that satisfies a discrete customer need. As a rule of thumb, two propositions that have different competitors can be considered distinct.

For example, consider a French outdoor equipment brand manufacturing three distinct propositions (sleeping bags, tents and cooking equipment for camping) to sell domestically to two customer groups (casual holidaymakers and outdoor enthusiasts). Taking this B2C (business-to-consumer) view, the brand would be operating in six distinct business segments, as illustrated below.

Figure 4.2 Business segments

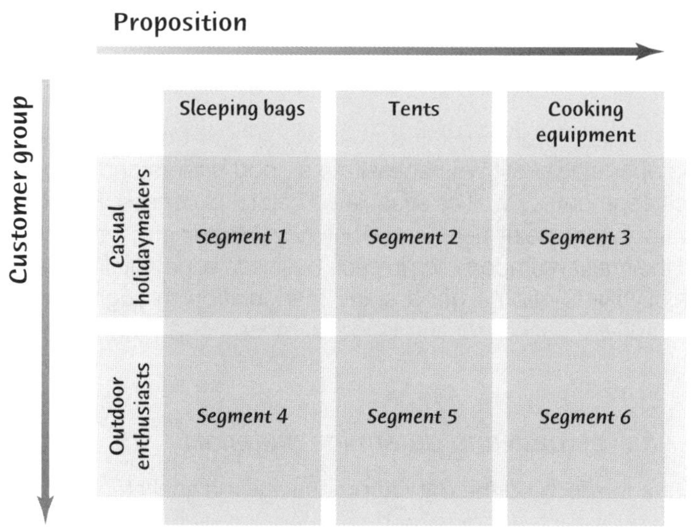

Developing understanding, agreement and alignment across your organisation on the business segments you serve, and their relative importance and attractiveness (see the next section), is key. For example:

[11] McDonald, M. and Payne, A. (2012) *Marketing Plans for Service Businesses: A complete guide*, Abingdon: Routledge.

- Apple spent considerable time exploring the use of its iPhones, iPads, Macs, services and other products (distinct propositions) across different customer segments defined by their usage location (e.g. education, workplace, home).

- In an amusement park, families, adult groups, schools and children's groups, adult individuals and corporations might be considered five (very basic) customer segments, with three distinct propositions: single-entry tickets, bundled tickets (including combinations of food, drink, priority access and gifts) and season tickets.

Step 3: Cut the financial data to align with these business segments

Having determined your business segments, the next challenge is to cut your organisational data so that they can be understood. This is rarely a straightforward task, as it is unlikely that your organisation's data has historically been captured that way.

Returning to the French outdoor equipment example, the profiles, requirements and dynamics of these segments may be very different, but they will be invisible to the organisation if it just looks at tent sales, without considering the customer groups they serve. Furthermore, taking a B2B (business-to-business) view, which many brands do, they might view sales through department stores and specialist retailers, without realising that the dynamics in those two channels are a consequence of a mix of six very different B2C business segments.

Even if allocating revenues is a relatively simple task, any calculations to determine operating profit will necessitate a good understanding of the cost to serve each segment, as well as associated capital expenses. In my experience, the most important point here is consistency. Mapping out the key drivers of cost, and their *relative* importance in each business segment, in order to allocate costs effectively, is often a good start. Triangulation through zero-budgeting exercises, activity-based costing or other means can then complement this approach.

Step 4: Analyse data and determine materiality

Having cut and allocated the data appropriately, the final step is to analyse the value created by each segment and to determine what is driving it. This often starts by creating a ROIC[12] vs. capital employed (profit pool) graph like the one shown in Figure 4.3, mapping each business segment on to it:[13]

---

[12] Calculated as Net operating profit after tax ÷ operating capital (see discussion later in this chapter.)

[13] Note that if this data cannot be accessed, substituting net operating profit for ROIC and revenue for capital employed is an alternative way of creating profit pools.

Figure 4.3 ROIC vs. capital employed

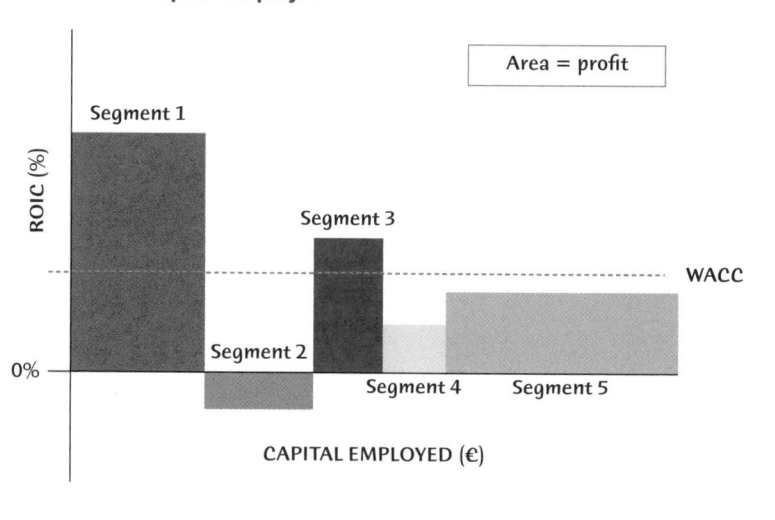

The area of each segment on the graph illustrates the contribution to value generation of the total business. Note the following:

- Segments 1 and 3 are the only ones where ROIC exceeds the company's WACC, showing that the others are destroying value in their current form. This raises questions about why this is the case (e.g. market issues, unappealing proposition, being sub-scale or at an early stage of maturity) and what can be done about it (e.g. cost reduction, exit, accelerate growth to reach scale).

- Segment 2 is loss-making (which may hitherto have not been visible to business). Can it be turned around? Does it contribute to the profitable delivery of other business segments? Can and should it be abandoned or shut down?

- Segment 4 uses the least capital, but is value-destroying at its current ROIC level. Would more investment drive up its profitability, or is it a distraction for management that should be exited?

- Segment 5 requires the most capital investment yet provides below-WACC returns. This again raises questions about the feasibility of improving its profitability or shifting resources to one of the profitable segments (depending on headroom for growth in those cases).

Why is value created?

To answer the questions raised above, you will need to understand *why* the business segments are performing in this way. Value creation is ultimately the function of one or both of two underlying factors: market/segment attractiveness and the organisation's competitive position within those markets. Figure 4.4 shows how these might be assessed for each segment.

Figure 4.4 Market attractiveness vs. competitive position matrix

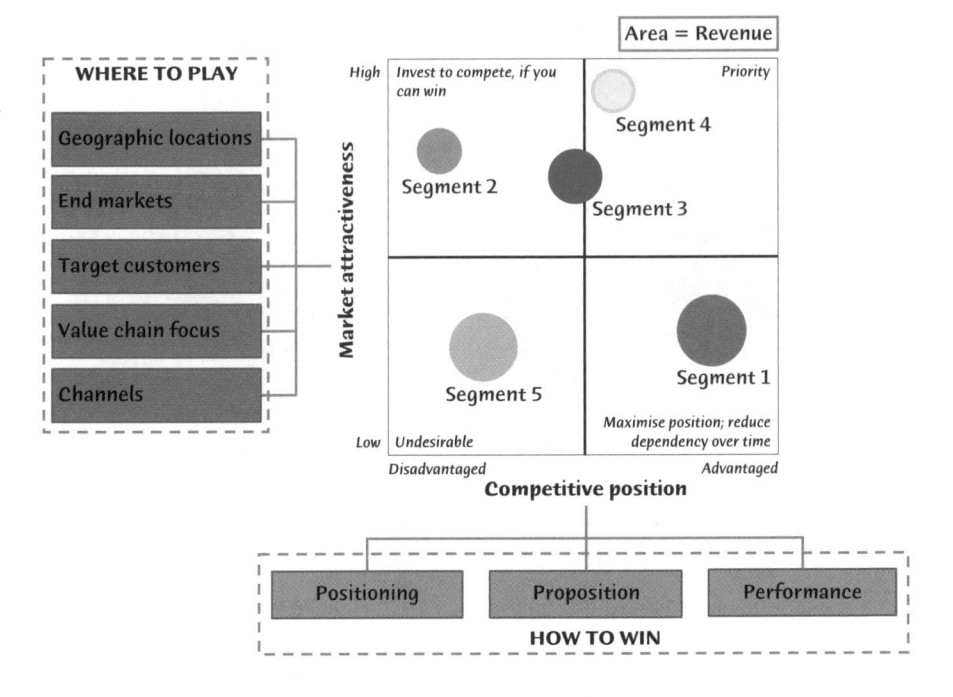

This matrix provides a high-level rationale for business segment performance and requires rigorous analysis of both dimensions. For example, exit barriers permitting (e.g. no major contractual or regulatory obligations), we would exit Segment 5 given it is value-destroying on account of both the market being unattractive and us having a weak position within it.

Business segment attractiveness (the X-factors)

The evaluation of business segment attractiveness is part art, part science, and typically involves the following elements.

In practice, to evaluate the market element of opportunity attractiveness requires a mixture of qualitative and quantitative assessment. Thus, evaluating competitive intensity involves both measurable indices (e.g. the Herfindahl–Hirschman Index – see later in this chapter) and qualitative judgements (e.g. relative substitutability of propositions). The art here is in finding specific data, or 'next best proxies', that can inform your views on all aspects of market attractiveness. Consider another example – growth projections in household furniture demand. The strong correlation between household furniture purchases and GDP means that projected GDP changes (e.g. using a consensus view from different economists' projections) can be a useful proxy for forecasted demand in that market.

Table 4.1 Dimensions of market attractiveness

Dimension	Description
Market size	All other things being equal, a larger market should be more attractive, as it offers greater opportunity. Calculating market size is usually through one or more of a range of top-down and bottom-up approaches.
Market growth	Ongoing growth in the market is another important factor in market attractiveness. Note that the projected growth of the TAM and SAM may be different, depending on which segments of the TAM are growing fastest. For example, the global music market TAM is growing, driven by streaming and developing market penetration; the SAM for music CD manufacturers in the USA, by contrast, is in decline.
Market profitability	Scale and growth alone are not attractive if the margins are too low – as exemplified by the rolling conveyor belt of sub-scale courier companies that have entered administration over the past five years, despite the significant growth in online retail and corresponding fulfilment. There are three main considerations when looking at market profitability: 1 **Scale:** the overall level of *current* profitability in the market. 2 **Spread:** the distribution of that profitability across the value chain and market participants. 3 **Shifts:** the trajectory of, and anticipated changes to, *future* profitability. These are, themselves, shaped by macro-economic and market factors.
Macro-economic factors	The PESTLE factors (political, economic, social, technological, legal, environmental) can have a significant impact on profitability. For example, consider the areas of policy and regulation where grants, subsidies, political shifts (e.g. towards prioritising national industries or greater interventionism to protect consumers) and regulatory stringency in production, sales and marketing can all contribute to changes in the relative attractiveness and profitability of markets (as we have seen in tobacco, for example).

(continued)

Table 4.1 Dimensions of market attractiveness (*continued*)

Dimension	Description
Market forces and trends	Porter's Five Forces (described later in this chapter) are key determinants of profitability. For example, the level and concentration of competition are important factors in evaluating profit potential, and Kim and Mauborgne's work on 'blue ocean strategies'[14] – searching for growth in uncontested market spaces – is one approach to addressing this. More qualitative analysis of key market trends and underlying market shifts are also important considerations for future attractiveness (e.g. the shift to online shopping that is affecting many retailers around the world).
Risk	Risk evaluation is subject to organisational context. If greater risk is accompanied by greater reward, an organisation's appetite for risk (and perhaps the role that opportunity plays in a wider portfolio) will determine the extent to which the market opportunity is considered attractive.

Importantly, it is the combination of these factors that drives attractiveness: a large market is not necessarily attractive if it is in decline (although it may be), or it may be less attractive than a smaller market with lower competitive intensity and higher profitability.

Market size

There are three broad approaches to market sizing that are commonly used:

1 **Top-down**

This is normally the place to start. If you are lucky, there may be government or trade association data that provides you with the size of the exact market you are considering (e.g. the IFPI for global music data). However, this is rarely the case. More likely, if you do find official or established data for a market, it will have either a broader or narrower definition than the market you are trying to size. Consequently, you will then need to make some assumptions to narrow or scale up the market size to reflect your market of interest. For example, to estimate the market for rap music in Germany, you might take data for the total German music market and apply an estimate of what percentage of that market relates to rap (which might come from a market survey).

[14] Kim, W.C. and Mauborgne, R. (2005) *Blue Ocean Strategy: How to create uncontested market space and make the competition irrelevant*, Boston, MA: Harvard Business School Press.

Sometimes, top-down estimation can be derived through collating and contrasting views of market experts to come to a consensus view.

2 Bottom-up: supply-side build-up

An alternative to the top-down data approach is to take a bottom-up view based on supply. In this scenario, you sum up the revenues of all providers supplying the market of interest. There is still an art to this in practice. For example, some companies will serve other markets in addition to the one of interest. In such a case, you might therefore start with the company's official revenues from its accounts but then estimate the proportion associated with the market you are sizing. Note that this approach has the limitation of sizing that part of the total addressable market that is being served, and does not account for currently unserved demand.

3 Bottom-up: demand-side build-up

The third, and perhaps most common, approach to market sizing is modelling the drivers of demand. Even if one of the two other approaches above has been used to get to an overall market size, this demand-side modelling can be used to break this number down into, for example, the required segments. The demand-side build-up typically follows a three-step process.

Figure 4.5 Market sizing process using demand drivers

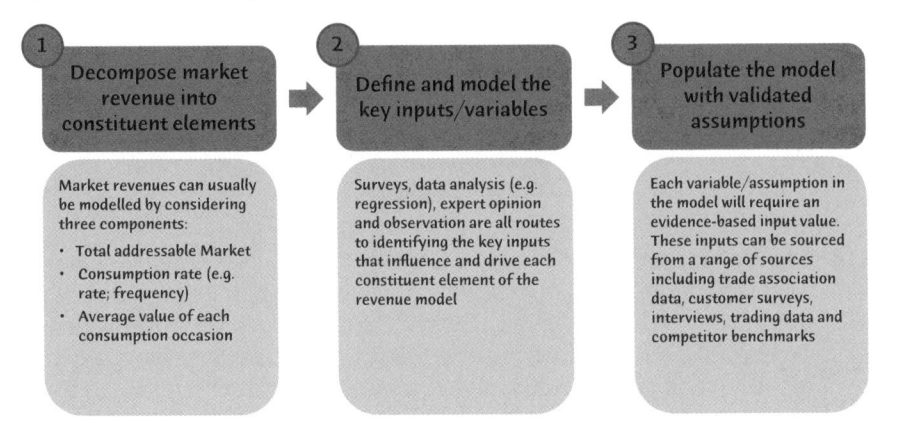

1. Decompose market revenue into constituent elements	2. Define and model the key inputs/variables	3. Populate the model with validated assumptions
Market revenues can usually be modelled by considering three components: • Total addressable Market • Consumption rate (e.g. rate; frequency) • Average value of each consumption occasion	Surveys, data analysis (e.g. regression), expert opinion and observation are all routes to identifying the key inputs that influence and drive each constituent element of the revenue model	Each variable/assumption in the model will require an evidence-based input value. These inputs can be sourced from a range of sources including trade association data, customer surveys, interviews, trading data and competitor benchmarks

For example, a very simple estimate of cinema market revenues in the UK might decompose market revenues into three revenue streams – tickets, concessions and advertising – and size them as shown in Figure 4.6.

The variables for these three revenue streams could then be estimated through surveys, historical transaction data, interviews with advertising agencies and other sources. The same method can also be used to size specific segments, adjusting the variables to reflect the values for that segment (e.g. for family groups, the number of admissions, percentage retail conversion and average transaction value may be quite different to the average for the cinema–going public as a whole).

Figure 4.6 Calculating cinema ticket revenues in the UK

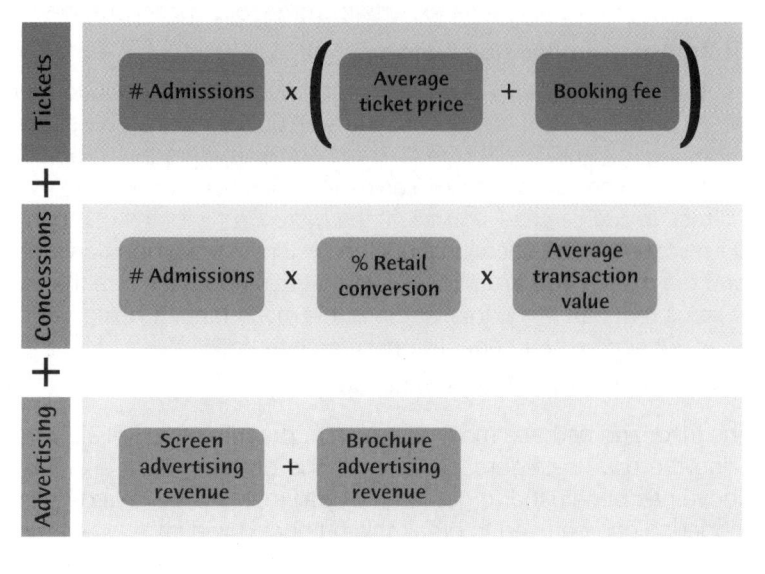

Triangulation – a principle introduced in Chapter 3 – is particularly important when market sizing. Given the assumption-driven nature of the exercise, comparing the number against other sources is very useful, if not essential. In the case of the UK cinema market, potential triangulations could include:

- **Top-down approach 1:** using official data from the UK Cinema Association (a trade body). Indeed, if you have data such as this, which is recognised industry-wide, it should serve as the starting point. Note, however, that this data does not give you a breakdown by segment, so you would still need to model this separately (e.g. informed by a survey of cinema-goers).

- **Top-down approach 2:** using a panel of experts from different functions within the organisation to challenge the numbers (e.g. through discussion or by using the Delphi method, where the experts are sent questionnaires and respond anonymously, several rounds of the questionnaire are issued, with everyone seeing everyone else's responses from the previous round and being offered the opportunity to revise their own, continuing until there is broad consensus).

- **Bottom-up approach:** summing the revenues of the three largest cinema chains – Cineworld, Odeon and Vue – who represent about 70 per cent of the market, and then scaling it up to 100 per cent of the market, giving you a supply-side view of the size of the market.

Whichever approach you take, always define clearly the purpose for sizing the market, and the use to which this market sizing will be put. For example, simply estimating the size of the potential market for biscuits may not be useful for a business which is new to the category and which does not have existing relationships with the large supermarket chains, given that this category will be fiercely protected by the large incumbent brands. In this case, considering the channels to which you are likely to have access in the early years, and sizing the market related to them, would be more useful data on which to base a market entry decision.

> ### Ten-pin bowling
> To estimate the size of the maintenance market for ten-pin bowling lanes, a range of options exists. An assumption-led estimate based on modelling the number of ten-pin bowling centres in the country, the average number of lanes in a centre, the frequency of the maintenance schedule and the average cost of maintaining a lane may suffice.
>
> This might then be triangulated with the revenues of suppliers that provide these services and the opinions of key stakeholders in the market (e.g. managers of bowling centres, suppliers of specialist bowling lane maintenance equipment) to get to a rough estimate. If this is insufficiently accurate for the requirements of the business (see the 'Good enough is good enough' principle in Chapter 3), a more comprehensive audit or survey may be required.

Market growth

As with market sizing, there is no one right way to forecast the future growth rates of a market. Instead, it is usually sensible to triangulate the results from two or more of the following techniques.

Table 4.2 Approaches to market growth rate estimation

Technique	Description
Historical extrapolation	Whilst historical market performance is no guarantee of future performance, trends and trajectories are a useful reference point. Such trends can then be dialled up or down based on more qualitative views of the future (e.g. for a cyclical business such as one selling white goods for the home, we might lower the growth rate relative to its recent historical levels if the economy is expected to enter a downturn following a recent period of economic growth).
Growth driver analysis	Having defined the constituent elements of your market sizing model, and the key inputs that drive it, regression analysis and other techniques can be used to model the shape and impact of these key variables on the market going forward. Thus, the forecast levels of housing transactions and house moves could be an important driver of fitted furniture.

(continued)

Table 4.2 Approaches to market growth rate estimation (*continued*)

Technique	Description
Market proxies	The future growth expectations of a market can be gauged by looking at proxy markets (typically either from other geographic markets or from other sectors). Thus, a Polish retailer of smart products for the home might look to North America's adoption of the internet of things, or its own country's adoption of mobile phones, as a proxy for how the technology might develop in Poland.
Expert forecasts	As with market sizing, expert opinion on the market outlook can be a useful guide to anticipated growth.
Buyer intentions or outlook	Interviews with buyers in a B2B environment, or surveys of consumers in a B2C one, can also generate data on the expected future growth rate. However, careful consideration must be given to the way in which the questions are asked to ensure responses are not skewed (e.g. a consumer responding to whether she intends to buy more, less or the same amount of a particular product will be influenced by her own economic outlook, which may not be aligned with what others are expecting, or what will actually happen).

One further wrinkle in the growth story is the extent to which your organisation feels it can affect the growth of a market or market segment through the introduction of an innovative proposition or marketing approach. For example, the popcorn market was relatively stable for many years until the introduction of premium popcorn through new channels (e.g. supermarkets, train stations, convenience stores, coffee shops) grew the whole market.

Market profitability

Growth without profitability is a fast track to bankruptcy. To understand market profitability, we must consider three related ideas:

1 **Scale:** the overall level of current profitability in the market.
2 **Spread:** the distribution of that profitability across the value chain and market participants.
3 **Shifts:** the trajectory of, and anticipated changes to, future profitability.

Scale: overall profitability

The overall profitability of a market is simply the average profitability of all the companies that operate within it.[15] Having defined your market, and the categories of companies that operate within it, you can compile a list of companies and

[15] As with market sizing, attribution judgements will need to be taken where companies operate across multiple segments and their financials are not split out.

collate their financial statements. Profitability is then calculated by summing the required figures to determine profitability, four common measures of which are shown below.

Table 4.3 Three common profitability measures

Measure	Description	Formula
Gross profit	The profit made after accounting for all direct costs associated with the sale (e.g. materials, labour to produce the product).	(net sales[16] – cost of goods sold) ÷ net sales
Operating profit/EBIT	The profit earned from core business operations. Operating profit or EBIT (earnings before interest and tax) excludes any profits earned from an organisation's investments, and is calculated before the deduction of relevant interest and taxes.	(operating sales – cost of goods sold – operating expenses – depreciation – amortisation) ÷ operating sales
Net profit	The bottom line once all costs (direct and indirect) have been substracted from sales.	(net sales – cost of goods sold – operating expenses – non-operating expenses) ÷ net sales
ROIC	Return on invested capital (ROIC) measures how much investors in a business are earning from the capital they have invested. It is arguably the most useful single measure of profitability when evaluating market profitability for the purpose of comparison across businesses either in the same industry or across industries.	net operating profit after tax[17] ÷ operating capital[18]

[16] Net sales = total sales – sales returns.
[17] Net operating profit after tax (NOPAT) = earnings before interest and tax (EBIT) x (1 – tax rate.)
[18] Operating capital = average debt liabilities + average stockholders' equity.

Although ROIC is typically seen as the best measure for evaluating value creation, its usage is limited by the availability of data (especially when assessing competitors) and net or operating profit is often used in its stead.

Spread: distribution of profitability

Even when a market is highly profitable in aggregate, the distribution of that profit across the different operators within it can vary significantly. As we described at the start of this chapter, establishing the 'perimeter' of the market is the starting point. Consider the airline industry. The International Air Transport Association (IATA) defines the air travel industry as comprising the participants shown in Figure 4.7.[19]

Having defined the types of participant, the next step is to estimate their relative profitability. This typically uses one of the profit measures listed above, taking a basket of companies to represent each type of participant. This can be challenging – data from pure players (i.e. organisations that only serve a specific part of a specific market) will need to be combined with that of mixed players (i.e. organisations that serve several parts of the market, or other markets as well). In the case of mixed players, the principle of triangulation is important again, with everything from expert opinion to news releases being used to estimate the relative proportion of sales and profitability of these sales. Consider again the case of air travel.

Figure 4.8 shows clearly that travel agents and computer reservation systems offer attractive potential returns in the air travel market, whereas manufacturers and airlines are, on average, value-destroying given that their ROIC is less than their weighted average cost of capital (WACC). Profit pool analysis is a common tool for assessing the spread of profitability in an industry and involves estimating the aggregate profits for an industry and then allocating them to key elements (e.g. value chain steps, distribution channels, customer segments). This approach requires the triangulation of top-down and bottom-up approaches (e.g. modelling profitability of key players in the market, incorporating expert opinion), mixing art with science.

Shifts: future profitability

Having understood the overall profitability of the market, and broadly how that is distributed, the final question to answer is how this profitability will shift and change over time – in terms of both absolute scale and the distribution across operators.

---

[19] Pearce, B. (2013) Profitability and the air transport value chain, IATA Economics Briefing No. 10.

Figure 4.7 Air travel participants

Manufacturers | Lessors | Services (e.g. maintenance) | Airports | Air navigation services | Airlines | Computer reservation systems | Travel agents | Freight forwarders

Figure 4.8 Weighted average ROIC for different parts of the air travel value chain

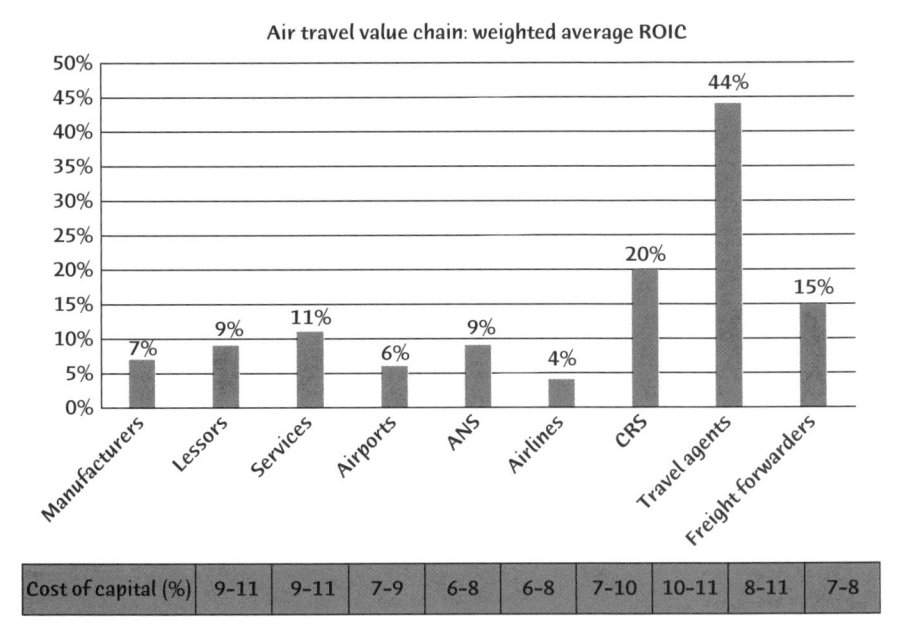

Air travel value chain: weighted average ROIC

| Cost of capital (%) | 9-11 | 9-11 | 7-9 | 6-8 | 6-8 | 7-10 | 10-11 | 8-11 | 7-8 |

Consider markets like recorded music or branded fast-moving consumer goods (FMCG), where power, and hence profitability, have shifted over time. The outlook for future profitability is shaped by the next two determinants of market attractiveness, to which we now turn: the macro-economic environment and market forces.

Macro-economic environment

The well-known PESTLE framework groups key external factors that could influence, or have an impact on, an organisation under six main headings.

Table 4.4 PESTLE factors for macro-economic analysis

Category	Description	Typical factors	Example
Political	Policies and practices of governments and other political institutions	Trade policies, political stability, industry regulations	Brexit
Economic	Economic performance, policies and structures in the markets in which you operate	GDP growth, exchange rates, interest rates, inflation, cost of living, consumer spending	Hyperinflation in Venezuela

(continued)

Table 4.4 PESTLE factors for macro-economic analysis (*continued*)

Category	Description	Typical factors	Example
Social	Social structures, norms, preferences, attitudes, beliefs and trends	Demographics, lifestyle trends, consumer attitudes, major cultural events, advertising	The ageing demographics of many Western cultures
Technology	Technological advances and digital developments	Research and development, automation, technology innovation	Tesla's electric cars
Legal	Legal and regulatory determinants or influences	Employment law, copyright, consumer law, discrimination law	The UK's introduction of the mandatory National Living Wage in April 2016 significantly changed the profitability of a number of British businesses
Environmental	Environmental protection and ecological impact	Legislation and consumer expectation on pollution, water usage and sustainability	US withdrawal from the Paris climate agreement in 2017

Up in smoke or basking in the sun?

Consider the PESTLE effects on the UK tobacco market, where the big five (British American Tobacco, China Tobacco, Imperial Brands, Japan Tobacco International and Philip Morris International) have seen core tobacco sales decline due to a combination of taxation, smoking bans in public spaces, public education on its health impact and ever-tighter sales and marketing regulations (e.g. standardised packaging, graphic images of the health impact of cigarettes printed on packets, putting tobacco out of sight in shops).

The reverse can also be true, as was the case where government subsidies to support greener energy sources drove a significant increase in the sales of solar panels. Once these subsidies were withdrawn, market growth quickly subsided.

Whilst PESTLE considers the impact of the external environment in areas other than just profitability, looking at these areas through this lens is a useful one when considering or anticipating the future profitability of your business. Such analysis will be primarily qualitative in nature but can be translated into 'real' numbers. For example, the World Bank Group's 'Doing Business' report[20] has, since 2004, empirically evaluated and ranked the ease of doing business in 190 countries, directly influencing the decision-making of governments and businesses alike.

Market forces and trends

Competitive intensity

A key determinant of market attractiveness, and long-term profit potential, is competitive intensity. The two classic ways of measuring it are:

1 Market share of the top 'n' companies (usually 5), by sales, employment or some other relevant indicator.

2 The Herfindahl–Hirschman Index (HHI), calculated by squaring the percentage market share of each company in the market and summing them. The lower the HHI, the more competitive the market. The highest value the HHI can have is 10,000 (where one company has 100 per cent share monopoly). UK merger guidelines characterise markets with an HHI of above 2,000 as highly concentrated. The US government classifies markets with an HHI below 1,000 as competitive (i.e. no dominant provider). Looking at the HHI over time can be particularly instructive. As a rule of thumb, calculate the HHI based on the largest companies that, in total, add up to 50 per cent of the market. Beyond that, research indicates the incremental change in HHI through further analysis becomes relatively immaterial.

Michael Porter's famous work on the Five Forces[21] supports qualitative analysis of competitive intensity.

Why am I covering Porter's Five Forces, one of the best-known and most widely used traditional strategy tools, in a book about agile strategy? Before you tweet, blog or email your righteous frustrations, please bear with me. Some do indeed argue that the dynamics of a networked economy, digitisation and globalisation are fundamentally altering the nature of competition. I do not disagree. However, as a framework for understanding an organisation's competitive context *at a point in time* (and this chapter is about baselining and context), Porter's Five Forces remain useful, and such dynamics can fit within it.

---

[20] See www.doingbusiness.org/reports [accessed 13 May 2018].
[21] Porter, M.E. (1980) *Competitive Strategy: Techniques for analyzing industries and competitors*, New York: The Free Press.

Table 4.5 Porter's Five Forces

Force	*Summary of its effect*
Competitive rivalry	The greater the competitive intensity (e.g. number, concentration), ease with which customers can switch (e.g. switching costs, loyalty), impact of losing customers (e.g. high fixed costs) and difficulty of exiting, the lower the attractiveness and more intense the profit (price) pressures.
Threat of entry	The easier it is for new companies to enter (e.g. capital requirements, customer switching costs, access to distribution) and differentiate (e.g. product, cost), the greater the competitive threat.
Threat of substitution	The greater the benefits from substitute propositions (e.g. product performance, cost) and the lower the cost of switching, the greater the competitive threat.
Supplier power	The more important the supplier is to the industry (e.g. availability of substitutes, concentration of suppliers), and the easier it is for it to forward integrate (e.g. switching costs, differentiation, policy and regulation), the greater the share of industry profits it can command (see the spread of profitability discussion earlier in the chapter).
Buyer power	The more important the buyer (e.g. buyer concentration), the easier it is to backward integrate (e.g. switching costs, differentiation, policy and regulation) and the greater the market transparency (e.g. pricing), the greater the share of industry profits it can command.

It is less adept as a *dynamic* tool for managing competitive dynamics and it does not reflect other aspects of market attractiveness or what matters most to a customer, but that is not its role. In the next chapter, when we consider a strategic intelligence system and the dynamic requirements of research and analysis, we will explore this in more detail.

Market trends

To understand future market attractiveness, you also need to gaze into the crystal ball of market trends (covering demand, supply and technology) and consider your potential to benefit from them. This is an art, but methods used can include:

- **Looking to proxy or reference markets:** understanding how other markets have developed, either as an indicator of how your market might change or to inspire you to lead a supply-led change yourself, is common practice. I know a marketer from a large Spanish food manufacturer who visits the UK

Figure 4.9 Porter's Five Forces

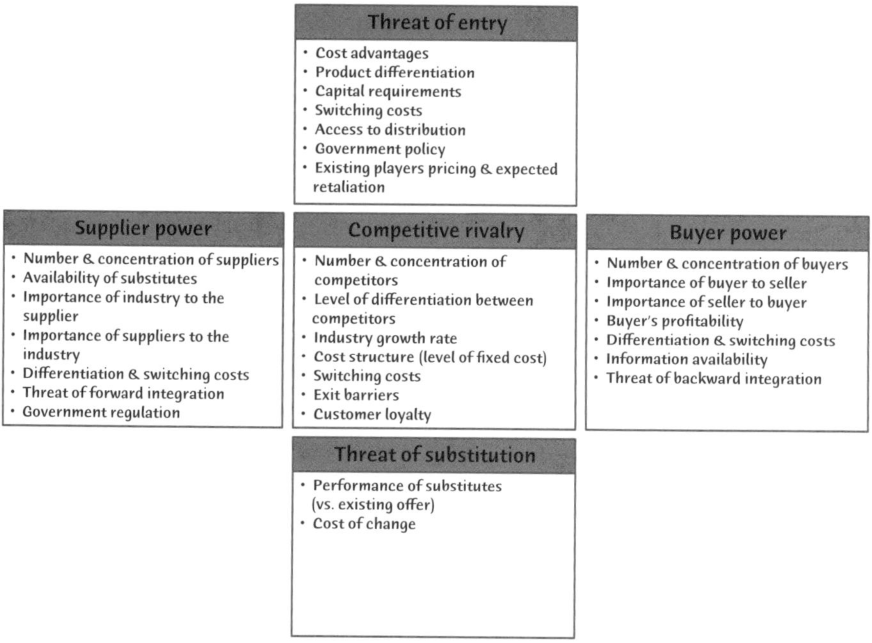

Threat of entry
- Cost advantages
- Product differentiation
- Capital requirements
- Switching costs
- Access to distribution
- Government policy
- Existing players pricing & expected retaliation

Supplier power
- Number & concentration of suppliers
- Availability of substitutes
- Importance of industry to the supplier
- Importance of suppliers to the industry
- Differentiation & switching costs
- Threat of forward integration
- Government regulation

Competitive rivalry
- Number & concentration of competitors
- Level of differentiation between competitors
- Industry growth rate
- Cost structure (level of fixed cost)
- Switching costs
- Exit barriers
- Customer loyalty

Buyer power
- Number & concentration of buyers
- Importance of buyer to seller
- Importance of seller to buyer
- Buyer's profitability
- Differentiation & switching costs
- Information availability
- Threat of backward integration

Threat of substitution
- Performance of substitutes (vs. existing offer)
- Cost of change

every six months to explore current UK food trends, as they see these as forebearers to subsequent trends in the Spanish market (UK businesses, in turn, often look to the US for the latest food and beverage demand trends). In a similar vein, public sector organisations often look to practices in the private sector in the hope of finding new means and approaches to serving the public more effectively. Identifying such opportunities early can change perspectives on the relative attractiveness of the market.

- **Applying and extrapolating megatrends in relation to your markets:** population growth, ageing populations in Western countries, the rise of the middle classes in developing ones, globalisation of trade (and resultant nationalist backlashes), technology advancements (e.g. mobile, artificial intelligence) and business model innovation are all megatrends contributing to the transformation of our personal and professional lives. Understanding how these trends could translate into attractive longer-term opportunities in your markets is a valuable exercise.

- **Consumer insight:** in an interview with *Business Week* in 1998, Steve Jobs stated: 'A lot of times people don't know what they want until you show it to them.' For B2C businesses, this creates a significant challenge. Pioneering work in human-centred design (HCD) by IDEO, amongst others, shifted the thinking from asking consumers what was needed to improve things to monitoring, observing or even being them. Techniques such as observation, digital diaries, social media listening, customer data analytics, in-context immersion (where you put yourself in the consumers' shoes) and co-creation (where products are developed in collaboration with consumers) are all leading to a better understanding of needs and trends in the marketplace, and with it a clearer understanding of its attractiveness. We discuss the role of 'design thinking' in defining your Horizon in Chapters 6 and 7.

- **Competitor intelligence:** an understanding of the objectives and R&D priorities of key competitors can provide some indication of their own assumptions on how the market is changing, and how they plan to accommodate these changes.

The value of understanding market trends lies in:

- Identifying opportunities that your competition has not.
- Determining effective ways to exploit them through your competitive position and AIR choices, which competitors find difficult to replicate.

The table below lists a wide range of primary and secondary data sources that can be used to get a qualitative view on market trends and dynamics.

Tracking trends over time is an important element of agile insight, and many of the sources listed in the table can be tapped into on a regular basis and used to feed the organisation's strategic intelligence system (addressed in the next chapter).

Table 4.6 Market insight data sources

Primary sources	Secondary sources
Competitors	Academic papers/journals
Conferences/trade shows	Analyst reports
Customers	Annual reports
Discussion forums	Company newsletters
Employees: current	Directories
Employees: former	Government publications
Industry/product/general wiki	Market research agencies
Industry professionals	Online databases
Internet blogs	Press (local, national)
Investment analysts	Promotional materials
Journalists	Subscription news feeds
Marketplace surveys	Syndicated research
Newsgroups	Trade organisations
Observations	Trade publications
Professional institutes	Websites
Social media (via social listening)	
Trade unions and associations	
Vendors and suppliers	

Risk

All this market potential can make a person giddy. However, the shadowy coun-terpart to the beaming light of opportunity is risk, which can take many forms, but is often broken down into four categories.

Table 4.7 Risk categories and definition

Risk category	Sources of risk	Example
Strategic	Economy, politics, society, market, competition	For a retailer of console games, the large console manufacturers (Sony, Microsoft, Nintendo) may move to a download-only model, eliminating the retailer's role in the value chain
Operational	People, processes, sys-tems, controls, externals (e.g. suppliers)	Inability to find skilled labour can be a constraint on growth for high-tech businesses
Compliance	Laws, regulations, policies, procedures	A business operating gaming (gambling) machines will be fined or even have its licence revoked by the regulator if machines are not compliant with strict market regulatory requirements
Financial	Treasury, tax, pensions, accounting and reporting	If local currency weakens against that of your largest markets, input costs will increase

The extent to which risks affect the attractiveness of a market is determined by four key factors:

- **Likelihood:** how likely it is that a risk will become a reality.
- **Impact:** the extent of the impact on the business if that risk does become reality.
- **Mitigation:** the efficacy of any risk mitigation, and the speed with which it would be put in place.
- **Uncertainty and volatility:** returning to the VUCA theme, there is so much uncertainty and volatility in some markets that the very act of identify-ing risks in the first place, or new ones suddenly appearing, is troublesome and itself a risk for the business. Early entry into developing markets is a classic example of this kind of risk.

Consider the examples of online clothing (Boo.com), pet care and food (Pets.com) and media (AOL Time Warner), where strategic (timing, market positioning, competition), operational (technology maturity and succession) and financial (large-scale, up-front cash investment in infrastructure) risks all played a role in burning investment capital with negative returns. Some of the approaches within the design and action phases of RADAR can help manage risk and defer 'binary decision points' (the big Yes/No decision) until more information is available, and thereby risk reduced. We will explore these in Chapters 7 and 8, when we discuss Horizon management, as it is one of the three components of your Horizon's ARC.

Competitive position

Taking all the above into account, and having determined the extent to which the business segments in which you operate are attractive, you are still only half way to understanding why value is created in the organisation. The other half requires analysis of the 3Ps of your competitive position:

- *Positioning:* the place your organisation or brand occupies in the mind of your customer.
- *Proposition:* the benefits of your offer (tangible and intangible, functional and emotional), and how customers access it.
- *Performance:* how well you operationalise the above elements (e.g. quality, consistency).

It is the interaction and alignment of these three elements that drives your competitive position. The organisation's unifying purpose (see Chapters 1 and 7) drives this alignment through its encapsulation of the organisation's reason for being (the why) and its role in guiding action (the how). For example, Walmart's proposition and positioning target the value-focused shopper and are designed 'to save people money so they can live better'.[22] To fulfil this, performance must focus on keeping costs to a minimum whilst preserving the requisite level of quality and service.

Assessment of competitive position is often clouded by focusing on what the organisation does well, regardless of whether it is truly valued by the customer. In practice, one key factor underpins competitive position: relevance. A competitive position is only useful if it is aligned with what your target customers need and value in that business segment or market. Relevance is shorthand for the extent to which what you represent, offer and are good at achieves this alignment.

Knowing needs is a 'need to know'

Relevance necessitates a thorough understanding of customer needs. The table below lists several sources organisations can tap into to achieve this.[23]

---

[22] See http://corporate.walmart.com [accessed 10 September 2017].
[23] See https://econsultancy.com/blog/66831-six-brand-case-studies-that-proved-the-value-of-customer-experience [accessed 21 January 2019].

Table 4.8 Sources for identifying customer needs

Source	Description
Customers	Customers themselves are the obvious starting point, although it is surprising how often the breadth of opportunities here is overlooked. Typical approaches include: **1 Focus groups** Focus groups are a useful way of gathering in-depth insight with a small number of existing, lapsed or non-customers. The ability to engage directly, probe, test (e.g. visuals, explore actual product) and contrast opinion is particularly helpful for developing or testing initial hypotheses. **2 Interviews** One-to-one customer interviews are often used in B2B, particularly where there are a small number of high-value customers. Where relationships are strong, and communication open, such interviews can provide a rich source of information on customers' needs and challenges, offering the opportunity to create new or improved propositions. **3 Self-documentation (e.g. digital diaries)** Longitudinal studies, where a group of customers capture their key activities, reflections, opinions and attitudes over a period of time, can provide useful raw material for understanding customer needs and issues. **4 Surveys** Surveys provide quantitative data that can be used to model the scale and attractiveness of potential opportunities. They usually benefit from doing some broader market analysis or qualitative work first (such as focus groups or interviews), to inform the questioning. **5 Feedback analysis** There are a wide range of sources of customer feedback that an organisation can use to identify opportunities. Communication directly with the company (e.g. formal customer feedback, contact centre calls, social media communications directly to the company, website enquiries) can be combined with other external sources (e.g. social media, forums, review sites) to provide a rich set of data. Social listening has grown as a discipline, as businesses and the technology have got better at separating insights from the noise.

(continued)

Table 4.8 Sources for identifying customer needs (*continued*)

Source	Description
6 Customer journey mapping	Ensuring all the customer touchpoints (the places where the customer comes into contact with your organisation) perform to a high standard has been a common focus area for many organisations. However, examining the customer's end-to-end journey – and the cumulative effect of all of these interactions and the activities and time between them – can offer significant additional insight and opportunities. It represents a shift from optimising silos to optimising the full customer experience.
	Consider Macmillan, the cancer support charity. Its research in 2012 identified that people affected by cancer needed additional help with everyday tasks (e.g. shopping, ironing), and that one in four of them lacked everyday support from family and friends. Its solution – to create a 'Team Up' online marketplace where support could be offered to people affected by cancer. This was not about optimising the touchpoints of people affected by cancer and Macmillan, but about addressing the customer journey from diagnosis to cure or end of life.
7 Customer observation	Observing how a customer goes about satisfying a need can lead to new ideas and solutions. Manufacturers of medical technology products have long subscribed to the process of observing surgical procedures to identify market and product improvement opportunities (e.g. the introduction of drug-eluting stents which significantly reduced a common surgical issue of restenosis – the re-narrowing of a blood vessel).
8 Be the customer (immersion in the customer context)	Rather than watch a customer, sometimes the best way to discover opportunities is to be one; spending time immersed in the customer context can lead to a broad range of insights. This technique is prevalent in service industries, particularly healthcare and hospitality, and in the retail industry in the guise of mystery shopping (where a company audits its retail experience by pretending to be a customer).
	All of these sources can help identify needs, prevalent attitudes, behaviours, opinions and issues that can be addressed.

Source	Description
Staff	Staff are a key source of customer information and insight. Whilst those that interact directly with the customer are typically the most useful in this regard (e.g. sales staff, customer service, store staff), do not overlook others who may offer insight from another perspective (e.g. operations staff, support staff).
Other stakeholders	Customers and staff are not the only stakeholders who can provide insight into customer needs and opportunities. Suppliers, competitors, regulators, consumer groups and a wide range of other stakeholders could all have information or insight that could lead to new opportunities.
Business analytics	Business analytics is a rich source for identifying opportunities. For example, analysing a customer database, transaction data or website activity can provide insight into customer segments, product complementarities, channel usage, timing of purchases or methods of payment, to name but a few. The act of understanding previous failures can also offer useful (albeit painful) insights on opportunities.
Competitor analysis	Analysing what competitors are doing, and how well received (or not) these offers are, can lead to opportunities for your own business. This can range from simple replication (e.g. the growth of the premium coffee market on the back of Starbucks shaping the market) to opportunism when your competitors are distracted (e.g. in the midst of an acquisition).
Trade press	Analysing the trade press, which covers market and competitor news, can be a valuable source for identifying opportunities.

When exploring customer needs, consider three categories:

- **Existing:** needs that already exist for such customers. For example, in the case of a coffee shop customer, coffee to drink in and coffee to take away are both existing needs.
- **Under-served:** needs that, whilst partially addressed in the market, are not fully satisfied. For example, environmentalist pressures on coffee shops are translating into mainstream concerns about disposable cups and waste, yet chains have been relatively slow to respond (the introduction of bring-your-own cup initiatives being the most notable effort to date).
- **Emerging:** needs that are only now becoming apparent or reaching critical mass. For example, with the rise of the freelance worker, the use of coffee shops as a working space has risen in importance. Some are flipping the coffee shop model on its head (see the Ziferblat example below), but others could emerge that embrace a 'work-first' positioning and proposition.

Ziferblat

Founded in Russia in 2011, Ziferblat is a coffee shop chain with sites across Russia, Europe and the UK that positions itself as offering 'a relaxing sitting room, shared office space, private meeting rooms and a full programme of events'. Rather than pay for coffees and cakes like a traditional coffee shop, Ziferblat charges by the minute for the time you spend there, and then everything you consume is free. It focuses on a customer's need for a space in which to exist – rather than refreshment – as the defining need that it serves.

A strong competitive position is about meeting identified customer needs better than the competition. To assess your organisation's competitive position requires consideration of the two ways in which target customers experience the 3Ps:

- *Psychologically:* what they think, understand and feel about you.
- *Functionally:* how well your offer meets their practical needs.

Let us explore each in turn.

Customer experience: psychological

The assessment of your organisation's psychological competitive position can be approached in several ways – from surveys and structured interviews through to analysis of unstructured data from social media and review sites. In the world of B2C, customer journey mapping has risen in prominence in the past decade; it offers a structured way of analysing how customers engage with a product category or service – exploring how customers feel and act at key touchpoints. At a more generic level, a simple approach is to consider your customers' typical buying cycle.

Figure 4.10 The 3Ps of competitive position

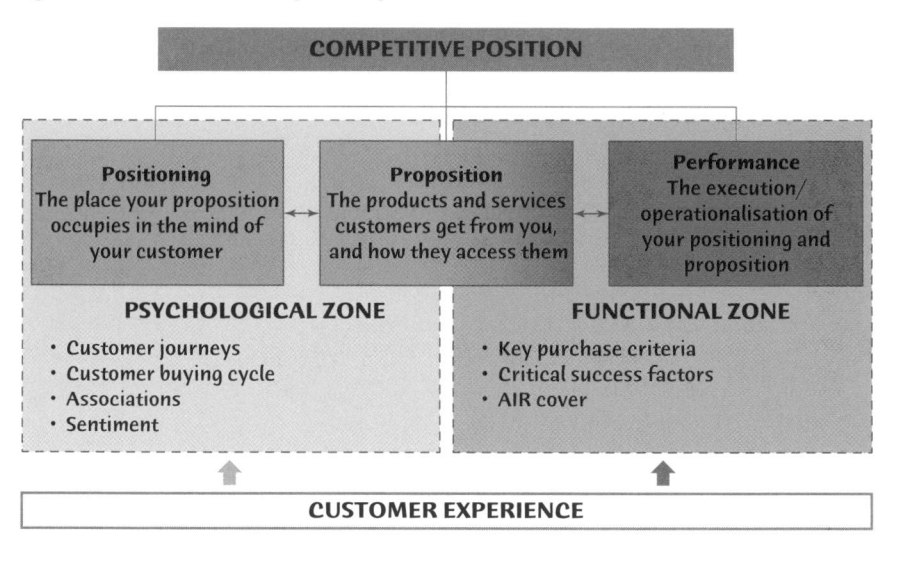

Figure 4.11 A typical customer buying cycle

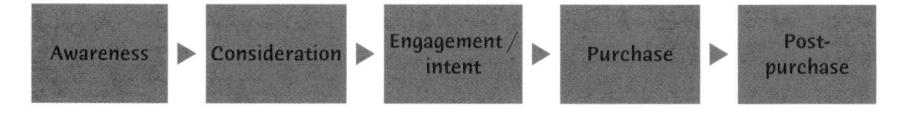

Along each step, there is analysis that can be done, and measures taken, that evaluate your competitive position. For example, the percentage of target customers who are aware of your offer, or would consider it for their next purchase, are key measures of 'share of mind'. Similarly, propensity to buy from your organisation, or measures of advocacy (such as net promoter score), are indicators of the level of positive sentiment customers have towards your organisation and what it offers. Beyond KPIs, there is value in understanding prompted and unprompted associations target customers attach to your organisation, brand or product, and sentiments expressed on social media and review sites.

Whatever approach you adopt, consider the following guidelines:

● Attribute your analysis clearly to the business segment(s) under consideration. Some aspects may apply across several or all segments (e.g. brand awareness) whilst others will be unique to one (e.g. intention to buy).

● Test depth of understanding as well as perceptions – the former is a question of marketing, communication and education and will significantly affect the latter.

● Use a combination of prompted and unprompted questioning to answer different aspects of awareness and association.

Customer experience: functional

Meeting customers' functional requirements is the yin to their psychological yang. To assess your organisation's ability to do so, follow three steps:

Step 1: Identify the key purchase criteria (KPC)

KPC are the key factors influencing a customer's purchase decision for a product or service, and they provide a yardstick against which you can measure your organisation and your competition. To understand them, consider how an individual or organisation experiences value through a purchase. There are five domains:

- **Personal:** this domain comprises two areas: first, confirming one's established sense of self (self-affirmation), second, realising the fullest version of yourself (self-actualisation). In a B2B context, a similar dynamic applies in terms of the organisation's identity.
- **Other people:** the twin benefits of fitting in (acceptance) and making an impression (admiration or appreciation) sit in this domain.
- **Societal:** the social, environmental and ethical impact of a purchase can be an important influencer in the decision-making process.
- **Proposition:** the functional benefits, and how it makes you feel (emotional impact), are the two key product contributions to value.
- **Economic:** from a purely economic perspective, a customer seeks ways in which a purchase will either save money, or generate it.

KPCs in B2C cases are typically identified through the range of customer insight data sources listed earlier. The five domains of customer purchase value are useful both to develop hypotheses to test through the consumer insight, and

Figure 4.12 Five domains of customer purchase value

VALUE DOMAIN	KEY COMPONENTS	
PERSONAL	Self-affirmation	Self-actualisation
OTHER PEOPLE	Acceptance	Impression
SOCIETAL	Environmental	Social & ethical
PROPOSITION	Functional	Emotional
ECONOMIC	Money saving	Money generating

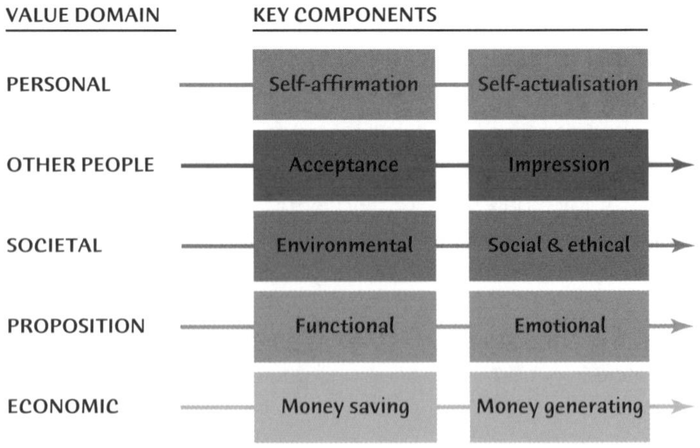

to frame the results of it. Clearly, the five domains will not all be equally relevant for every B2C and B2B situation and environment, and an individual element can mean very different things in different contexts (e.g. consider the functional component of a proposition in B2B bid evaluations, where innovation is often an important criterion).

Following their identification, there is a final, vital stage in understanding KPC: assessing their relative importance. In a B2C environment this is often tested through consumer research (e.g. rating or ranking factors); in a B2B environment, detailed discussion with the customer, or a request for a proposal (RFP), if issued, will bring a level of clarity to this.

Depending on your market, your competitive position within it and timing, KPC can be relatively stable or rapidly changing. Furthermore, new competition, technology or innovations can fundamentally change KPC, as was seen in the early days of smartphones.

Virgin

Richard Branson's Virgin Group oversees a broad set of businesses ranging from trains to mobile operators, healthcare providers to radio stations. What binds this organisation together is its relentless focus on, and satisfaction of, customer need. For example, Virgin Care, a healthcare business, has a monthly 'You said, we did' programme in each of its clinics, which takes regularly collected patient feedback, acts on it and then tells them what has changed. Virgin Atlantic took a decision several years ago to recruit cabin crew not from other airlines, where they felt that the training and focus was wrong, but from other hospitality and customer-centric industries to drive a different level of service. Primacy was given to attitude and mindset. In each case, the priority is on meeting under-served or emerging need.

Step 2: Determine the critical success factors (CSF)

CSFs are the critical things your organisation must get right to satisfy customers' KPC and future shifts in the market. They are shaped by four elements:

- **Customer KPC:** each customer KPC will have associated CSF that drive them. For example, if product durability is a KPC, this raises potential CSF relating to product design and specification, manufacturing, quality control, packaging, storage, and even delivery and after sales service.
- **Market trends and regulations:** markets are dynamic, powered by demand and supply trends and regulatory change (e.g. the introduction of the EU's General Data Protection Regulation in May 2018). These dynamics can introduce new CSF and make current ones redundant.

- **Competition:** new competition, or new manoeuvres from existing competitors, can 'rebase' CSF. For example, Tesco's introduction of its Clubcard (loyalty scheme) in the UK, and its widespread adoption by customers, made a loyalty scheme a CSF for many grocers.
- **Technology:** new technologies can transform CSF – from 24/7 customer service through to next day or even next hour delivery.

Figure 4.13 The shapes of CSFs

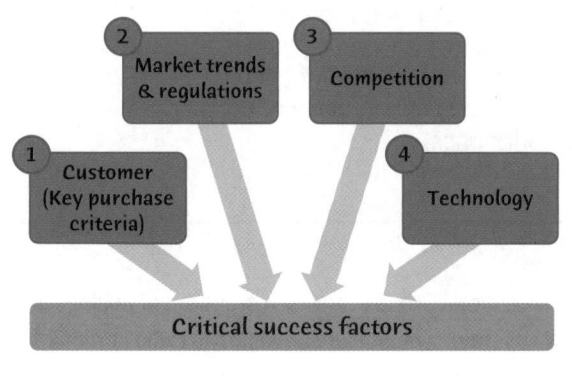

Non-standard standards

The ISOFIX standard for children's car safety seats (introduced by Britax in partnership with Volkswagen in 1997) changed the CSF for this category, but only in certain markets. All US cars manufactured since 2002 have been mandated to include the fittings for ISOFIX, and yet in Australia the use of ISOFIX was only legalised in 2014.

CSF provide a focus for where to invest resources, as they link to what matters to the target segments of the market in which you operate, now and in the future, so think of them as the barometer of relevance. To visualise CSF, it can be helpful to map them on to a value chain (a visual representation of the activities by which an organisation adds value to a product or service). The figure below shows a generic example for a traditional retailer.

Figure 4.14 A traditional retail value chain

Design	Source & procure	Inventory management & distribution	Store operation	Marketing	Sales	Fulfilment	Customer support

However, be cautious when considering CSF, as they can change, sometimes very quickly. The importance of a free meal on a flight rapidly diminished as a new business model, and value proposition was introduced by value airlines. Management of the Horizon, and the monitoring of its ARC, is therefore an ongoing control on the definition of CSF.

Step 3: Calculate your 'AIR cover'

With the CSF clearly defined, the final step in determining your functional competitive position is to evaluate how well your AIR choices address them. To do so:

1 Map your AIR factors to each CSF

A cornerstone of RADAR is the systematic design and management of AIR factors (see Chapters 1 and 7). The important step here is to match them to the CSF, noting that any one individual AIR factor can be relevant to more than one CSF.

2 Calculate your AIR cover score for each CSF

Having aligned your AIR factors to the relevant CSF, you can then quantify the level of AIR cover offered by your current Horizon. AIR cover expresses the extent to which your current Horizon addresses the CSF you have identified. An example for product quality is shown below.

Figure 4.15 Example of AIR cover assessment for one KPC

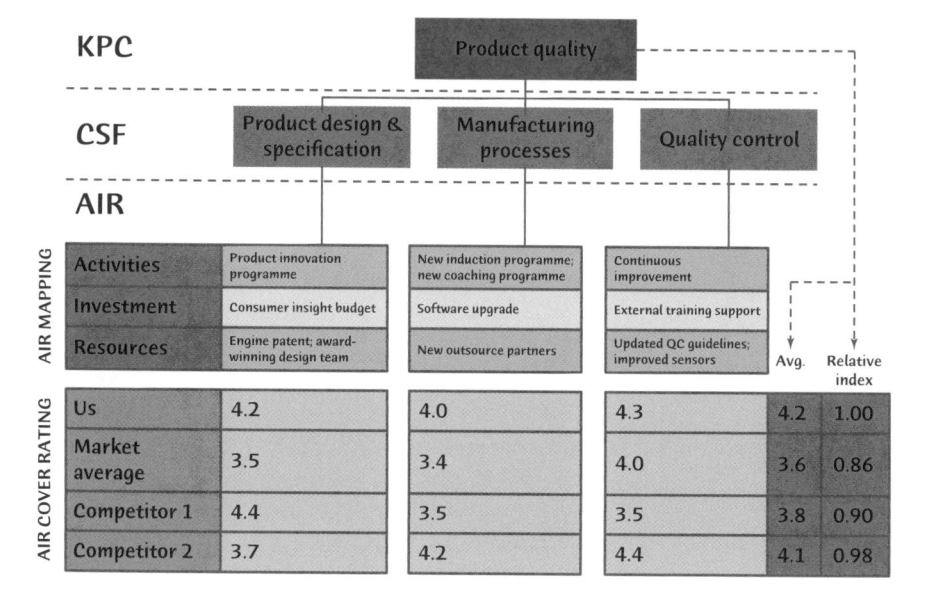

In the above example, the following activities would take place:

● Having identified the product quality KPC and associated CSF, consider the AIR factors within your organisation that contribute to the fulfilment of each CSF. In this example, under Product design and specification, activities include a company-wide programme to develop the next-generation product; investment includes a new consumer insight budget, and key resources include patents and an award-winning design team.

- Next, score your AIR cover out of five. Depending on time and resources, the level of detail can range from a high-level assessment via discussion with internal and external stakeholders through to a more structured and rigorous assessment of the key factors underlying each CSF. In the example above, the rating of 4.2 against Product design and specification was calculated by scoring the following criteria out of five, and then averaging the result.

Table 4.9 Example of AIR cover calculation for one CSF

CSF: product design and specification	
Constituent factors	Score (out of 5)
1. Quality of insight used to inform design	4
2. Quality of design processes, systems and tools	4
3. Capability and capacity of design team	4
4. Alignment with wider organisation (e.g. manufacturing)	5
5. Financial 'return on innovation'	4
TOTAL	**21**
AVERAGE	**4.2**

In this example, a straight average was used, but the factors could be weighted if appropriate.

- Repeat the above for each CSF under that KPC, and then average them to get a total KPC figure. Again, a straight average was used here, but the factors could be weighted if appropriate.
- Next, estimate a similar AIR cover score for the total market and for any significant specific competitors (in this example, it has been done for two competitors). If you are unable to do this for each CSF, estimate it at a KPC level. Data sources to use can include buying and deconstructing the product (often done by technology and furniture manufacturers), mystery shopping (possible for both B2C and B2B), customer surveys, interviews with suppliers or ex-employees, trade press or publicly-released company information and announcements.
- Finally, create a relative index by dividing the total market's and each specific competitor's average KPC rating by the highest score achieved (in this case, your organisation was highest with an average of 4.2, so it achieves an index of 1.00).

3 Create an 'up, down, in, out' plan

By replicating the above for each KPC, you can get a view of the relative strength of your AIR cover. This, alongside the relative importance rating given to each KPC, will give an indication of where to focus, as shown below.

Figure 4.16 AIR cover vs. importance matrix

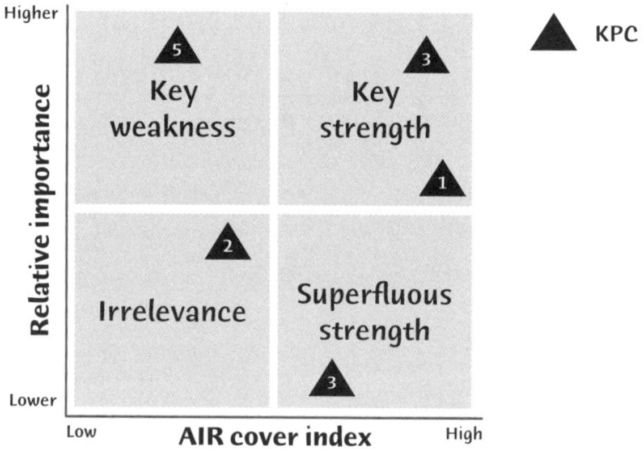

The AIR cover/importance matrix reveals four zones, with one or more of five choices available.

When evaluating your strategic options for AIR cover, consider the following:

- **5KQs:** Regularly refer the discussion back to two sets of choices expressed in the five key questions model:

  - Where can you truly differentiate yourself? (The 'What makes us great?' question.)

  - Where must you make changes either to raise performance to meet at least minimum performance levels in key areas or to lower investment in unimportant areas? (The 'How should we adapt?' question and ADAPT areas introduced in Chapter 3.)

- **Interdependencies between KPC:** Although a specific KPC may not be valued by the market, the AIR factors supporting it may also be supporting other KPC that are. For example, a new warehouse management system supporting vendor-managed inventory, which in this example has limited appeal to an organisation's customers, may also significantly reduce the time and cost involved in returning items - another KPC that is highly valued.

- **Alternative application of the same AIR factors:** Linked to the idea of interdependency is that of alternative applications for the AIR cover that is supporting an unvalued KPC. There are some interesting examples of products (resources) being repositioned to meet a different need. Listerine was originally a surgical antiseptic and a cure for gonorrhoea before being

Table 4.10 The four zones of the AIR cover vs. importance matrix

Zone	Description	Strategic choices
Key weakness	Your competitive position is materially weaker than that of the market/key competitors in an area important to customers	● **Up:** build up AIR cover to minimum threshold or beyond to compete (e.g. strategic initiatives, training, technology). This can include building on an existing key strength to extend further leadership in an area of established excellence
Key strength	Your competitive position is materially better than that of the market/key competitors in an area important to customers	● **Down:** reduce investment in activities and resources supporting superfluous strengths or irrelevance, if they are not supporting other CSFs ● **In:** bring in new resources or capabilities to shore up organisational weaknesses or further consolidate strengths (e.g. partners, acquisitions)
Superfluous strength	Your competitive position is strong in areas that customers value less	● **Out:** divest activities and resources supporting superfluous strengths or irrelevance, if they are not supporting other CSFs in the business
Irrelevance	Your competitive position is weak in areas that customers value less	● **Do nothing:** take no action initially, and revisit further down the line if circumstances change

repositioned as a mouthwash. In other cases, resources that did not find success in their original guise were hugely successful in another. See the example below.

- **KPC positioning may vary by target business segment:** AIR factors that are not wanted by one part of the market may be highly valued by

---

Better the Snowdevil you know

When Tobias Lutke, Daniel Weinand and Scott Lake looked to launch Snowdevil, an online snowboard equipment store, they could not find an e-commerce platform they liked, and decided to build their own. The Snowdevil store was not successful, but the storefront they created was – they renamed it Shopify, started to sell it to others who needed a better e-commerce platform and it now powers over 500,000 businesses in 175 countries.

another. For example, a fully staffed customer installation support helpline may be highly valued by DIY enthusiasts, but not by trade buyers who would rather have the product without that additional cost factored in.

Results

The SCORE component of the RADAR results framework is another important aspect baselining performance. I cover it in detail in Chapter 9, so I mention it only briefly here for completeness.

Table 4.11 SCORE baseline considerations

Component	Considerations
Social	• Addresses equality and welfare, ethical trading, communities and philanthropy • Where measures or evaluations do not currently exist in these areas, an initial audit of them will provide a baseline for further improvements
Commercial	• Financial outcomes are typically analysed through the prisms of customer, channel and product/service, and 'cut' by market, business segment and organisational unit (e.g. group, business unit, division) • Equal focus should be placed on understanding the performance of the 'commercial engine' (product development, marketing, sales and business development)
Operational	• Operational performance analysis typically focuses on five key areas: cost, quality, speed, dependability and flexibility[24] • In addition to baselining performance, you must also baseline existing resources (e.g. people capabilities, physical assets, intangibles such as brand and IP), including suppliers • Data is fundamental to operational effectiveness and efficiency, and any operational baselining must also evaluate the gaps between the data needed and the data available and readily accessible to run the business (we cover this in the next chapter)
Reputational	• An organisation's reputation in the eyes of customers, employees, suppliers, partners and other key stakeholders underpins long-term organisational success • If data is not captured on this, it is imperative that a programme of capturing it begins (e.g. customer feedback)

(continued)

[24] See Chapter 2 of Slack, N., Brandon-Jones, A. and Johnston, R. (2013) *Operations Management*, 7th edn, Harlow: Pearson Education Limited.

Table 4.11 SCORE baseline considerations (*continued*)

Component	Considerations
	• Whilst typically more qualitative in nature, there are certain measures that can be usefully captured and compared over time (e.g. net promoter scores, social sentiment scores, awards received, volume and proportion of positive press coverage)
Environmental	• This typically covers emissions and pollution, resource usage, conservation activities and safety and regulation

Note that the act of reviewing and baselining your organisation's SCORE inevitably necessitates:

- Deeper reflection on where the organisation wants to focus its efforts in the future (informing or challenging its definition of UP).
- A focus on trends over time as well as current position (i.e. longitudinal analysis – understanding historical inflection points and what drove them).
- Benchmarking, where possible, against competitors and best-in-class examples from across industries and markets.
- The setting of targets or aspirations against each area.
- Refinements to data collection and analysis (see the discussion of minimum enterprise data sets in the next chapter).

Where are you not?

Understanding the context and baseline of your organisation through analysis of where value has been created, why it was created, and the results it generated is critical. It is also incomplete. Once in the throes of such analysis, an organisation risks biasing its activity towards those business segments in which it currently competes (i.e. existing propositions into existing markets). However, strategy is not just about where you are, but also where you are not. Kim and Mauborgne's work on Blue Ocean Strategy[25] does an excellent job of driving this point home, and searching for 'blue oceans' (i.e. uncontested market spaces) is an important element of any context and baseline analysis.

In practice, this means identifying and assessing the broader market opportunities available to you, and your ability to exploit them, by looking:

- within existing markets (through new propositions);
- at new markets (either through existing or new propositions).

[25] Kim, W.C. and Mauborgne, R. (2006) *Blue Ocean Strategy, Expanded Edition: How to create uncontested market space and make the competition irrelevant*, Boston, MA: Harvard Business School Publishing Corporation.

In both cases, you are asking yourselves the same set of questions focused on the opportunity framework introduced in the last chapter.

Figure 4.17 Key questions when exploring potential market opportunities

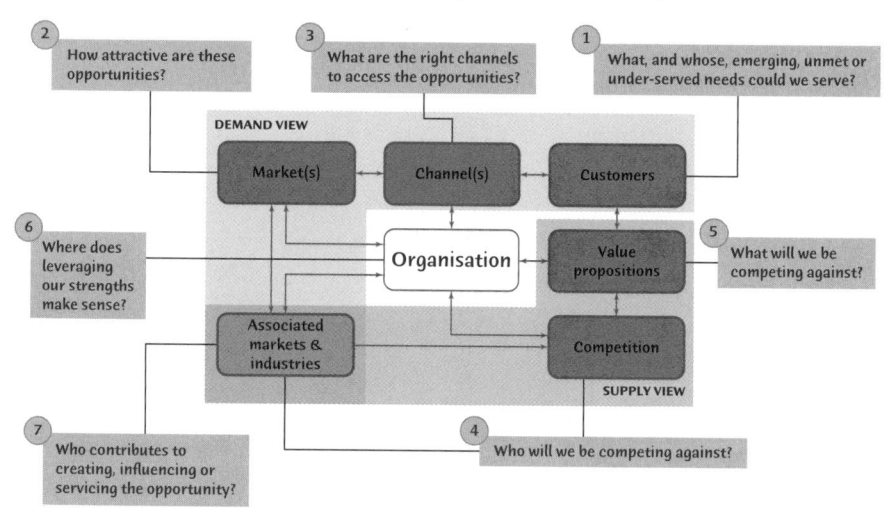

Channel your thoughts

Opportunity identification starts with customer need and evaluating market attractiveness, both of which we discussed earlier in this chapter. The question that naturally follows is 'What are the right channels to access the opportunities?', which requires analysis of several interrelated questions:

MARKET

1 What is the channel mix currently used to meet the opportunity?
2 How effective is this mix in meeting customer needs?
3 How has this mix evolved, and how will it evolve in the future?
4 Why is it evolving in this way?

ORGANISATION

5 How well matched are your organisation's current channels to the above?
6 To what extent will you be able to exploit the opportunity, or gain an advantage versus competitors, through your existing channels or a new channel strategy?

Answering these questions typically involves developing and validating a clear view of channels through market reports, trade body or government information, customer insight, analysis of existing players and expert interviews. The principle of triangulation applies here – combining these different sources will give you greater confidence in the existing and emerging channel mix.

When analysing your own organisation's channel footprint and performance, and how it maps to that of broader consumer needs, key purchase criteria and the market, there are five key areas to explore.

Figure 4.18 Key areas of channel performance

Whilst not exhaustive, the above list highlights the key areas of focus. Whilst financial performance is the starting point, key operational areas (such as inventory or order-to-cash effectiveness) or customer service (e.g. the number of issues or complaints and the percentage of first-time resolution) will provide a greater understanding of what is driving these financial metrics. The relative competitive position of the organisation in each channel is also key and is addressed through various market coverage and marketing analyses and metrics.

Channel analysis is often further complicated by other factors:

- There are often several partners or suppliers involved, so getting a common and comparable view across channels can be hard.

- Objectives may vary by channel, or even by circumstances relating to specific components within a channel. For example, the chief executive of a well-known retailer spoke to me about stores which, when examined purely in terms of in-store sales, should be closed. However, the volume of click-and-collect online orders, and their roles as pre-purchase showrooms, meant that some of those stores needed to be understood in a different light, and alternative models identified to make them more profitable.

- Actual or potential channel conflict (i.e. where channel partners are selling the same product in the same market with potentially different pricing), and the existence of grey markets, can further cloud figures on sales and profitability by channel.

Tesla Motors[26]

In the US, Tesla's direct-to-consumer (DTC) distribution model is shaking up an industry in which the use of franchised dealer networks is not only the norm, but legally protected in some states. Indeed, this channel debate is highly politicised, as members of state legislatures try to balance the interests of existing car dealerships with the draw of new tax revenues from DTC activity.

But this channel approach is not just about disrupting car dealerships. Tesla produces its cars to order, so there is no requirement for stockpiling in large dealership forecourts, and the DTC approach also provides a valuable platform through which to educate customers on the new technology, provide a personalised service (e.g. installing power points at home) and offer ongoing direct marketing.

Competition and value propositions

Whilst our earlier discussion of Porter's Five Forces provided a high-level view of the competitive forces at play, we can go considerably deeper with competitive intelligence. Identifying actual or potential competitors, and gathering the relevant information on their goals, strategy and competitive position, is typically done by looking through six lenses.

Figure 4.19 Lenses through which to identify actual or potential competitors

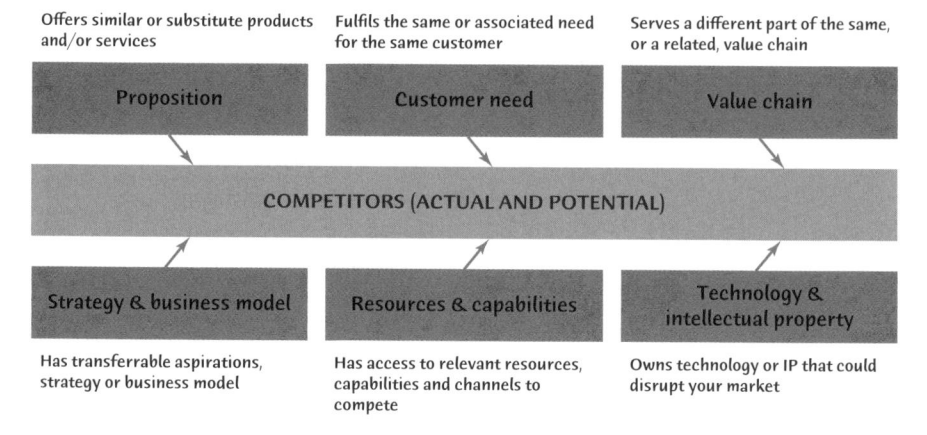

The sources for identifying your competitors are rich and varied: customers (yours and those of competitors), suppliers, your own sales and marketing team, other key market stakeholders, web searches, web analysis tools (e.g. SEMrush, Similarweb, Google Analytics), trade bodies and market reports are just a few examples. Having done so, the next step is to understand their goals, strategy, positioning and proposition, indicators of which can be found through the following sources.

[26] See http://www.autoremarketing.com/retail/direct-to-consumer-sales-debate-goes-way-beyond-tesla [accessed 13 January 2017].

Table 4.12 Competitor information sources

Category	Area	Key questions
Proposition	Product features	● What customer needs are they emphasising or prioritising?
		● What new products/features are 'coming soon'?
		● What patents or IP have they registered?
	Services	● How do services feature in the proposition?
	Channels	● What channels are they using to access customers?
		● What are these touchpoints communicating about the brand?
	Partners	● With whom have they partnered to support or develop their proposition or go-to-market approach?
Marketing, communications and PR	Website	● What does the copy on the website suggest about positioning, proposition, plans and priorities?
	Marketing materials	● What do they emphasise in their marketing messaging?
	Corporate publications and press releases	● What information do they provide on strategic intent and longer-term objectives?
		● What do announcements on new markets, customers, propositions and partners suggest about their strategy?
	Events	● What events are they attending or sponsoring?
		● What do they communicate at these events?
	Social media	● What can you intimate from their usage of social media (channel usage and content)?
		● With what types of customers do the company positioning and proposition resonate (e.g. followers, likes)?
		● What do customers say about them on social media?
	Email	● What messages are they pushing through email?

Category	Area	Key questions
Resources and capabilities	Executive team	● Who have they hired? ● What do the backgrounds of the executive team say about likely plans?
	LinkedIn	● How is the organisation structured?
	Recruitment	● What types of employees are they looking to hire? ● What does this tell you about their strategic intent?
	Investments	● What major investments are they making (including acquisitions)?
Customers	Reviews	● What do customers say about them in reviews and on social media?

We come back to proposition (see Chapter 7), but the key here is to determine 'next best alternatives' for customers, how your proposition compares and where the differentiation lies.

Getting the most from your organisation

The discussion on opportunity has, thus far, been market-focused. However, opportunity is not all about outward-looking considerations, and there are organisational considerations that will shape an organisation's views on an opportunity:

Strategic fit

Even when a clear opportunity exists, your organisation may not be the right one to exploit it. Strategic fit is the extent to which the competitive position and AIR of the organisation match, or could be credibly extended into, the available opportunity. The fact that a Ferrari Segway or Colgate microwave meal ever existed (they both failed in the market) should be reason enough to factor strategic fit into your thinking when evaluating a range of market opportunities.

Strategic assets

Sometimes an opportunity can be created by an organisation leveraging its existing strategic assets (distinctive resources and capabilities):

● **Alternative use for a product:** sometimes, an organisation's existing product can be extended into a new application.

● **Alternative application of resources and capabilities:** notwithstanding the 'strategic fit' caveat addressed above, there are many examples of using intangible resources (especially brand) to extend into new areas of opportunity. Amazon's cloud server farms – originally developed out of

Amazon retail's need for large-scale computing power – are marketed as Amazon Web Services to customers requiring access to cloud-computing services. For a long time, this part of the business has been significantly more profitable than the retail business that begat it. Sometimes, these alternative applications are more serendipitous than planned.

(Re)apply yourself to succeed

Play-Doh started life as a wallpaper cleaner in the 1930s, before becoming, since the 1950s, an enduring and well-loved children's toy. Similarly, WD-40 has extended into many household uses since its original conception as a solution to avoid corrosion in nuclear missiles. Another famous example is Pfizer's Viagra – a global hit product for treating erectile disfunction – which was originally developed by Pfizer as a treatment for high blood pressure and chest pain caused by heart disease.

Fortune favours the Flickr and Slack serendipity

Stewart Butterfield, whilst developing a massively multiplayer online game, realised that part of the platform which enabled photos to be shared could be marketed as a separate service. Through that, Flickr was born. A decade later, he repeated the trick when an in-house messaging app, developed to enable better coordination between developers of a new online game, was launched as a separate app. The app – Slack – was valued at $1bn in 2016.

Risk

We covered risk briefly earlier in our discussion of market attractiveness. Clearly, an organisation's appetite for risk, expressed in everything from entering new areas through to taking on debt, will influence which opportunities it pursues.

Ultimately, it is the interaction between market opportunities and organisational capabilities – i.e. the Horizon – that determines the priorities for an organisation, with risk appetite an important influencer.

RAC up the results

The elements discussed thus far in the chapter act as a snapshot to contextualise and baseline current organisational performance, market conditions and potential opportunities. But how do you baseline the ability of the organisation to adapt to changing conditions over time? The introduction described the three criteria by which to judge organisational agility – responsiveness, adaptability and control (RAC) – and an organisation's RAC rating evaluates these through ten statements.

Table 4.13 RAC rating evaluation questions

Criterion	Topic	Evaluation statement
Responsiveness	Anticipatory data	The right data is available at the right time to anticipate new or changing requirements
	Analysis	People with the right skills consistently access and analyse this data and define and prioritise action appropriately
	Execution	The organisation has the skills, technology and capacity required to act on anticipatory and performance data in a timely fashion, and empowers people appropriately, both formally and through its culture, to do so
	Competition	The organisation's service levels rank in the top 10% of its competitor set
Adaptability[27]	People	The employment models, people development (e.g. multi-skilling), organisational structures and incentives across the organisation encourage operational flexibility
	Processes	The working practices, use of suppliers, outsourcing and automation, and planning approach encourage operational flexibility across core, support and management processes[28]
	Technology	The organisation fully exploits relevant technologies to create a more adaptable operating model

(continued)

[27] This is based on the four key dimensions of 'Dynamism by Design' – people, processes, technology and data – which are outlined in Chapter 7.
[28] Business processes are commonly grouped under three headings: first, core processes that deliver value directly to the customer and which are essential in realising the organisation's goals (e.g. research and development, manufacturing); second, support processes that enable the core activities by providing resources and infrastructure, but which do not directly deliver value (e.g. accounting); and third, management processes used to plan, measure, monitor and control business activities (e.g. strategy, planning and budgeting, compliance.)

Table 4.13 RAC rating evaluation questions (*continued*)

Criterion	Topic	Evaluation statement
	Optionality	Optionality is factored into the organisation's planning and practices to ensure appropriate adaptability (e.g. capacity redundancy, parallel development and other real options – see Chapter 6 for a brief introduction to real options)
Control	Performance management and governance	The right performance data is available to the right people at the right time, integrating different sources if necessary, analysed in a timely fashion at each level of the organisation and actioned appropriately
	Measurement system control	Data requirements are evaluated periodically and systematically to ensure that the measurement system remains in line with business needs

To calculate your organisation's RAC rating, each of these statements is scored from 1 (strongly disagree) to 5 (strongly agree), summed and multiplied by two to get to a rating out of 100. Determining the score for each of the RAC criteria depends on the commitment, time and resources available to you, and can typically involve the following:

● commercial, operational and process analysis;
● cross-functional team evaluation (e.g. via workshop);
● customer survey;
● employee survey;
● management reporting and control assessment (governance review);
● Minimum Enterprise Data Set (MEDS) assessment – see Chapter 5;
● organisational capability audit;
● technology audit.

An additional benefit of this exercise is to drive focused discussion on what is constraining the organisation's agility, identifying areas to develop 'Beyond the Horizon' (see Chapters 5 and 7).

Conclusion on context and baselining

Much of this chapter has been about traditional strategic analysis, understanding where you are in terms of your business and market opportunities. The resultant fact base provides the context for the design of your Horizon. The management of that Horizon, however, requires a more dynamic approach to research and analysis that reflects the agile insight characteristics described in Chapter 3. That is the subject of the next chapter.

Summary

- Before you can set your Horizon, you must first understand where and why your organisation creates value. Value creation can be defined in purely financial terms as earning a return on the money you invest (return on invested capital) that exceeds what it costs you to secure that investment through a mixture of debt and equity, having accounted for risk (expressed as the weighted average cost of capital).

- To identify *where* value is created within your organisation typically requires four steps: first, define your market, second, define your business segments, third, cut your financial data to align with them, and finally, analyse the data and determine materiality.

- Determining *why* value is created involves the analysis of two underlying factors: market attractiveness and the organisation's competitive position within those markets.

- To baseline organisational performance, focus on the SCORE elements of the RADAR results framework (social, commercial, operational, reputational, environmental).

- Baselining and context also involves considering the current market opportunities that you are not exploiting, identified through the systematic review of customers, markets, channels, competition, value propositions, associated markets and industries, and the organisation's own resources and capabilities.

- Your organisation's agility, as measured by its RAC rating, can itself be baselined through the evaluation of ten statements associated with responsiveness, adaptability and control. Doing so will help you identify further areas for organisational development 'Beyond the Horizon'.

Case story: Separating the ChIC from the chaff

'Know thyself' muttered Emma to herself, somewhat archly, as she looked at the data that had been prepared by the team. Sitting down with Simon, the lead commercial analyst, to discuss the hypotheses and available data sources had been a useful first step. Thankfully, the investment in systems over the past five years, including the replatforming of their transactional website, meant that they had access to some 'half-decent data' (Simon's words). There were, of course, limitations, and the CRM had 'never been used in anger' (Simon again), but overall the basics were in place and there was opportunity to get far more out of what they had.

The hypotheses the team had developed, and the subsequent analysis undertaken, had thrown up some interesting results and had caused heated debate.

Channel

Once some of the less immediately visible day-to-day channel costs were considered in aggregate (e.g. period-end channel rebates, returns, marketing and promotional spend), channel profitability looked somewhat different to what Emma and Sam had originally expected. For example:

- Return rates for online were more than three times the average of store-based purchases, and online customers were 60 per cent less likely to purchase a replacement item upon completing the return than their store-based counterparts. Taken together, this made the online part of the business significantly more costly to serve than it appeared at first blush – yet it was by far the fastest growing channel for reasons of customer convenience. Focusing on reducing returns, encouraging replacements when returns do happen, customer lifetime value (LTV) and the CRM opportunity, and encouraging store visits through improved store theatre and services would be important in addressing these challenges.
- Own-store click and collect, which had been a real volume growth area for Leisurious, was value-destroying once all costs were accounted for. Yet the business knew that the multi-channel customer was one of the most attractive in terms of lifetime value (their data suggested up to 30 per cent higher than a store-only customer). Clearly, they would need to find a way to innovate with this offer.
- Emma and Sam knew drop-shipped orders through third-party websites were costly, but customer analysis showed that there was a 40 per cent overlap of customers with their own website. These third-party sites had been useful routes to market in the early days but, given Leisurious' prominence in the market now, this was a margin that did not need to be given away. Transitioning these volumes to their own website would be a priority in increasing online profitability.

Looking beyond existing channels, the business modelling of the outlet opportunity had been very encouraging. For it to be successful, the team had agreed on five potential locations that minimised the cannibalisation risk and maximised returns, and which would enable the outlets to function successfully for both clearance and special make-up (SMU) product. The latter would be a potentially useful brand entry point for previously unserved consumers.

The channel analysis had also shown that there was significant overstocking in certain channels, whilst stock-outs for the same SKUs were happening too often in others. This suggested that there was a significant opportunity to reduce costs, and increase service levels, across all channels, by moving to a single stock pool. This would require accurate inventory records and investment in ensuring the best possible returns management. It would also require switching on more of the company's ERP functionality, enabling real-time stock file updates. Emma and Sam concluded this was a longer-term project that should be planned for and robustly tested in parallel to current operations before making any switch across.

Innovation of the proposition

The cost of goods (CoGs) benchmarking analysis against competitors had been somewhat inconclusive – as the teams, and the buyers in particular, had got lost in debates about what was truly comparable. Despite this, the output of this exercise had proved extremely useful when combined with the channel analysis and stock-out issues:

- The CoGs analysis had necessitated a mapping of the broader sourcing of product and had revealed that the business had an average lead time of nearly 18 weeks. This compared poorly to some of its fast-fashion competitors, who were achieving turnarounds of closer to six weeks.
- The implications of this were important. Leisurious was unable to respond to stronger than anticipated (and planned) demand for certain SKUs, and the resultant loss in margin far outstripped any potential CoGs reduction benefits.
- Emma and Sam concluded that supply chain responsiveness, rather than cost reduction, should be prioritised. By splitting manufacturing between its current Vietnamese suppliers and a new, near-shored partner in Turkey, Portugal or maybe Eastern Europe, they could be more responsive and replenish if required.
- This notwithstanding, they knew that planning would also have to be improved and, together with improved terms with their suppliers, which were originally negotiated on far lower volume projections, there was plenty of scope for reducing CoGs.

Analysis of competitors' accessories propositions, and requests from Leisurious' own customers, showed some obvious opportunities for the brand in areas such as bags, hats, scarves, gloves and socks.

The review of the customer journey and experience (Cx) had also proven enlightening, and Emma and Sam had both done accompanied shops with customers in person to understand their thinking. It was clear that not enough was being done to inspire their customers both in store and online. The products were well-loved, but customers were looking for more – advice, ideas, encouragement. This really got Emma and Sam thinking about the role of the store and online in different terms, with a focus on offering more 'content' to customers.

Customer engagement

Linked to the Cx work had been an exploration of who their customer truly was, and with it a segmentation of the market. Calculating Leisurious' AIR cover against the resultant key purchase criteria and critical success factors had given the team clarity on what to prioritise. Key items on the 'up, down, in, out Plan' were:

- Maximising Leisurious' position as providers of stylish, durable items that fit well and offer great technical performance.
- Addressing some range weaknesses (with the fleece offer in tops the most important).
- Strengthening the brand's relationships with its customers.

'Know thyself' is fine as an adage, said Emma to Sam one evening in the pub, 'but right now I feel like I know too much!'. 'The list is long,' conceded Sam, 'but we need to stay focused on the Horizon.' And with that, they settled down to discuss the recent market insight that had just been completed.

In your organisation

Exercise 4: Hypotheses development

1 On your own, and considering in turn each element of the 5KQs as described in the section 'Insight and the five key questions' in Chapter 3, create a list of hypotheses that you believe hold true for your organisation and the market, and which you consider to be drivers or shapers of its current performance.

2 Ask the members of the core group to do a similar exercise individually.

3 Bring everyone together for a workshop, and undertake the following tasks:

3.1. Compare lists, starting with organisation. Pay special attention to hypotheses that are:

- common to all or most of the lists;
- unique to one or two of the lists.

3.2. Eliminate duplicates and prioritise hypotheses within each of the two domains. Criteria for prioritisation should be agreed as a group, but could include:

- Impact on the business (financial and non-financial, e.g. reputation).
- Relevance to your organisation's strategy or current Horizon.
- Level of uncertainty, particularly where different outcomes would have very different effects on your organisation.

3.3. For the top 10 to 15 hypotheses, use the HAD framework to identify what types of analysis you would do, and the sources of data required to do it.

3.4. Consider the frequency with which you would want to test these hypotheses, which ones can be answered through discrete research, and which would benefit from ongoing strategic intelligence.

4 Execute the analysis required to test the hypotheses.

This work will feed into the design, action and results exercises that follow in the later chapters.

5

Use your intelligence – how to track market and organisational performance

'A wise man proportions his belief to the evidence'

David Hume

In this chapter we do the following:

- Define what a strategic intelligence system (SIS) is, and what it comprises.
- Understand how to define your minimum enterprise data set (MEDS).
- Consider the process and systems implications of a SIS.

Where the previous chapter described how to take stock of an organisation and its environment at a moment in time, this chapter explores how to analyse and track its onward path. This is the essence of agile insight and to do it, RADAR uses strategic intelligence (SI) (see Chapter 3).

What is a strategic intelligence system (SIS)?

A SIS is the mechanism through which RADAR's agile insight requirements are managed and met. It sits at the core of Horizon management and comprises:

Data

To determine your organisation's strategically critical data, known as its minimum enterprise data set (MEDS), you must consider three elements.

Table 5.1 The data elements of strategic intelligence

#	Consideration	Description
1	Market and organisational dynamics	These represent the full range of potential data sources available for anticipating, diagnosing and prescribing required action.
2	Strategic intent	This is determined by four elements: your unifying purpose, Horizon, key considerations 'Beyond the Horizon', and target outcomes (expressed through the SCORE and ERA elements of the results framework.)
3	The objectives of strategic intelligence	The four objectives – anticipate, control, communicate and improve – further focus your data priorities

Processes

The SIS feeds, draws on and adapts the MEDS over time through a continuous cycle of anticipating, analysing, acting and adapting (the A-cycle). This creates the dynamism at the heart of agile insight.

Systems

A SIS requires technology and systems to capture, store, process, analyse, visualise and disseminate the MEDS. The nature of the A-cycle means that these systems must be readily extensible, enabling them to adapt to changing requirements.

These SIS components are summarised in Figure 5.1, and this chapter explores each in turn.

Data: take your MEDS

Diagnosis: a poor diet

Increasingly, the data challenge within organisations is not one of paucity, but of 'skewed abundance' (i.e. a lot of certain types of data, and not enough of others). The risk is that decisions will be *biased* by the data available, rather than *based* on the data needed (a classic challenge for marketing professionals investing across online and offline channels).

Moreover, this voluminous data is often not joined-up. Even more advanced organisations, which may have a dedicated 'insight' function focused on customers, competitors and the market, typically fail to adequately blend this insight with the internal analysis of their performance and capabilities.

Figure 5.1 The components of a strategic intelligence system (SIS)

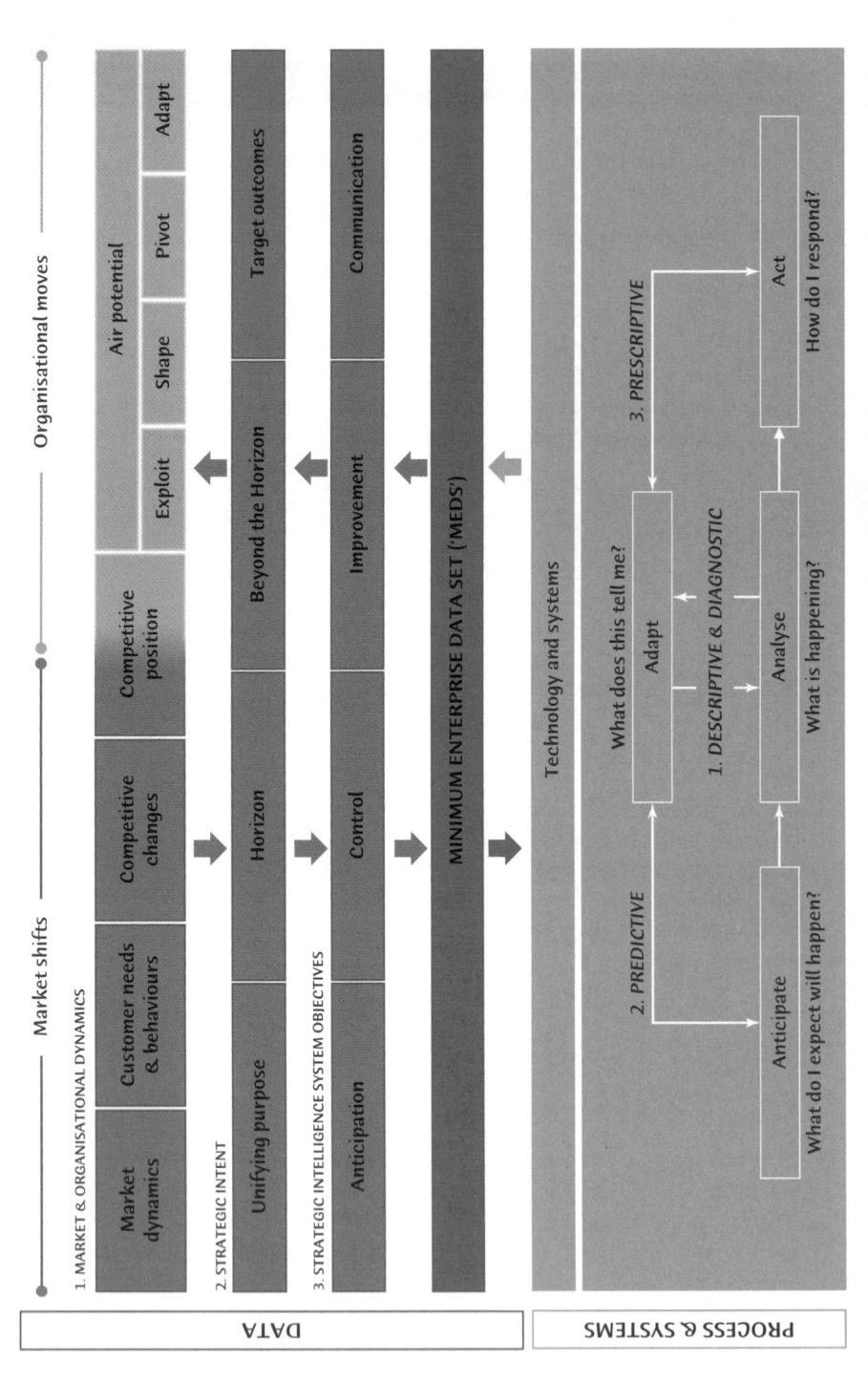

We need to avoid this unbalanced diet – gorging ourselves but gaining little nourishment. The MEDS is the prescribed remedy – a focused, integrated set of strategically critical quantitative and qualitative data and insight.

Determining the prescription

The MEDS considers a wide range of sources relating to market and organisational dynamics.

In the face of this broad range of considerations, narrowing down the MEDS focus requires the application of two filters – strategic intent and SIS objectives.

Strategic intent
Strategic intent is the starting point for focusing your MEDS. As described in Chapter 1, it is determined by four elements:

1. Unifying purpose
This provides a directional imperative for all Horizon choices. For example, Marks and Spencer's commitment to social and environmental sustainability (its 'Plan A'[29]) has significant implications for its overall Horizon, and the organisation's MEDS.

2. Horizon
Expressed through Horizon statements, the Horizon defines where the organisation will play, and how it will win. Chapter 9 illustrates how these Horizon statements link to data requirements via RADAR's results framework.

3. Considerations 'Beyond the Horizon'
Whilst RADAR focuses on the Horizon, there is a requirement to look selectively beyond it. There are three reasons for this:

- *Lead times:* the lead time required to prepare for certain potential Horizon shifts effectively rules them out if they are not explored and anticipated in parallel. This reflects some of the characteristics of venturing seen in both start-up and corporate environments.

- *Emerging market developments:* there are aspects of a market's development, such as emerging technologies or new entrants, whose impact may not be fully understood but which must be tracked given the potential impact they could have on the existing Horizon.

- *Broader organisational change requirements:* there may be required changes, only indirectly related to the current Horizon, which improve the organisation's underlying agility and RAC rating (e.g. multi-skilling staff or leveraging automation).

[29] See https://corporate.marksandspencer.com/plan-a [accessed 7 June 2018].

Table 5.2 Market and organisational dynamics considered under MEDS

Consideration	Description	Example sources
Market dynamics	Having baselined the market as discussed in Chapter 4, these are the trends and developments which develop over time (both quantitative and qualitative)	● Analyst reports ● Analogous or more advanced markets ● Business analytics
Customer needs and behaviours	The evolving needs, wants, attitudes and behaviours of customers	● Competitor publications, marketing and press releases ● Customer feedback and reviews ● Customer observation
Competitive changes	The developments of existing competitors, new entrants and substitutes (including companies doing it themselves in B2B)	● Expert opinion and consensus ● Organisational initiatives
Competitive position	● *Position:* the image the organisation enjoys in the eyes of its customers, and how it is differentiated from competitors ● *Proposition:* the relative appeal of the products and services offered, and of the channels through which they are accessed ● *Performance:* the organisation's operational performance (SCOREcard) and resources and capabilities (AIR cover) relative to its competitors	● Precursor events, signalling a forth-coming change (e.g. regulatory review, change of government) ● Predictive analytics ● Published market data
AIR	● Having analysed your AIR and baselined your AIR cover as described in the last chapter, four options feed into MEDS: – *Exploit:* how can you exploit existing AIR to win in serving existing, new, emerging or under-served needs? – *Shape:* how can you use existing AIR to shape future market demand? – *Pivot:* how can you pivot on existing AIR to apply it to new business segments? – *Adapt:* where must you adapt or transform existing AIR to meet changing market requirements? (see ADAPT in Chapter 3)	● R&D/innovation pipeline ● Social listening ● Staff feedback ● Suppliers and partners ● Surveys ● Technology news ● Trackers (market, brand) ● Trade data, news and events ● Web analysis tools

Ultimately, these relate to optionality – both short- and long-term:

- The longer-term areas of potential or anticipated market developments (e.g. applications of artificial intelligence) and AIR developments (e.g. infrastructure developments) necessitate their own insight to inform decision making and the development of real options (see Chapter 6).

- Some shorter-term areas, relating to major organisational changes, good or bad, that fundamentally alter an organisation's competitive position (e.g. R&D breakthroughs, acquisitions) or RAC-specific adaptations (e.g. implementing process automation) will also require data to inform choices and track progress.

Both these areas can lead to adding items to your MEDS, determining what should form part of the Horizon design, which we address in Chapter 7.

Figure 5.2 Areas driving commitment 'Beyond the Horizon'

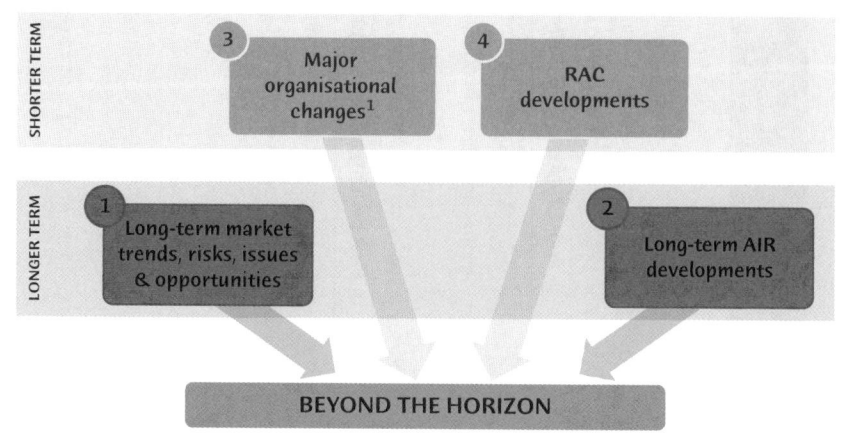

4. Target outcomes

These are expressed through the SCORE and ERAs of the results framework (Chapter 9).

Each of these four elements will contribute to determining what should be included and excluded from your MEDS.

SIS objectives

The MEDS' focus can be sharpened further by considering the four objectives of a SIS.

Through engaging the relevant organisational and external stakeholders in the two areas above, you can develop a MEDS data model, including data dictionary, documenting the required data elements (both quantitative and qualitative), the sources for them and how they integrate. Note that MEDS is not created to the exclusion of all other data in the organisation – it defines the *minimum*

Table 5.3 How strategic data objectives sharpen the MEDS focus

Objective	Overarching question	Questions to sharpen the focus for meds
Anticipation	What, if it changed, would necessitate a Horizon shift?	• Which assumptions, risks or choices in our ARC would have the most impact if expectations are defied?
		• Which ERAs would have the most impact if delivered late or not at all?
		• What sits 'top right' in the volatility/impact matrix (i.e. high volatility and high impact) for market trends, customer needs and behaviours or competitor changes?
		• Where does our current or developing AIR offer the greatest potential to exploit or shape market changes?
Control	What do I need to evaluate and control performance?	• What are the key SCORE measures that demonstrate the overall performance and success of the Horizon?
		• What are the key performance indicators (KPIs) further down the organisation that have the greatest influence on these?
		• What are the key compliance requirements (regulatory, contractual) to which we must adhere?
		• What are the key market performance assumptions that underpin our Horizon?
Improvement	Where can I make improvements, and what will the impact be?	• Which elements of our AIR cover have been identified as key weaknesses? (see Chapter 4)
		• What data would provide us with the best understanding of where our proposition is falling short of customer expectations?
Communication	What do I need to communicate, and to whom?	• Which customer segments and other key stakeholder groups are most important to the current Horizon?
		• What data, information or messaging is required or would have most relevance and impact if shared with them?
		• What dialogues or experiments would most enrich these relationships?

data and insight 'must haves' to support RADAR. Furthermore, the definition of your MEDS will necessitate a review of the process, governance, systems and technology requirements to support it, leveraging existing resources and supplementing them where needed – the topic to which we now turn.

Process, systems and technology

Technology and systems

In the context of RADAR, technology and systems need to be considered from two viewpoints:

1. How they are shaping the market
Technology is driving market, customer and competitor changes on a massive scale. Keeping on top of technology developments and making informed choices in line with your unifying purpose and Horizon are critical. For example, two very different retail brands I know explored the use of Google beacons in their stores to track customers and their behaviours and came to different conclusions. One rejected them as too intrusive given the brand's positioning as championing individuality and free spiritedness, whilst the other is pursuing widespread adoption.

2. How they are used internally to support a SIS
Technologies available to support data management, analysis and ultimately decision making and execution, are advancing rapidly, bridging the divide between structured (e.g. relational databases) and unstructured (e.g. email) data and enabling the rise of the 'data adhocracy'. To take just one example, consider data storage:

- Data vaults, a next-generation take on the enterprise data warehouse, store data from multiple sources, to which additional sources can be added over time, without having to change existing designs. This extensibility, together with an architecture that allows for unstructured data, combines flexibility and responsiveness with the rigour of a well-established methodology and architecture (comprising hubs, satellites and links).

- Data lakes, unlike data vaults, store data in its original format, from structured databases through to unstructured emails, offering a single store for all organisational data. They can be particularly effective when managing very large but relatively simple data sets but lack the more prescriptive methodology associated with data vaults and therefore require an experienced team to manage them.

Both technologies offer the potential to tap into different data sources as requirements change, enabling a greater level of adaptation than systems have previously allowed. Similarly, analytical tools (e.g. SAS, Splunk, Alteryx) and visualisation technology (e.g. Tableau, QlikView) are evolving quickly, enabling a wide array of static and interactive visualisation options to support decision making.

However, there are trade-offs to be made when adopting a more agile approach to data processing. These relate primarily to the six criteria of data quality.[30]

Table 5.4 Data quality criteria

Criterion	Definition: the extent to which the data. . .
Completeness	. . . is present
Consistency	. . . is in sync across the organisation
Uniqueness	. . . is recorded only once
Validity	. . . conforms to its definitional syntax (e.g. format)
Accuracy	. . . correctly describes its corresponding real-world object or event
Timeliness	. . . is available at the time it is needed

Where timeliness is given primacy, compromises are often required in areas such as completeness and uniqueness. In some organisations, 'agile data science teams' are forming, integrating cross-functional business and technology expertise under the oversight of a scrum master (Scrum being a well-known framework for agile software development). There are limitations to this approach – you cannot release a 'minimum viable product' for data analysis in the same way you can for software – but many of the practices can be applied (e.g. user stories, iteration) and adapted (e.g. releasing documented metadata as an interim output at the end of a 'sprint' or development cycle).

Being able to adapt your MEDS requires systems and a data architecture that are themselves responsive to change. The extensibility of data vaults is an example of this, but there are more prosaic examples too. In some cases, a stand-alone pilot system may serve as a starting point until such a time as the data can be rolled into existing production systems. Whilst this is not ideal, it is often preferable to waiting months for a production system's modifications to come online.

Such 'transitional' data architectures require careful planning and risk management and must be developed knowingly. Agile is not an excuse for sloppiness or ill-considered haste. Robust data management is important, for once the data is no longer sufficiently accurate, or even if it is merely believed not to be, the whole approach fails. Clear policies and direction on data architecture, metadata, governance, input controls and validation can significantly improve data quality. Furthermore, by having a data governance board that oversees all data projects and their outcomes, and approves policies and procedures, there is focused accountability for this critical function.

[30] DAMA UK Working Group (2013) The Six Primary Dimensions for Data Quality Assessment, available at https://www.whitepapers.em360tech.com/wp-content/files_mf/1407250286DAMAUKDQDimensionsWhitePaperR37.pdf [accessed 21 January 2019].

Performance management: agile insight in action

Data and systems are but servants to the control and action that a SIS drives. Each step in its continuous A-cycle of anticipating, analysing, acting and adapting plays a unique role:

- *Anticipate:* to anticipate future Horizon changes made possible by changes in the market or organisation.
- *Analyse:* to determine the performance and validity of your current Horizon and potential for future Horizon changes.
- *Act:* to make informed design choices and performance actions.
- *Adapt:* to adjust the Horizon (small-scale change) or Horizon Shift (large-scale change).

Figure 5.3 The A-cycle at the heart of a strategic intelligence system

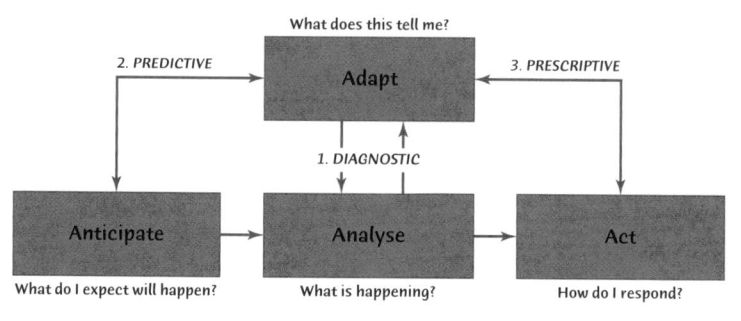

The design principles that inform agile strategy start by putting people and customers at the centre of everything the organisation does (see Chapter 6). Consider how this focus on the customer can express itself across the A-cycle:

Anticipate and analyse

The predictive capacity of analytics can be incredibly powerful, and occasionally an ethical challenge. One former supermarket employee claimed that their data analytics systems could predict with reasonable accuracy whether a person would become pregnant several weeks in advance of being so, simply based on their basket contents and historical purchasing profile. Less intrusively, commonplace sales mechanisms like customer profiling based on historical purchase behaviours (e.g. People who bought this also bought. . .) can serve to develop new segments on the fly.

Anticipating and analysing customer behaviour is informed by the regular pulse-taking of existing customers through feedback mechanisms, whether active (e.g. focus groups, satisfaction surveys, front-line staff interactions) or passive (e.g. customer database analysis, social listening, feedback from your sales and marketing teams). The focus should look beyond composition (e.g. 12 per cent of visitors to our coffee shop brought their own cup) to address trends and the pace of change (e.g. the percentage of customers who brought their own cup is rising at an increasing rate each month). 'Inflection detection' becomes the mantra by which you explore data to determine emerging needs at the earliest possible opportunity.

Act

Understanding is only useful if it is acted upon, and your ability to do so reflects your RAC rating. For example, a bicycle retailer might email its customer base highlighting a new type of road tyre and analyse open and conversion rates to refine its segmentation. It can then adjust the messaging and proposition based on this segmentation, providing it has the operational flexibility to do so.

This also illustrates the dialogue aspect of agile insight – the act of understanding is also an act of engagement. By interacting with customers, whether through surveys, social media or experiments, you are drawing them closer to your organisation.

Going further, you should maximise opportunities to enter into dialogue with potential needs, testing new concepts and adopting an experiment mentality (e.g. A/B testing a variation on your offer in a discrete area of your business). This has the additional benefit of providing opportunities to engage your customers in a controlled and positive act of responding to their needs. Underpinning all of this is the idea that need is dynamic and changing, sometimes rapidly, over time.

Para bailar La Bimbo[31]

Bimbo is a baked products manufacturer with brands including New York Bagel Company, Sara Lee, Mrs Baird's and Marinela. Its headquarters are in Mexico, where its Gansito product (sold under the Marinela brand and similar to a Twinkie) has been popular for over 50 years. In 2015, the brand launched a special red velvet flavour edition of the Gansito bar in the US but did not consider doing so in Mexico. Once Mexican consumers got wind of the US version of the product, they took to social media to vent their frustration that it was unavailable in their own country, 'Gansito Red Velvet' became a viral trending topic across the whole of Mexico. The subsequent launch of the product in two test markets – Mexico City and Guadalajara – led to a 12 per cent increase in the sale of Gansito products, beating the sales target by 71.4 per cent.

Adapt

A SIS allows you to adapt to change with greater speed and control, redirecting AIR to where it can have the greatest positive impact on customers.

---

[31] Source: https://www.brandwatch.com/blog/bimbo-case-study/ [accessed 9 March 2018].

> ### Loyalty, expectancy, maternity
> At a business serving the parents of 0–4-year-old children across a number of key categories, analysis showed that over 80 per cent of the total customer lifetime value was realised in the first two years of the customer relationship, and indeed most of that before the child was even born, through the pre-natal big shop of first-time parents (e.g. cots, changing tables, prams, car seats). This small window of opportunity led the business to de-prioritise the traditional and costly loyalty schemes rolled out by many retailers, and instead focus marketing investment on accessing and engaging expecting parents in order to maximise the share and conversion of that big shop.

Where are the humans?

By focusing on the data, technology, systems and processes, it can be easy to underestimate the role of people in ensuring a successful SIS. Do so at your peril – capabilities, leadership and culture are the lifeblood of a well-managed SIS.

Capabilities

As with any integrated intelligence platform, the challenge with a SIS lies in both integrating the various data sources and interpreting them correctly. Collectively, this will involve the following capabilities from across the organisation:

- **Finance:** the finance team is typically the owner of the 'one version of the truth' within an organisation, ensuring that all numbers reconcile and accurately reflect business performance.
- **Operations:** operations staff typically use a range of operational databases to support their work. Their knowledge of the systems, and how they are used, is important.
- **Sales and marketing:** sales and marketing are often the repository for broader market and customer data, some of which may be relevant for your MEDS.
- **Customer services:** a customer services team typically controls a wide range of customer-related data, from enquiries through to orders, support calls, feedback and complaints.
- **Technology:** systems integration skills in particular are key given the nature of the data requirements, cleansing and integrating data from diverse sources (e.g. from simple extract-transform-load procedures through to the implementation of middleware and the use of Flume, Kafka and other data management approaches).
- **Market intelligence:** increasingly, organisations have (typically out-ward-facing) insight functions either in-house or via a third party that pro-vide ongoing insight on consumers, markets and competitors.

- **Data science:** robust statistical methods for determining, for example, 'inflection points' in the data (i.e. where a change in trend is occurring) or the underlying drivers of performance require skilled analysts.

As a minimum, a cross-functional multi-disciplinary 'Virtual SIS unit' should be established to ensure the Horizon management data requirements are met effectively and efficiently. In time, I strongly recommend that you set up a dedicated, integrated team managing both internal (organisational) and external (market, customer and competitor) insight.

Leadership and culture
The attitudes, behaviours, social and power structures (culture) and leadership that shape the organisation overall also shape its ability to implement and exploit a SIS. Like any other significant organisational change, successful adoption of agile strategy practices requires both championing from the top, and staff recognising its benefits and pulling it through the organisation. RADAR draws contributions to strategy development from a wider audience both inside and outside the organisation, and this requires both governance and mindset changes. We address these topics further in Chapter 10.

Final thoughts on SIS

Creating your SIS, and an environment in which it can be acted upon efficiently, is about more than just data. Clarity of strategic intent, technology, clear governance and processes, leadership and culture all play important roles.

Furthermore, the machine feeds itself: as Horizons adjust and shift, so too does the SIS adapt to capture different data, embracing new sources and stakeholders. To act on the direction this provides, however, requires the operating model of the organisation to be flexible and responsive. That is our next topic.

SUMMARY
- A strategic intelligence system (SIS) is the mechanism through which RADAR's agile insight requirements are managed and met. It comprises three elements:
  - *Data:* an integrated set of strategically critical quantitative and qualitative data and insight, known as its minimum enterprise data set ('MEDS').
  - *Processes:* the A-cycle of anticipating, analysing, acting and adapting which feeds, draws on and adapts the MEDS over time.
  - *Systems:* the technology and systems required to capture, store, process, analyse, visualise and disseminate the MEDS.

- An organisation's MEDS is a focused, integrated set of strategically critical quantitative and qualitative data, performance metrics and insight on trends and opinions. It draws from a wide range of market and organisational sources, with its focus determined by the organisation's strategic intent and the four SIS objectives: anticipation, control, communication and improvement.
- Each step of the A-cycle plays an important role in a SIS:
  - *Anticipate:* to anticipate future Horizon changes made possible by changes in the market or organisation.
  - *Analyse:* to determine the performance and validity of your current Horizon and potential for future Horizon choices.
  - *Act:* to make informed design choices and performance actions.

    Adapt: to adjust the Horizon (small-scale change) or Horizon shift (large-scale change).
- Technology and systems need to be considered from two viewpoints: how they are shaping the market and how they are used internally to support a SIS.
- A successful SIS is also about people, and specifically capabilities, leadership and culture. If these are not well managed, the SIS will fail.

Case story: The escape from adhocracy

Since their last meeting with Simon, the lead commercial analyst, the team had done a lot to clarify not just Project ChIC but also Leisurious' overall purpose and direction. Defining UP, their Horizon, key elements beyond the Horizon, the AIR required to support it and the target SCORE, ERAs and ARC of the results framework had been tough but satisfying. Now, they were sitting with Simon, Mike, the retail operations director and Claire, the head of IT.

Emma: To run a successful retail business requires a mix of good information, judgement and instinct. I have great faith in our instinct and judgement but feel we have an opportunity to help ourselves with better information.

Simon: I will second that! We actually have access to a lot of good data and information in the business, but the team and I are rarely able to spend time considering how to best use it as we are constantly bombarded with ad hoc requests.

▶

Mike:	That is the nature of the beast in retail, I am afraid. It is a quick-moving world, and ad hoc data requests are par for the course.
Sam:	I half agree, Mike. It is certainly fast-moving, but I think if we were more systematic in our approach, we could reduce ad hoc requests significantly, and have more timely data on the areas that matter most to us.

Over the next four hours, the team worked through their true ongoing data requirements, based on market and organisational dynamics and what was relevant to them when focusing on the Horizon and the key areas beyond it. In the case of the latter, the longer-term initiative to reduce time to market by two-thirds, from 18 weeks to six, would require significant internal data, analysis and resource to support it. To avoid this dominating the discussion, Emma requested that Mike produce an outline business case and project proposal – they would need to run that as a separate, dedicated project.

Emma had also asked Simon to bring along a list of all the major ad hoc data requests that his team had received over the past 12 months and comparing it to what they had discussed as core aspects of their MEDS was both enlightening and encouraging. About half of the list were items that they had identified to include in the MEDS, and systematising access to those would greatly reduce the work for Simon and his team. The remainder broadly fell into two categories:

1. Genuine 'Beyond the Horizon' requests: the challenge here was that a good proportion of them were not aligned with the newly defined UP – they were a function of what they *could* do, rather than what they *should* do. These would not have been required 'in the new world'.
2. Unfocused requests: in the absence of a clear understanding of the organisation's focus and direction, data and insight relating to a broad range of topics had been requested. All were reasonable in themselves, but none were aligned with the Horizon that the organisation had now set.

'I am guilty for creating some of those', admitted Sam. 'I think we all are', replied Emma. 'Does that mean ad hoc requests are no longer an option?' asked Mike somewhat incredulously. 'I don't think that would be realistic', replied Simon uncertainly.

'This is not about stifling creativity or an explorative spirit – quite the opposite, and I think our Unifying Purpose is clear on that', replied Emma. 'Adopting this approach is intended to support rather than constrain creativity and innovation. We must, however, channel it into the right areas.'

She looked down the list of requests and added, 'I mean, we are not looking to expand our footprint in mid-market department stores under the current Horizon, so let's not waste time and resources tracking their performance, when we could more usefully divert that resource to areas where we do want to grow.'

There was discomfort in the room. It sounded like the right thing to do, but Mike and Simon in particular were worried about some of the potentially unintended consequences. Emma picked up on this feeling and addressed it head on. 'I understand your concerns. This exercise has been useful for us, but it warrants a workshop with a broader cross-section of our team, both to ensure that we have not missed anything and to gain their buy-in. Simon, can you arrange it?'

Simon was more than happy to arrange it – he felt they were on the right track, but his intuition and experience told him that refinements would be needed and getting input from the right stakeholders was the quickest way of identifying them. The escape from adhocracy would need to be taken one step at a time.

In your organisation

Exercise 5: Define your MEDS

Like a bad school-band drummer, this exercise is painfully out of sync. It requires you to have defined UP, your Horizon, the key elements that lie 'Beyond the Horizon' and your target outcomes (see Chapters 7 and 9). I suggest that you read those chapters and their associated exercises first, and then return to this one to get the full value from it. Having done so, please do the following:

1 Circulate the following documents to the core group for pre-workshop review:

- *'Data state' output:* documentation from the audit you undertook at the end of Chapter 3, which identifies the data available and any key gaps.
- *Strategic intent:* the definition of the organisation's unifying purpose, current Horizon (Horizon statements), key considerations beyond the Horizon, target outcomes (SCOREcard, ERAs) and the ARC tracker that underpins them.

2 Run a workshop in which the following questions are addressed:

- What data does the organisation's strategic intent demand? Explore the areas for consideration in the right-hand column by discussing in turn what each strategic intent element means for them.

Strategic intent element	Areas for consideration
1. Unifying purpose 2. Current Horizon (including regulatory and compliance requirements) 3. Target outcomes (SCORE, ERAs) 4. Considerations beyond the Horizon	• Market dynamics (quantitative and qualitative) • Customer needs and behaviours • Competitive changes • Competitive position (3Ps) • AIR

Review and update the ARC tracker as you go through this exercise.

- Does your list reflect a good mix of quantitative and qualitative data? If not, what other data might redress the balance?

- How will this data be used?

Consider the four key objectives of a SIS: anticipation, control, communication, and improvement:

  - Who will be using this data, and in which contexts (e.g. meetings, news releases)?

  - For each data element, under what conditions would action need to be taken? (E.g. if manufacturing volumes increased above 10,000 units/week for three months in a row, production expansion would be required.)

  - How do these different elements relate to each other?

  - Which elements would you want to combine to provide further insight?

- How does this data set map to what is currently available in the organisation?

- Where there are gaps, how significant are the process, people, systems and technology changes needed to close them?

  - What changes are required?

  - How long would these changes take to implement?

  - How expensive will they be?

Following the workshop, translate the output into a MEDS data model, documenting the required data elements (both quantitative and qualitative), the sources for them and how they integrate.

[PART THREE]

Design and action

How to foster agility in your organisation

6

'The future depends on what you do today.'

Mahatma Gandhi

In this chapter we do the following:

- Introduce the 'test and learn' approach and describe its relevance to RADAR.
- Explore how key design principles inform the RADAR approach to agile strategy.
- Introduce and define real options, a key enabler of strategic agility.

Research and analysis can show you the way, but it is design that builds the path, and action that walks it. This introductory chapter to the design and action components of RADAR is appropriately short. The two chapters that follow – the first on design, the second on action – are predominantly about tools and techniques, in keeping with their activity-based nature. This chapter is about grounding these tools and techniques in the foundational concepts and context which underpin them. Specifically, we will address three topics: test and learn, design thinking and real options.

Test and learn: a time of action

Discrete research and strategic intelligence will indicate the need for shifts in direction. The timing of these required shifts will rarely align with the annual planning cycle of traditional strategy development. So how should we respond?

In the start-up world, much is made of creating minimum viable products and 'failing fast'. The primacy of action, and a test and learn mentality, fit well with the dynamics of a free-flowing environment, constrained only by available funding. In more established businesses, failing fast often creates challenges, and the various mechanisms and approaches adopted are all, in part at least, unsatisfactory (e.g. appointing a chief innovation officer, creating a separate innovation department or unit, apportioning self-directed exploratory time into an individual's working week).

A common thread to many of these approaches is the inferred need to separate 'innovative' or 'disruptive' activities from the daily running of 'business as usual'. Yet as lines are blurring between innovation and business as usual, we see a similar blurring between design and action, which are no longer simply sequential steps in an annual process, but rather iterations of ongoing management control and business as usual.

The roots of this trail all the way back to the formulation in the 1950s of the 'Plan-Do-Check-Act' (PDCA) or Deming cycle. Originally devised for the continuous improvement of processes, it appears increasingly relevant in the context of strategy in the modern business environment, where responding quickly to market changes has become a source of differentiation, or even a prerequisite for survival. Furthermore, whilst the cycle remains true, the speed with which one moves through it has seemingly increased. Like the colours of the spinning top that it resembles, this increase in speed causes the individual elements to blur into one continuous block of activity.

The lean entrepreneurship movement of recent years, as spearheaded by Steve Blank and Eric Ries, has reinvigorated this approach for a new generation of entrepreneurs with its similar 'Build-Measure-Learn' cycle. For RADAR, its importance lies in the principles of building a plan (the Horizon), evaluating

Figure 6.1 The PDCA or Deming cycle

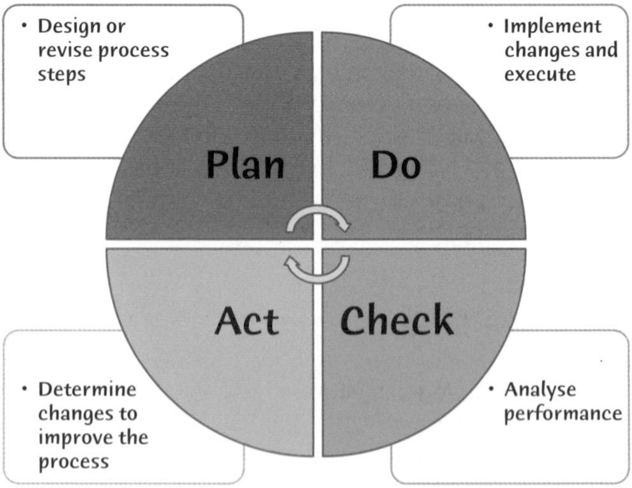

its performance and validity through the SIS and the results framework and then learning and acting through Horizon adjustments or shifts (discussed in Chapter 8). The A-cycle of agile insight, introduced in Chapter 5, echoes this in the research and analysis area.

The principles of design thinking and their role in RADAR

Alongside the lean entrepreneurship movement, design thinking, and its role in broader business strategy, has become a trending topic in recent years. There is more to this than simple hyperbole; if you strip away the worst excesses of its neologisms (for the record, idea generation *did* exist before 'ideation') and the keynote presentations high on lustre and low on content, there is still substance to this union. Many of the underlying principles of design thinking have an important contribution to make to the field of strategy, and RADAR specifically. Let us consider six in particular:

Principle 1: Put people and customers at the centre of everything the organisation does

Design thinking is sometimes referred to as human-centred design (HCD), a more expressive term embodying its core principle. Whilst marketing and sales account teams are typically the voice of the customer within their organisations, chanting their mantra of 'identifying, anticipating and satisfying customer requirements profitably',[32] HCD goes further by seeking genuine empathy with its subjects. Rather than focus groups and surveys (tell me what you think), HCD places greater emphasis on immersion, observation and co-creation (let me experience what you do). In the world of HCD, you understand the life of a fish not by visiting the aquarium, but by swimming in the sea.

In the world of RADAR, this has implications for how customers are incorporated into the organisation's strategic activities – from how customer insight is gathered (see Chapters 4 and 5) to how customers are engaged in the act of strategy development itself (see Chapters 7 and 8).

Principle 2: Needs first, solutions second

Linked to the first principle of customer-centricity is the tenet that exploring and identifying needs opens up possibilities, whereas jumping directly to a solution may result in overlooking brand new ways of doing things and potential step-changes in performance.

---

[32] The Chartered Institute of Marketing's official definition of marketing.

The tale of the sensor and the slipper

Working with a healthcare provider, I once explored options to reduce the risk of falls for the elderly – a serious issue for any healthcare system. Falls are the second leading cause of accidental or unintentional injury deaths worldwide, with adults over 65 years old suffering the greatest number of fatal falls.[33]

Working with one of the world's most respected technology firms, I spent time in their innovation labs as they demonstrated the latest sensor equipment, which could detect, and algorithmically profile, the microscopic changes in temperature at a person's house over the day, inferring from it their daily routine (e.g. tea-making, cooking dinner). By taking this data and combining it with other sensor data sources (e.g. carpet sensors), the technology could profile when the pattern of behaviour in the house was following the daily norm for that person, and when there was an abnormal divergence from it, and the likelihood that a fall had caused that divergence. The technology was impressive, and the company's initial proofs of concept had shown encouraging results.

A nurse I was working with at the time, with typical matter-of-factness, replied with a simple question: 'What about slippers?' Other research had shown that a significant proportion of those who had fallen were not wearing rubber-soled slippers that would have prevented the fall in the first place. Both methods were effective, but in the tale of the sensor and the slipper, that latter was far simpler and more cost-effective. I chalked it up as a lesson learned.

For RADAR, the lesson lies in the fact that truly understanding customers is key, and simply asking them what they want often does not yield the right answers. A good strategy is designed to meet clear needs and deliver specific outcomes.

Principle 3: Be holistic and multidisciplinary in your thinking

The role of design in modern business practice is truly multidisciplinary, encompassing a wide range of domains and disciplines including graphic and industrial design, production and software engineering and human sciences, to name but a few. The rise of the user experience (UX) movement over the past decade, the goal of which is to improve customer satisfaction and loyalty through the utility, ease of use, and pleasure provided in the interaction with a product',[34] is testimony to how far commercial design's influence now extends.

[33] World Health Organisation (WHO) Factsheet: Falls, available at http://www.who.int/mediacentre/factsheets/fs344/en/ [accessed 21 January 2019].

[34] Kujala, S., et al (2014) UX Curve: A method for evaluating long-term user experience, *Interacting with Computers*, 23(5), pp 473–83.

For RADAR, a multi-disciplinary approach is essential: strategic agility is meaningless if the business cannot support it operationally. Data and analytics are not useful add-ons to business as usual, they *are* business as usual. Furthermore, being 'holistic' (another over-used but necessary term) involves looking beyond your own organisation to understand how all influences on your organisation, and the influence it exerts on the wider world, are understood and incorporated into your decision making.

Principle 4: Use clear principles to guide and drive consistency through the design process

In our daily lives, the notion of principles has noble and ethical overtones – someone who sticks to their principles does the right thing, even when it is easier to do something else. In business, principles are used in a vast array of different circumstances, from business modelling to organisational values and culture. One area in which I have frequently used them is organisational design, and for three main reasons: first, to agree the overall direction and goals for the exercise; second, to drive consistency when making a range of interrelated decisions (e.g. macro structures, roles definitions, accountability and responsibility allocations); and third, to introduce objectivity into what can otherwise become very emotive subjects (e.g. the allocation of responsibilities and budgets, the redundancy of certain roles).

In RADAR, principles are the building blocks of your unifying purpose and, as with their use in organisational design, serve the three purposes of defining overall direction, guiding decision making and providing an objective basis against which to evaluate options.

Principle 5: Find and iterate solutions

Design thinking encourages cyclical prototyping and continual improvement, with each iteration resulting in both greater clarity of the customers' requirements,

Figure 6.2 Iteration in design thinking

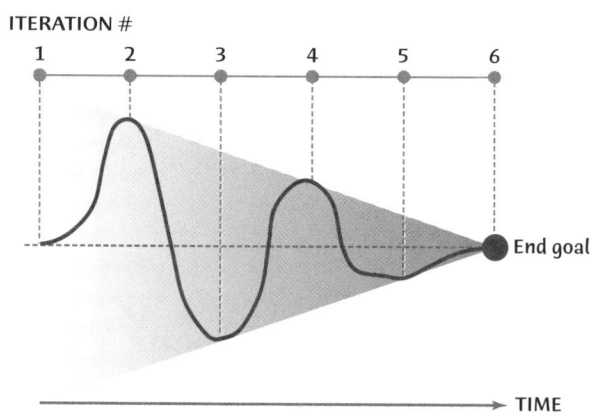

and a product that more closely addresses them. This iterative 'homing in' on customer needs is illustrated in the figure opposite.

In RADAR, defining the Horizon (Chapter 7) and Horizon Management (Chapter 8) embrace this iterative approach.

Principle 6: Translate insights into actionable solutions

Ultimately, design thinking seeks to develop useful, practical and desirable products. Tim Brown, Chief Executive of IDEO, defines design thinking as 'a discipline that uses the designer's sensibility and methods to match people's needs with what is technologically feasible and what is viable as a business strategy, so it can be converted into customer value and market opportunity'.[35] Thus, the IDEO model of human-centred design seeks the intersection between three interlinked questions:

- **Desirability:** in line with Principle 2, the approach starts with need – do customers want a solution to the need or want that has been identified?
- **Feasibility:** this addresses whether the organisation can serve the identified need (e.g. has the resources and capabilities to do so), i.e. can we do this?
- **Viability:** finally, even if it can be done, can it be done profitably and in line with the organisation's broader goals? In other words, *should* we do it?

In the context of RADAR, decisions regarding setting the Horizon (Chapter 7), and Horizon adjustments and shifts (Chapter 8) need to reflect this tripartite view.

Figure 6.3 Desirability, feasibility and viability

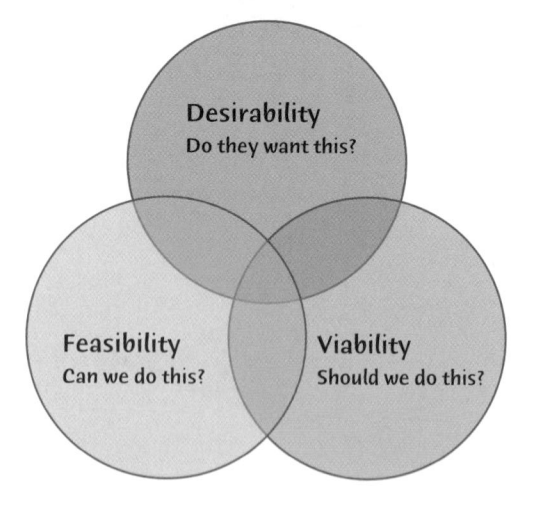

[35] Brown, T. (2009) *Change by Design*, New York: Harper Collins.

The short discussion of these six key principles above may leave you with the impression that I consider HCD a universal panacea, and at times others have almost presented it that way. It is not. There are limitations to it, of which the three most important from my perspective are:

- HCD is sometimes used as a substitute for strategy. However, despite its name it tends to be proposition-focused, and broader considerations of both where to play (e.g. relative attractiveness of end markets) and how to win (e.g. positioning) are only dealt with incidentally, if at all, in the core approach.

- In a similar vein, HCD is a process and set of tools, not a fully fledged system of management. It cannot replace the old way of doing things. However, it can enhance and contribute to a new way.

- HCD risks slaughtering the calf of step-change business model innovation at the altar of incremental innovation (e.g. improved propositions). There is room, and a need, for both in an organisation.

Apple is often held up as the exemplar for design thinking. However, in Steve Jobs it had a unique individual who was both an astute and driven businessman and a champion of the power of design. It was this combination, rather than design thinking on its own, that drove this. Indeed, I doubt Steve Jobs would even have considered his approach to be design thinking.

Another risk of HCD is justifying all failure as learning, whether it was avoidable or not. Whilst failing fast is justifiable in start-up environments, where the cost of failure can be relatively low, in established businesses it can be punishing and therefore must be parameterised. I am not saying it does not have a place in an established business – it does – only that it cannot be the sole method of working or used as justification for poor planning or thinking.

Get real

The final topic for this section is real options, as defined by Chris Matts and Olav Maassen. For these two practitioners, real options are about 'deferring decisions to the last responsible moment'[36] ('last responsible moment' being a term used to describe delaying commitment to an important, costly, irreversible and unclear decision until the point where the cost of not making the decision becomes greater than the cost of making it).[37]

The modern work environment makes this increasingly possible not only in software development, where it has been a mainstay of agile development for some time, but also in the real world. For example, the growth in skilled freelance staff, the evolution of third-party logistics outsourcing, software as a service,

---

[36] Matts, C. and Maassen, O. (2007) 'Real Options' Underlie Agile Practices, available at https://www.infoq.com/articles/real-options-enhance-agility [accessed 21 January 2019].

[37] See Rubin, K.S. (2013) *Essential Scrum*, New Jersey: Pearson Education, Inc.

remote working and cloud computing technology, temporary office space and even 3D printing are all enablers for reducing the lead time in building capacity and capability, and for trialling proof of concepts before committing to large-scale capital expenditure outlays.

A real option comprises four main components.

Table 6.1 Key components of a real option

	Component	Description
1	Value	The benefit that exercising the option will bestow on the business (e.g. financial, time)
2	Expiry	The point at which the option can no longer be exercised (e.g. due to time passing)
3	Purchase cost	The costs associated with creating the option (e.g. retainer fees)
4	Exercise cost	The cost of the option once you commit to it (e.g. new staff hires, capex investment)

The two key points here are:

1 Real options are a value equation, evaluating the relative benefit of each fork in the road by weighing up the collective cost of having these options with the benefits of exercising the right one when the time comes.

2 Real options are timebound (have an expiry date), after which they are no longer valid. Delaying production on two different types of Christmas lighting no longer has a value for that year once Christmas has passed.

In RADAR, real options play a role in designing the Horizon (enabling 'Dynamism by Design' – Chapter 7), considerations beyond the Horizon and Horizon shifts (Chapter 8).

What we cover in the next two chapters

Having laid down some basic tenets of lean entrepreneurship, design thinking and real options, the next two chapters show how RADAR incorporates them in the very design and execution of strategy, dissolving the barriers between designing and doing. We start with design.

Summary

- The test and learn approach of lean entrepreneurship, with its Build-Measure-Learn cycle, has a role in RADAR through defining the Horizon (build), measuring the impact of the Horizon choices over time (measure) and then implementing Horizon adjustments and shifts if required (learn and build).
- There are six key principles of design thinking that are incorporated within RADAR:
  - Put people and customers at the centre of everything the organisation does.
  - Needs first, solutions second.
  - Be holistic and multidisciplinary in your thinking.
  - Use design principles to guide and drive consistency through the design process.
  - Find and iterate solutions.
  - Translate insights into actionable solutions.
- Real options are about deferring decisions to the last responsible moment, enabling organisations to keep their options open and therefore to be more agile. The breadth, depth and quality of available resources and capabilities that can be brought into the organisation at short notice to enhance both capacity and capability are shifting real options from conceptual plausibility to practical reality.

Case story: Life is a (customer) journey

Sam had just spent a couple of hours going back through the customer research and analysis that had been undertaken to test their original hypotheses. It had been worth the time she had devoted to it, despite her initial feelings of guilt that there were other pressing items on her to-do list, as she now had before her a long list of insights grouped under the three areas of Project ChIC: channels, innovation of the proposition and customer engagement.

From a channel perspective, around 80 per cent of their customers would browse online before going into the store. That was not in itself particularly surprising. However, what and where they chose to browse, and how that varied by mission (i.e. their reason for looking) provided food for thought. For example, feedback on Leisurious' website was clear: it was too transactional – customers wanted it to reflect more fully their lifestyle and offer editorial and community content as well

▶

as product. In addition, browsing Instagram played a big role in discovery for the younger members of Leisurious' target audience, yet the organisation's commitment to that channel was limited to posting the same images it had on its website. Could it be more active and current in how it used social media? The recently introduced option to purchase directly from Instagram without leaving the site certainly warranted tracking as a 'Beyond the Horizon' opportunity and threat.

The customer survey feedback had also shone a light on a perennial theme that the company had only recently parked: sub-brands. Given their new Horizon, this might serve as an elegant solution to address the margin challenge whilst improving the overall appeal of the range and managing value for money perceptions. Sam had scribbled the words 'premium performance fabrics' in the margin of her notebook, the rash of athleisure offers that had flooded the market in recent times had opened consumers' minds to the benefits of performance fabrics. Could Leisurious incorporate them more effectively into its own product range as a premium product and market them accordingly? It could also manage assortment across channels to offer a more limited value-for-money range in certain third-party and outlet channels, whilst maintaining a more premium positioning in their own and in a limited number of other third-party channels. It was also clear that the lead-time reduction initiative that Mike was managing would become increasingly important for a customer base that had been weaned on to fast fashion at one end of the spectrum, and the 'see now, buy now' trend in high fashion at the other.

This line of thinking, alongside feedback from the survey, focus groups and accompanied shops, also talked to a different conceptualisation of customer engagement and loyalty. Whilst no customer was going to turn down promotions and money off, the bigger opportunity for engaging their core customer lay in exclusive content, priority access (e.g. to product launches or sales), limited editions and the growing trend of personalisation. The latter also provided an opportunity to make more of the store experience, with a personal stylist option (supported online and in store) and customisation of clothing. There were some interesting start-ups that could potentially serve as partners to accelerate the execution of some of this.

Sam leant back on her chair and paused. 'We all talk about being customer-focused', she thought, 'but how often do we truly follow through on the words?' There was plenty to share here with the rest of the team, and she would walk through the summary findings as the key part of the next monthly company meeting.

In your organisation

Exercise 6: Understand your customer

How much does your organisation know about its customers? This exercise looks at the data sources available to you to understand your customer and considers what more could be done.

1 With representation from key functions across the business, build a list of the sources of customer insight available to you. Potential sources may include:

- data captured through customer service interactions;
- feedback submitted by the customer directly to the company (e.g. feedback forms);
- feedback, comments and reviews on third-party platforms (e.g. social media, review sites);
- customer-facing staff feedback;
- one-off or regular surveys undertaken by the organisation;
- third-party reports and data sets.

2 For each source:

- Give a rating of 1 (low) to 5 (high) for its quality, based on the six dimensions discussed in Chapter 5 (completeness, consistency, uniqueness, validity, accuracy, timeliness).
- List both who currently has access to it, and who should have access to it.
- List what actions it drives, and what actions it should drive.
- Identify what would make the data more useful (e.g. combining with other data sources, including additional data elements).

3 Where quality ratings are low, distribution gaps exist or other actions could be taken, agree steps to address these issues.

4 What additional customer data sources would be useful?

- What value would they bring above and beyond the data already available?
- How would their usage change the actions taken in the organisation?

5 Develop a definitive list of customer data improvements based on the above analysis:

- Are these captured in the MEDS developed in the previous chapter's exercise?
- If not, why not?

For those that are deemed strategically critical, set to work implementing the required changes.

7

How to develop strategic intent and operational flexibility

'Design is a funny word. Some people think that design means how it looks. But, of course, if you dig deeper, it's really how it works.'

Steve Jobs

In this chapter we do the following:

- Explore the practicalities of defining UP.
- Outline key considerations when designing your organisation's Horizon.
- Understand the role of 'Beyond the Horizon' in design.
- Introduce dynamism by design and its contribution to your RAC rating.

Design sits at the very centre of RADAR – both literally (bridging analysis and action) and figuratively. The design principles we saw in the previous chapter – needs-focused, multi-disciplinary, principle-driven, iterative, actionable – find their expression in the two key areas of RADAR's design approach:

1 *Strategic intent:* as defined by your unifying purpose, Horizon, key considerations beyond the Horizon and target outcomes (SCORE and ERAs).

2 *Operational flexibility:* increasing the responsiveness and adaptability elements of your RAC rating by embracing dynamism by design.

This chapter digs deeper into each.

Designing good intent

As we saw in Chapters 1 and 5, RADAR's design of strategic intent addresses the following areas.

Table 7.1 Key elements of dynamism by design

	Area	*Description*
1	**Unifying purpose**	Your unifying purpose guides the two main Horizon decisions: which opportunities to pursue and how to win. It comprises a set of principles used to set direction and drive consistency and objectivity in decision making. In the context of your organisation's RAC rating, it primarily contributes to control, but also directs how you will adapt and the prioritisation of different changes.
2	**Horizon and target outcomes**	To define your Horizon, you must define the following: • **Horizon statements:** these are simple but substantive statements that define your Horizon, derived by distilling down your responses to the 5KQs. They are the levers of your agility, the hinge on which the direction of your organisation swings; if the Horizon Statements are no longer valid, then new ones must be defined (a Horizon Shift – see Chapter 8). • **Competitive position (3Ps):** the 3Ps of competitive position (positioning, proposition, performance) express how you intend to win and how you want your customers (actual and targeted), and the wider market, to experience your Horizon choices. This is where any design choices affecting customers need to find their expression. • **ARC (assumptions, risks, choices):** the Horizon's ARC is used to anticipate change. The definition of the ARC – translated into a set of measures and focus areas that can be validated on an ongoing basis – is part of the design process. • **AIR:** AIR (activities, investments and resources) makes your unifying purpose and Horizon real and must adjust to support Horizon shifts; without flexibility designed into your AIR (e.g. real options, use of third-party providers to inject capacity and/or capability), the strategic choice to Horizon shift cannot be fulfilled. • **Target outcomes (SCORE and ERAs):** the numbers and milestones you want the Horizon to deliver.
3	**Beyond the Horizon commitments**	Developing options for longer-term opportunities and taking other enabling actions to improve the agility of the organisation are reasons to design beyond the Horizon.

Together, the above fulfil the objectives of strategy outlined in the introduction – setting direction, creating meaning, determining choice and ultimately creating value. It all begins with defining UP.

Unifying purpose

We defined a unifying purpose as a set of principles whose role it is to:

1 Define the why and guide the how of the organisation – unifying aspiration and action.
2 Provide a directional imperative for all Horizon choices.
3 Provide criteria by which to assess all strategic choices (i.e. how to respond to the 5KQs in areas such as positioning, proposition and AIR choices).

In addition, we described the ABCD factors that shape it.

Table 7.2 ABCD factors

	Influence	Description
A	**Authentic beliefs**	Genuine, consistent beliefs that do not change unless the bases for them do
B	**Business strengths**	Resources or capabilities that differentiate your organisation from the competition
C	**Competitive/market space**	Untapped, emerging or under-served 'meta-needs' in the market (e.g. poor service, uninspired product designs)
D	**Desired outcomes**	What you want the organisation to achieve beyond simple financial success

Figure 7.1 Influencing factors when defining UP

To define UP for your organisation, observe the following principles:

1 **Be meaningful:** as discussed in the introduction, one of the four objectives of strategy is to create meaning. This is a critical aspect of a unifying purpose, as it must extend beyond simply achieving functional goals (i.e. be successful) to engage, inspire and enable people to make the right choices consistently (i.e. be meaningful, however you choose to define that term in your organisation).

2 **Consider multiple stakeholders:** to paraphrase a cliché, meaning is in the eye of the beholder. You must define UP not just with consideration for your actual or target customers, but also for other key stakeholders, most notably employees, suppliers and investors (or trustees in a charity). The table below outlines some of the key questions that relate to the meaningfulness of a unifying purpose for different stakeholder groups.

Table 7.3 Example stakeholder questions influenced by an organisation's unifying purpose

Stakeholder	Key questions
Employees	1. Why should I work for you?
	2. Will I be content or even proud to be associated with your organisation?
	3. How does what I am doing fit into the bigger picture?
	4. Why does what I do matter?
Customers	5. Why should I buy from you?
	6. Do your values, principles and self-image match mine?
Investors	7. Why should I invest in you?
	8. Does your risk profile match my risk appetite?
	9. Does this organisation have long-term value-generating potential?
Suppliers	10. Why should I supply you?
	11. Why would I treat you better than other companies I supply?

When defining UP, consider what you would want the responses to these questions to be. This will go a long way to directing your initial thoughts.

3 **Be principled and practical:** to ensure UP is not too narrowly defined, it should be defined as a set of principles, where each principle meets the following criteria:

- **Brief:** each principle should capture a single idea, concept or theme.
- **Grounded in a market need, business strength, authentic belief or desired outcome:** a principle must align either to a market need

(e.g. an under-served market segment or uninspiring career options for new graduates), a genuine organisational strength (e.g. leveraging an established brand), an authentic belief (i.e. a belief that will genuinely affect decision making, not something stated for marketing effect e.g. 100 per cent organic ingredients) or a desired outcome (e.g. achieving top decile ratings for customer satisfaction).

- **Necessitates trade-offs and directs action:** the principle must be specific and meaningful enough to drive genuine choices and actions. For example, the principle 'Make excellent products' does not qualify, because its opposite 'Make terrible products' is meaningless. By contrast, the principle 'Good design and function at a low price' (one of IKEA's governing principles) does fit this criterion, as its alternative 'Good design and function at a high price' is a viable alternative and the principle does drive choice and action (e.g. materials used, manufacturing complexity).

A unifying purpose typically comprises no more than seven principles or statements. This principles-based approach is key when defining UP and serves both to define overall direction and guide decision making by providing an objective basis against which to evaluate options.

4 **Consider what got you here:** unlike start-ups, an established business has a history, existing customers, established competitors and a competitive position. A unifying purpose should consider these, with emphasis on what makes the organisation great and its positioning and capabilities relative to its competitors. This is not to say the defining UP cannot mark a break from the past – there are plenty of examples where this has worked for organisations (e.g. Marvel transitioning from magazines to movies). However, any such break from the past needs to be an active choice.

5 **Combine the why and how:** my definition of UP talks of 'unifying aspiration and action'. To do so, consider the following questions.

Table 7.4 Aspiration and action considerations when defining UP

Category	Questions
Aspiration *What do you* *want to be?*	1. Who are your target customers (existing and desired)? 2. How would you want them to describe your organisation? 3. What are the key 'moments of truth' between you and them? 4. How is excellence expressed through these moments of truth? 5. Why will they choose you over your competitors? 6. How would you want other key stakeholders (e.g. employees, suppliers, investors) to describe your organisation? 7. Beyond this, why else does your organisation exist? 8. What does this all imply about the target outcomes you want to achieve?

Category	Questions
Action *What must* *you do to* *become and* *sustain that?*	9. What is the right positioning to adopt to support the above aspirations, given the market and competitive context? 10. How should this be expressed through the proposition? 11. What does this mean for how and where people access the proposition? 12. What does this mean for how your customers experience your proposition (i.e. what aspects of its performance are most important)? 13. How does this play to your current strengths? 14. How should AIR choices be made in the future to support this? 15. How will your organisation retain or further its advantage?

By considering these topics, you will produce a well-written unifying purpose that is specific, concise and necessitates choices. It will colour and shape your responses to the 5KQs, guiding and prioritising how the organisation changes. This unifying purpose, and the competitive position through which it finds expression, must be genuine and embraced with conviction, as it will invariably be tested hard at times, and posturing does not typically survive such tests.

Dunkin Donuts

With over 11,700 franchise restaurants in 33 countries, Dunkin Donuts is a major player in the global Quick Service Restaurants (QSR) market. Consider how the following statements could be used to define UP for the company:

- Unique everyday indulgences for individuals, families, friends and colleagues to enjoy.
- Food and experiences that are fresh and fun.
- 'Distinctively Dunkin', whether in store, at home, at work or on the go.
- The best donuts. Period.
- Considerate, straightforward and responsible in how we act.

Defining UP in this way fulfils three roles:

- **Define why and how:** creating foods and experiences that are fresh and fun and distinctively Dunkin, accessible in store, at home, at work and on the go, and acting in ways which are considerate, straightforward and responsible (e.g. in how to address healthy eating) all point to the why and how of Dunkin Donuts.
- **A directional imperative:** everyday indulgence, food and experiences, uniqueness, individuals, families, friends and colleagues, and best donuts all build on Dunkin Donuts' strengths and provide focus.

▶

- **Criteria for strategic choices:** the UP defined above places emphasis on uniqueness, freshness, fun, consideration, straightforwardness and responsibility – packaged as being distinctively Dunkin. This will guide everything from new product development to channel strategy, staff development to marketing.

This example highlights an important distinction between mission and vision statements and a unifying purpose, mentioned in Chapter 1. UP is defined exclusively for internal use (and shared with key partners and suppliers). The translation of what UP means for customers is then the role of those with a customer-facing role (most notably marketing, sales and customer-facing operations). Contrast this with mission and vision statements such as the ones above, which are often communicated directly to the end customer, clouding their objectives.

Horizon setting

Make a statement

The Horizon summarises the market opportunities you are targeting (where to play) and how you intend to succeed (how to win). In the design part of RADAR, the responses to the 5KQs that define the Horizon, informed by research and analysis, are distilled down into Horizon statements – simple but substantive expressions that encapsulate your Horizon. Horizon statements must reflect both the targeted market opportunities and your competitive position.

Figure 7.2 Considerations when creating Horizon statements

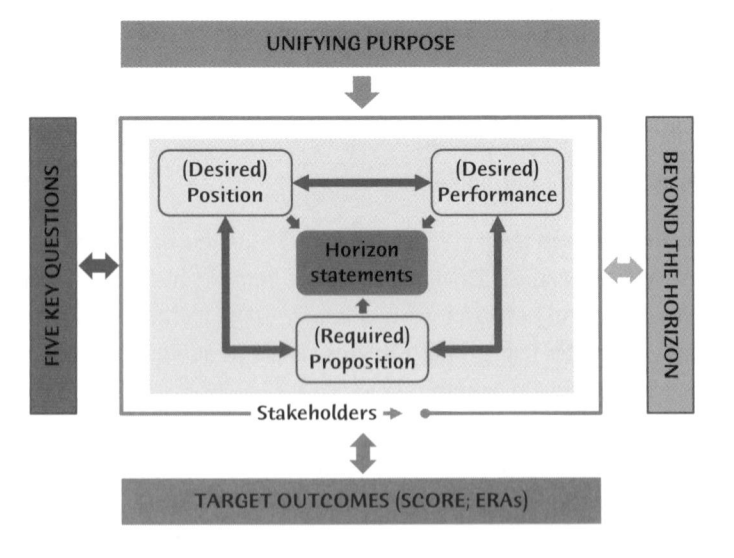

When creating your Horizon statements, do the following:

1 **Discuss all the 5KQs:** as a team, do not just jump directly to the Horizon questions 'Where do we play?' and 'How do we win?' A meaningful discussion, underpinned with research and analysis, that debates 'Where is the opportunity?', 'What makes us great?' and 'How should we adapt?' is critical to developing a shared understanding, richness and depth.

2 **Be guided by your unifying purpose:** given the potential opportunities identified (both internal and external), what does UP tell you about which to prioritise and how to address them?

3 **Debate target outcomes:** typically, target outcomes will be a mixture of those set independently of the Horizon statements (e.g. sales or profit targets to fulfil shareholder expectations, regulatory requirements) and those set as a result of defining them (e.g. entry into a new market). Regardless of their origination, target outcomes must clearly link to the Horizon statements. It there are target outcomes without associated Horizon statements, or vice versa, then this must be resolved.

4 **Consider current areas beyond the Horizon:** you may already be investing in long-term changes (e.g. R&D in new product categories) or exploring how to exploit emerging market opportunities or technologies (e.g. use of artificial intelligence). These are typical 'Beyond the Horizon' considerations (even if they are not currently labelled as such) and need to be discussed when setting the Horizon, principally to determine which of the following three roles they will play:

● Remain a formalised 'Beyond the Horizon' consideration.

● Become part of the new Horizon.

● Cease to be actively considered or pursued.

5 **Adopt multiple perspectives:** ensure that the mix of people discussing the Horizon is suitably diverse in terms of function, experience, hierarchy, etc. As with defining UP, incorporating multiple stakeholder perspectives is fundamental to defining Horizon statements.

6 **Use the 3Ps starting with position:** in Chapter 4 we considered the 3Ps of competitive position:

● Position leads the 3Ps in this case, as it defines how the organisation wants to be perceived (i.e. the effect it will have on its stakeholders).

● Performance is the desired level to be achieved on measures that reflect this target positioning. This is where you define your Horizon-specific target outcomes (SCORE) and how you will get there (ERAs). It also informs your AIR decisions.

- Proposition, the final P, is the means through which the targeted position is experienced by the customer, and the target performance realised, and is therefore subordinate to them both.

For example, a restaurant's desire to be considered the finest in fine dining (position), reflected in Michelin stars and high levels of customer satisfaction (performance), requires a proposition that bears certain characteristics (e.g. innovative and delicious recipes, the finest ingredients, a great atmosphere in the restaurant, excellent service).

7 **Create balance across the Horizon statements:** the Horizon statements, when considered collectively, should be:

- **Cohesive:** all statements are reinforcing and complementary (e.g. an entry-level positioning for a car brand should not have a top-of-the-market product specification).
- **Compelling:** the combined 3Ps, as defined by the organisation's principles, should have intrinsic appeal for its target stakeholders (e.g. customers, employees, investors, suppliers).
- **Competitive:** as well as intrinsic appeal, the combined statements should have distinctive appeal and meaning within the context of the organisation's competitive set.

Making a statement with value hotels

Consider the example of an established value hotel chain that is looking to consolidate its position and drive future growth. Example Horizon statements might include the following:

- Further enhance our reputation in the market for offering great value through investment in the areas that customers value highly (e.g. comfortable beds, quiet surroundings, a decent shower).
- Roll out further hotels in catchments that reflect the local dynamics driving our current success.
- Create a premium economy offering in our larger city centre hotels to increase share of business visitors and revenue per available room (RevPAR) by 5 per cent in implemented hotels.
- Offer a new range of fresh and healthy meals for each daypart and a greater focus on food origin.
- Introduce a revised loyalty programme with enriched content and benefits extending beyond the walls of the hotel.

Describe your competitive position

To answer the 5KQs and design its Horizon, an organisation must reflect on its competitive position (particularly 'What makes us great?' and 'How should we adapt?'). Documenting each of the 3Ps is a key element of the design process, providing the blueprint for how the organisation can compete and win.

Positioning

Positioning directly addresses an organisation's target customers, creating in them thoughts and feelings and describing benefits that directly address their needs, wants, behaviours and attitudes. Marty Neumeier talks of 'onliness' – a market space in which you can claim as an organisation to be the only one.[38] Thus Zara, the international clothing retailer, might position itself as 'The only international fashion retailer that both sets and sells the latest trends hot off the runway at affordable prices to fashion-loving customers of all ages who want to feel current and stylish in the era of fast-fashion.' Noted, that is quite a mouthful, but it captures:

- What it is (a fashion retailer).
- How it is different (setting and selling the most current styles at affordable prices).
- Who it is serving (fashion-loving customers of all ages).
- Why it is important (people want to feel current and stylish in the era of fast fashion).

Proposition

An organisation's proposition is the bundle of products and services that are offered to an intended target customer or mindset,[39] and how they access it. It is the embodiment of the organisation's position and comprises the following elements:

Figure 7.3 Elements of a proposition

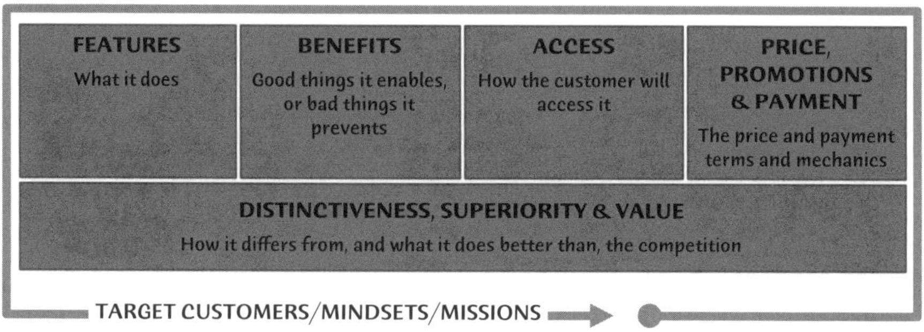

FEATURES	BENEFITS	ACCESS	PRICE, PROMOTIONS & PAYMENT
What it does	Good things it enables, or bad things it prevents	How the customer will access it	The price and payment terms and mechanics

DISTINCTIVENESS, SUPERIORITY & VALUE
How it differs from, and what it does better than, the competition

TARGET CUSTOMERS/MINDSETS/MISSIONS ➡ ⬤

---

[38] Neumeier, M. (2007) *Zag: The number-one strategy of high-performance brands*, Berkeley, CA: New Riders.

[39] Note a target customer can have different 'mindsets', e.g. prioritising convenience in the morning rush and high service levels in the evening.

- *Features:* this describes what it is and does. For example, a lawnmower has sharp blades, a basket for grass cuttings, offers adjustable heights for the blades, etc.
- *Benefits:* the benefits are the good things that the proposition does for the customer (e.g. cuts wet grass as well as it does dry), or the bad things that it prevents (e.g. easy maintenance). These can be experienced through the senses (e.g. a great looking lawn) or emotionally (e.g. a garden you are proud of).
- *Access:* whilst channels have traditionally been discussed separately, and we did so ourselves when exploring opportunities in Chapter 4, they are such an integral part of how 21st-century companies compete on their offer, from cloud computing through to internet banking, that I consider them an integral part of the proposition discussion. For our lawnmower, this could include access to annual maintenance checks at major garden centre chains.
- *Price and payment:* the price paid, and the terms and mechanisms of that payment (e.g. monthly payments, interest-free credit for 12 months) are key components of the proposition and the customer's perception of value – ask any car dealer.
- *Distinctiveness, superiority and value:* this defines what it does differently and better than the competition. This can originate from any one, or combination of, the other elements of the proposition. For example, the lawnmower may be cordless, which, combined with its revolutionary body shape and wheel configuration, gives it market-leading manoeuvrability and enables it to get into even the tightest nooks of your garden.

A strong proposition typically meets the following five criteria:

1 Aligned with what matters most to the target customers (e.g. performance, price, quality).
2 Focused on emerging, unmet or under-served needs.
3 Distinctive and differentiated from the competition (and superior in at least one aspect).
4 Supported by the organisation's broader competitive position and business model.
5 Difficult to copy (e.g. due to the combined capabilities required to produce it, patent protection).

When designing your value proposition, explicitly compare it with the target customer's next best alternatives, so that you can understand where the true differentiated benefit lies.

> **John Lewis**
>
> John Lewis first launched a Click and Collect offer in February 2009. At that time, it had 28 full-line stores and a further two John Lewis at Home sites in the UK, limiting the reach of its proposition. However, over 2010 it trialled the extension of Click and Collect into Waitrose supermarkets (owned by the same group, which had a total of 223 stores in 2010). By transforming the access component of its proposition, it was able to do the following:
>
> - Increase John Lewis' online sales significantly by making 130,000 products accessible via Click and Collect to a far wider audience.
> - Enhance Waitrose's appeal – supermarket shopping could now include the collection of a wide range of other goods – increasing footfall and encouraging grocery sales.

Performance

The final P of competitive position – performance – reflects the execution or 'operationalisation' of the positioning and proposition, for example, delivering minimum or target levels of performance. Therefore, in the case of the lawnmower, customer feedback on the manoeuvrability of the machine or data on the mean time between repairs will reflect elements of the competitive position. These then feed into the minimum enterprise data set (see Chapter 5).

ARC

The moment of defining the Horizon is also the best time to capture the assumptions, risks and choices or consequences (ARC) that underpin it. Voicing and documenting these as you go is a necessary discipline, and for each Horizon statement you should ask yourselves as a group what assumptions, risks and choices or consequences are bound up in that Horizon statement. Whilst this might feel repetitive, the answers are often instructive, and can draw out potential underlying conflicts between the Horizon statements (see my earlier point on Horizon statement cohesiveness). Chapter 9 gives an example of documenting an ARC.

AIR design

With the Horizon set and the competitive position defined, you need the AIR behind it to deliver the required results. Chapter 3 described the

ADAPT framework, and Chapter 4 AIR cover. Together, these can be used to determine and design organisational change. This requires the following steps:

1 As part of Horizon setting, debate each of the areas of the ADAPT framework (aim, drivers and trends, AIR, positioning and proposition, technology) in relation to both your market opportunities and organisational situation.

2 Having created your Horizon statements, determine the critical success factors (CSF) that underpin them and any Beyond the Horizon requirements (see next section).

3 Determine the AIR cover for these CSF, noting where:

   ● it differs from that relating to the current Horizon;

   ● additional capacity (rather than capability) is an issue.

4 Determine the associated AIR modifications, creating an 'up, down, in, out' plan (Chapter 4).

5 The scale and sequencing of change in your 'up, down, in, out' plan determines whether it is an adjustment to your existing Horizon or a full-blown Horizon shift (see Horizon planning, Chapter 8).

Figure 7.4 AIR elements

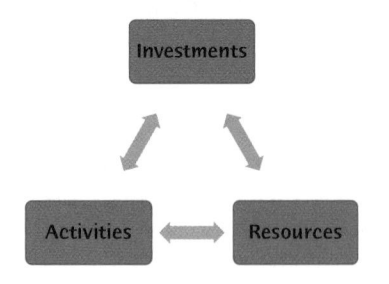

Note that, whilst this approach does not necessarily involve a wholesale redesign of the operating model, it often raises areas that require substantial change or investment (often relating to people, data, systems and technology). The practical challenge lies in balancing and prioritising these changes, guided by the unifying purpose and the anticipated demands of the market.

Target outcomes

Defining your Horizon will include setting the numbers (SCORE) you wish to achieve and the milestones (ERAs) you will hit along the way. The three broad steps involved are:

1 For each Horizon statement:
- Think across the SCORE elements and identify the most relevant measures that would express that statement's performance.
- Use 'backcasting' (see Chapter 9) to determine the ERAs and associated measures required to track them over time.

2 Once completed for all Horizon statements, identify overlaps and opportunities to rationalise the total number of SCORE measures and ERAs whilst still retaining full coverage of target outcomes.

3 Set targets for each measure informed by a combination of historical performance, market norms or requirements, expert stakeholder opinion, modelling and aspiration (see Chapter 9).

This topic is addressed in detail in Chapter 9.

Looking Beyond the Horizon: timing and S-curves

We have introduced the long- and short-term elements that inform considerations Beyond the Horizon (see Chapter 5). Whilst RADAR focuses on the Horizon, it must also look selectively beyond it given the longer lead times associated with certain organisational changes, the need to manage emerging market developments and the requirement to enable broader organisational changes that are only indirectly related to the Horizon.

Figure 7.5 Areas beyond the Horizon

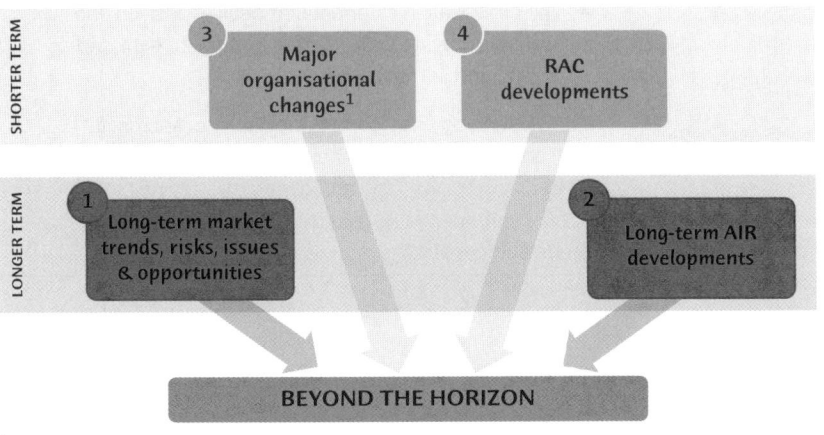

[1] e.g. R&D breakthroughs, acquisitions, disposals, loss of key staff

Clay Christensen[40] elegantly summarises the challenge of industry S-curves (the growth, maturity and phasing out of a technology or chosen path) and the lead time required to prepare for new directions:

'If a company has ignored investing in new businesses until it needs those new sources of revenue and profits, it's already too late. It's like planting saplings when you decide you need more shade. It's just not possible for those trees to grow large enough to create shade overnight. It takes years of patient nurturing to have any chance of the trees growing tall enough to provide it.'[41]

From a design perspective, the implication for potential Horizon shifts is clear. Like a strategic Eugene O'Neill, you must selectively ask 'What lies beyond the Horizon?' in parallel to the existing Horizon. This question can be answered through four key methods.

Table 7.5 Four methods for reaching beyond the Horizon

	Method	Description
1	**Insight**	In determining your Horizon and its ARC, you will have collated significant market and organisational insight to support your Horizon statements, including future-looking trends, risks, issues and opportunities. Exploring how these could change the current Horizon and ARC under different scenarios is an important starting point.

This analysis should include consideration of:

- Opportunities not currently addressable by the organisation (e.g. because they are sub-scale, or because the organisation does not have the relevant capability).

- The organisation's current competitive position and AIR, and how they might be further leveraged, exploited or augmented in the future.

Many technology companies (e.g. Google, Microsoft, IBM) and increasingly companies from other sectors (e.g. trend-driven fast-fashion and general merchandise retailers) employ teams to track, evaluate and transform emerging trends and capabilities into viable ventures.

[40] Christensen, C.E., Raynor, M.E. and McDonald, R. (2015) What is Disruptive Innovation? *Harvard Business Review*, available at https://hbr.org/2015/12/what-is-disruptive-innovation [accessed 3 May 2018].
[41] Christensen, C.M., Allworth, J. and Dillon, K. (2012) *How Will You Measure Your Life?* London: HarperCollins.

	Method	Description
2	**Testing**	Where the potential warrants it, market lead time permits it and the organisation has the capacity and capability to do so, testing new (minimum viable) propositions to gain a better understanding and validate the potential or requirement for longer-term changes beyond the current Horizon can work. This can be particularly effective where you are building off an existing positioning or product platform, as has been the case with Kellogg's development of its Crunchy Nut product using a test and learn approach.[42]
3	**Venturing**	Venturing on a small number of potential future options represents the next step up in terms of cost, commitment and risk. Again, this would be informed by insight and initial testing where possible, run in parallel to the current Horizon activity and reviewed in each Horizon gateway.
		It can take different forms, from straight 'big bets' through to incremental venturing. In the latter's case, consider an approach where, adopting the 'segmentality' of Chapter 3, you break down different potential big bets and identify 'Perspective connectives' or common elements (Chapter 2) that could be used to support any of them. By combining this with the use of real options, you could de-risk the venture by investing incrementally in areas that could be put to a range of potential future uses. For example, consider an organisation exploring the development of an online holiday accommodation marketplace, which could comprise either or both of individual privately owned sites (e.g. an aggregator for villas) or professional multi-unit sites (e.g. holiday parks). Its AIR development requirements would include the following:

- Elements that are unique to either individual or multi-unit sites (e.g. a property services team for cleaning and prepping villas would not be required on multi-unit sites, which will have their own professional cleaning service on site).
- Perspective connectives that are common to both options (e.g. a flexible online portal where it is easy to browse, book and pay).

Developing elements that progress these perspective connectives and prioritising those elements with a long lead-time, whilst maintaining the option to adapt later, would offer the greatest flexibility as the organisation explores which option to pursue (see Figure 7.6).

(continued)

[42] See http://www.ibbusinessandmanagement.com/uploads/1/1/7/5/11758934/kelloggs-edition-15-full.pdf [accessed 3 May 2018].

Table 7.5 Four methods for reaching beyond the Horizon (*continued*)

Method	Description

Figure 7.6 Example holiday marketplace portal considerations

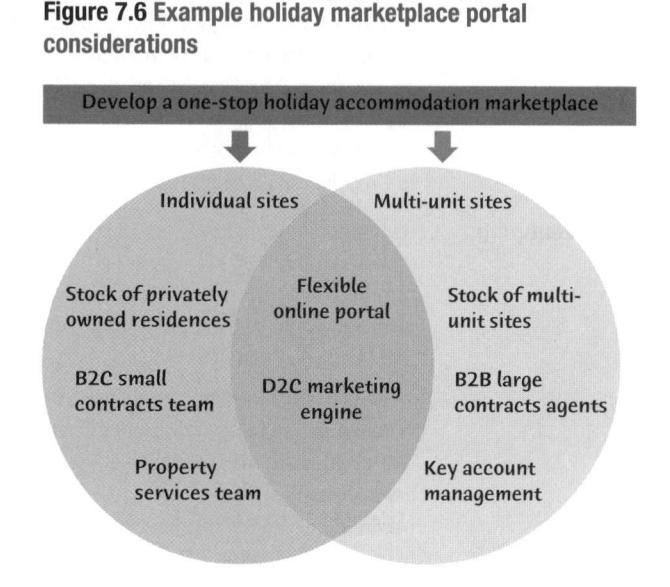

4	**Acquisition**	Sometimes, tracking and acquiring businesses may be the right course of action to manage transitions in the market. However, it can be an expensive and risky endeavour. Facebook spent $1bn acquiring its mobile-first rival Instagram in 2012, and then $19bn for WhatsApp two years later – a high price to pay for coming to the mobile party late.

The key takeaway from this short discussion of beyond the Horizon is that the understanding methods of longer-term opportunities (insight, testing) soon morph into delivery (through venturing and acquisition). Therefore, managing these alongside the current Horizon necessitates dedicated resources, the extent of which will be limited by the three-headed Cerberus that guards the gates of all investments: cash, organisational capacity and risk appetite.

Redesigning the engine whilst flying

The discussion of strategic intent so far has focused on the Horizon's initial design. However, RADAR adapts this intent to its changing circumstances, whether through modest adjustments to the existing Horizon or full-blown

Horizon shifts. This is covered in the next two chapters, but 'designing in' the operational flexibility required to make it work is the topic to which we now turn.

Dynamism by design

Strategic agility necessitates operational flexibility: the RAC criteria of agility (responsiveness, adaptability, control) must be embedded in the design of the Horizon itself. I call this 'Dynamism by Design', and there are an increasing number of levers available across the domains of people, process, technology and data that can be used to embed agility within an organisation:

Figure 7.7 Example dynamism by design levers

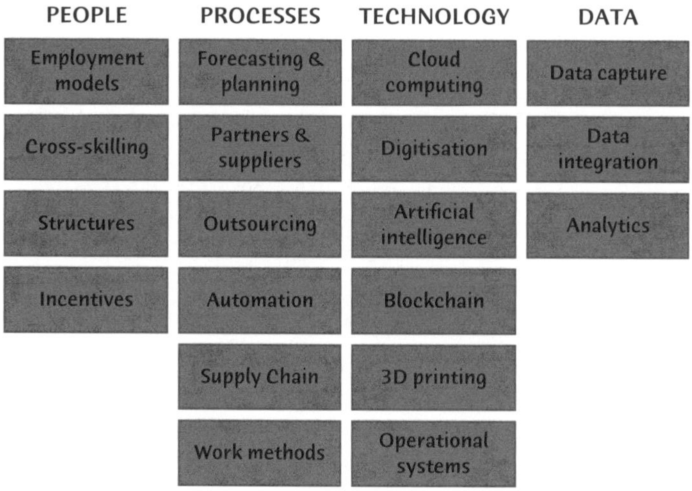

PEOPLE	PROCESSES	TECHNOLOGY	DATA
Employment models	Forecasting & planning	Cloud computing	Data capture
Cross-skilling	Partners & suppliers	Digitisation	Data integration
Structures	Outsourcing	Artificial intelligence	Analytics
Incentives	Automation	Blockchain	
	Supply Chain	3D printing	
	Work methods	Operational systems	

The list above only skims the surface of options available to design greater agility into your organisation, and others will no doubt appear over the next few years. The intent here is simply to whet your appetite for the possible and encourage you to think through the different ways in which your people, processes, technology and data can be managed to drive the responsiveness, adaptability and control underpinning greater agility. If agility and the capacity to change is not designed into the operations of the business, then inflexibility will have to be managed out as it is encountered, and that will slow you down.

A final thought on not changing

One consequence of the more vigorous proselytising on agility is the widespread misperception it can create that staying the same is for losers and associated

Table 7.6 Levers to embed agility in the design of an organisation

Lever	Description
PEOPLE	
Employment models	A 2018 report by the World Economic Forum[43] identifies five sources of workforce input:
	1 **Core workforce:** permanent employees filling a range of (changing) roles.
	2 **Company affiliates:** external associates with a good understanding of, and strong association with, the organisation (e.g. alumni).
	3 **Partners:** talent provided by outsourcing/managed service providers.
	4 **Publicly available talent:** specialised talent sourced and/or managed by a third party.
	5 **Consumers:** crowdsourcing talent to solve problems, get ideas, gather data and complete field work.
	Every category other than the core workforce offers the opportunity to 'plug and play' capacity and capability when required, allowing companies to scale and skill up temporarily when circumstances demand it. The rise of experienced freelancers and next-generation temp agencies are making this opportunity increasingly accessible.
Cross-skilling	Cross-skilling core staff is a long-established practice to manage the vicissitudes of demand in the short term. It is most effective where the diversity of activities and/or the depth of skill and experience required to do them is more limited. Collaborative working and team stability are key enablers of cross-skilling.
Structures	When exploring agile practices in software development, much is made of small, dynamic cross-functional teams. Three principles govern such structures:
	• **Organise around the customer journey:** hierarchies, business units, divisions and products are the mainstays of organisational structures, but agile software development focuses instead on organising around the customer journey.
	• **Be cross-functional:** each team contains all the capabilities and domain knowledge required to complete the task.
	• **Self-organise:** teams are 'self-organising', meaning that they have the responsibility and authority to add, remove, retrain or reorganise team members as required.

[43] World Economic Forum (2018) Operating Models for the Future of Consumption, available at https://www.weforum.org/reports/operating-models-for-the-future-of-consumption [accessed 1 May 2018].

Lever	Description
	Whilst these principles may be difficult to transpose wholesale into a larger corporate entity, replicating aspects of the customer focus, cross-functional integration and autonomy can contribute considerably to a more agile structure. Satya Nadella, CEO of Microsoft, explained the importance of organising into capabilities that can be applied to different customer problems in an interview in 2018: 'In the long run, we [in the technology sector] are much more capability-driven. I want a silicon capability. I want a cloud-computing capability. I want an AI capability. I want great product aesthetics in devices. Then we want to be able to take [these capabilities] and apply them to different markets at different times. Without this strategic flexibility, it's very, very hard.'[44]
Incentives	Incentives can be a barrier to organisational agility. They can also be a catalyst, where shared metrics relating to, for example, responsiveness or collaboration form an important part of recognition and remuneration.
PROCESSES	
Forecasting and planning	The role and purpose of forecasting and planning in an agile organisation requires careful thought. In the face of Horizon management, traditional organisational-level forecasting is less meaningful (although financial goals must still of course be set for key stakeholders including investors, shareholders and banks). However, a SIS can contribute to targeted and more informed forecasting and planning, regularly updated as more data becomes available. The impact of this can be felt in other areas listed in this section, such as lower inventory or more effective service from partners.
Partners and suppliers	Increasing partner and supplier responsiveness and adaptability through better systems, processes, data, governance, communication and contracting, typically achieved through greater inter-company integration, can have a material impact on an organisation's agility.
Outsourcing	Outsourcing, when done well, can increase an organisation's agility significantly. Take for example customer services, where a good (and scaled) outsource partner is able to increase short-term capacity to maintain service levels, flexibly bring in multi-lingual support and increase productivity through focus, specialism and systems to adapt as the business grows.

(continued)

[44] McKinsey Quarterly Podcast (April 2018) Microsoft's next act, available at https://www.mckinsey.com/industries/high-tech/our-insights/microsofts-next-act [accessed 1 May 2018].

Table 7.6 Levers to embed agility in the design of an organisation (*continued*)

Lever	Description
Automation	From basic marketing automation through to intelligent process automation, which combines process redesign, robotics and machine learning, automation is being used to initially mimic activities currently undertaken by humans, and then improve on them over time. From banking to warehousing, the potential impact is significant: one report estimates that up to 45% of employee activities can be automated by adopting current technologies, reducing errors and increasing responsiveness.[45]
Supply chain	System thinking and the theory of constraints reflect the idea that 'a chain is as strong as its weakest link'. The rewording 'a supply chain is as agile as its least agile element' equally applies. Lean practices, from better information and process integration across partners through to more dynamic sourcing (e.g. increasing near-shore sourcing for high sell-through items), more responsive inventory management (e.g. single pool of stock, consignment models) and quicker fulfilment, can significantly improve the agility of an organisation.
Work methods	Agile working practices such as Scrum, and their 'scaled' counterparts such as SAFe,[46] LeSS,[47] Disciplined Agile (DA)[48] and XSCALE,[49] share some common traits such as co-location, cross-functional teams, iteration, short 'sprints', autonomy, minimum viable products, activity visualisation, failing quickly and empowerment. Deploying these practices, where appropriate, can increase responsiveness and adaptability; the challenge remains ensuring that it does so whilst maintaining the levels of control required in a larger organisation. We touch on this in Chapter 10.
TECHNOLOGY	
Cloud computing	The rise of cloud computing and open source systems has lowered the investment and time required to build systems infrastructure and enter or scale new business areas. From open source eCommerce platforms such as Magento or Shopify through to Salesforce's suite of software as a service (SaaS) customer management tools and even advanced AI tools through IBM Cloud, there are a wide range of scalable and extensible options available.

[45] McKinsey (January 2017) Introducing the next-generation operating model, available at https://www.mckinsey.com/business-functions/digital-mckinsey/our-insights/introducing-the-next-generation-operating-model [accessed 2 May 2018].
[46] See https://www.scaledagileframework.com [accessed 21 January 2019].
[47] See https://less.works [accessed 21 January 2019].
[48] See http://www.disciplinedagiledelivery.com [accessed 21 January 2019].
[49] See http://xscalealliance.org [accessed 21 January 2019].

Lever	Description
Digitisation	As technology advances, the range of activities and resources subject to digitisation – from newspapers to nanosurgery – continues to grow. Certain objectives of digitisation appear to be similar across industries and use cases (e.g. speed, transparency, searchability, quality, convergence), and many of the benefits can support all three RAC criteria.
Artificial intelligence	Artificial intelligence (AI) is a big bet investment for many of the tech giants (Google, Apple, Facebook, Amazon, IBM, Microsoft). Its commercial applications are still nascent (e.g. chatbots on customer service sites, driverless cars, decision support in insurance claims), but its potential to drive greater agility is clear: it can transform responsiveness (as seen in the use of chatbots), adaptability (learning from large data sets about emerging patterns is at its core) and control (as seen in driverless cars).
Blockchain	Originating as a distributed ledger for cryptocurrencies, blockchain has the potential to transform a broad range of activities, from banking and music services through to voting for government. Its champions maintain that the distributed nature of its structure and its resistance to modification (i.e. it is highly secure) creates opportunities to reduce costs and increase responsiveness by eliminating human intermediaries. We are still in the very early days of this technology, but opportunities to drive greater agility through it will come.
3D printing	3D printing has existed for decades, albeit with use limited to a small number of manufacturing industries. As the technology has matured, its growth has come mainly from business process applications rather than consumer usage (e.g. component manufacture in aeronautics, customer implant and drugs in the medical and pharma arena, even 3D printed shoes[50]). There is potential here for greater responsiveness (e.g. print on demand products, already available for books) and adaptation (e.g. co-creation and personalisation).
Operational systems	Not all systems are in the cloud (see above), and there are agility improvements to be gained from managing existing systems more effectively, whether that be through better architecture, improved workflows, greater integration (see data integration below) or simply improved maintenance.

(continued)

[50] See https://techcrunch.com/2017/04/07/adidas-latest-3d-printed-shoe-puts-mass-production-within-sight [accessed 21 January 2019].

Table 7.6 Levers to embed agility in the design of an organisation (*continued*)

Lever	Description
DATA	
Data capture	To repeat that hackneyed management mantra: if you do not measure it, you cannot manage it. Designing and managing your MEDS (Chapter 5) is a key part of both baselining and improving your organisation's agility.
Data integration	Data integration applies within an organisation (e.g. linking together different functional or channel data sets) and across organisations (e.g. with partners and suppliers) and extends out to broader market data. The use of increasingly sophisticated middleware, data vaults and data lakes (see Chapter 5) can drive better use of internal and external data, and with it greater agility as the organisation learns to connect key data types (e.g. a 'single view of the customer' across all channels) and adapt its products and services to respond more quickly (e.g. ensuring complaints on social media can be quickly associated with orders and customer records, leading to faster resolution).
Analytics	There has been no shortage of coverage over the past few years of how analytics can be used to diagnose, predict or even prescribe activity and, in doing so, lead to a more responsive organisation which is primed to adapt to emergent trends.

with failure. This is simply not true. Jeff Bezos provides an interesting perspective on managing change, or more specifically managing 'not change':

'*It helps to base your strategy on things that won't change. When I'm talking with people outside the company, there's a question that comes up very commonly: "What's going to change in the next five to ten years?" But I very rarely get asked, "What's not going to change in the next five to ten years?" At Amazon we're always trying to figure that out, because you can really spin up flywheels around those things. All the energy you invest in them today will still be paying you dividends ten years from now. Whereas, if you base your strategy first and foremost on more transitory things — who your competitors are, what kind of technologies are available, and so on — those things are going to change so rapidly that you're going to have to change your strategy very rapidly, too.*'[51]

[51] Kirby, J. and Stewart, T.A. (2007) The institutional yes, *Harvard Business Review*, October 2007.

When designing your Horizon, do consider what the research and analysis tells you about what will not change, as well as what will, and ensure that both are reflected in your Horizon choices.

Gatorade goes back to first principles[52]

Back in 2008, Gatorade was in the throes of decline. Faced with stiff competition from Coca Cola's lower-cost Powerade, it had seen sales drop by 10 per cent whilst its rival's grew by 13 per cent. Its initial response of launching new flavours, low- and no-calories variants and exploring new channels was not fuelling the required turnaround.

It returned to the first principle of design and focused on customer need. It discovered that its core customer, the serious athlete, carb-loaded before an event and drank protein shakes to recover after it. This showed a clear opportunity to offer three complementary products: energy chews and drinks to 'prime' before an athletic event, core hydration drinks to help the customer 'perform', and protein shakes and bars to 'recover' after an event. With fewer flavours, less discounting and innovating around the current product rather than away from it, sales returned from a low of $4.5bn in 2009 to $5.6bn in 2015.

Summary

- RADAR's design approach focuses on two areas: strategic intent and operational flexibility.
- Strategic intent is expressed through an organisation's unifying purpose, Horizon, key considerations beyond the Horizon and target outcomes (SCORE and ERAs).
- A unifying purpose defines the why and guides the how of the organisation – unifying aspiration and action and providing a 'directional imperative' for all Horizon choices. A well-written UP is specific, concise and necessitates choices.
- The Horizon summarises the market opportunities you are targeting (where to play), and how you intend to succeed (how to win). It is expressed through Horizon statements which, collectively, must be cohesive, compelling and competitive.

▶

---

[52] See https://hbr.org/2017/08/how-gatorade-invented-new-products-by-revisiting-old-ones [accessed 10 May 2018].

- Whilst RADAR focuses on the Horizon, it must also look selectively beyond it given the longer lead times associated with certain changes, the need to manage emerging market developments and the requirement to enable broader organisational changes that are only indirectly related to the Horizon. Insight, testing, venturing and acquisition are four mechanisms through which this can be done.
- Strategic agility necessitates operational flexibility: the RAC criteria of agility must be embedded in the design of the Horizon itself. Dynamism by design is the ethos that supports this and reflects multiple levers available across the domains of people, process, technology and data.

Case story: Changes on the Horizon

Emma was doing what she had done countless times before: sitting at her desk and ruminating on the new ideas that Sam had presented at that morning's company meeting. She had taken much encouragement from the consumer insight – there was clearly a path to be navigated. It had also reiterated the need for the business to make clear and consistent choices, and to prioritise those areas that would deliver the greatest long-term value.

Their recent efforts to baseline and contextualise the business, define UP and set their Horizon were all supportive of this, and had brought home some hard truths regarding their Horizon:

- The Portuguese market, which they had entered four years ago, was proving to be an unprofitable distraction. The analysis of the attractiveness of both the total and serviceable addressable market, and Leisurious' ability to address it, had led to the inevitable conclusion that they should exit.
- It seems they had misjudged who their core customer was. Emma and the team had been labouring under the pretext that their most important customers were the fashion-first twenty-somethings, whereas it was the slightly older career mums that had really driven growth over the past two years. Moreover, some of the edgier styles they had introduced in the most recent collection had proved unpopular with this group. Whilst those items were still important for the brand's positioning, they had to balance that with enough classic staples in the core range to satisfy their true core customer. Sam's ideas on sub-brands made sense in this context and reflected what some of their closest competitors were doing.

- Sam was also right in her analysis of collection refresh frequency – their AIR cover analysis had shown it was something that customers valued and competitors were managing far better than Leisurious. The 'Beyond the Horizon' initiative to reduce lead times would need to be brought into the next Horizon shift.

However, it was not all about addressing downsides, as there were also positives upon which the business could capitalise:

- Initial analysis suggested that the outlet opportunity would indeed be incremental to the business. They could further reduce the risk through special make-up product as an entry level into the brand. Mike had proposed a pop-up experiment in a major outlet park, enabling the brand to trial an outlet proposition and observe the impact on their own shops in the surrounding area as well as online purchasing in the catchment around that park.
- Focusing on how they should ADAPT, there was also the opportunity to partner and develop an exciting design offer that went beyond simple personalisation to create genuine co-creation of garments, being true to their unifying purpose, which included the principle of being 'a mass-market innovator of style, fit and comfort'.
- Finally, the customer insight had shown that the brand certainly had permission to engage more closely with its customer base but needed a new approach. Emma was up for the challenge.

What gave Emma strength was that she felt the team was firmly behind her and the purpose they had defined. Changes were on the Horizon, and she would not want it any other way.

In your organisation

Exercise 7: Defining UP

What should your unifying purpose embody? To define UP for your organisation, do the following:

1 Interview key customers and suppliers and explore their views of you as an organisation. Explore in particular:
   - Why customers choose you.
   - What associations your organisation triggers in their minds.
   - What they consider to be your strengths and weaknesses.

- What needs they feel are untapped, emerging or under-served in the market.
- What they would do if they were in charge of your organisation.

2 Using this data as input to the session, bring together the core group to discuss the following topics:

- What are the key beliefs that underpin the organisation?
- What does the organisation want its customers and stakeholders to say about it?
- What unifies the different staff members that work within the organisation?
- What has driven the success of the business up until now?
- What can you learn from the customer and supplier feedback?

3 Given the above, split into two or three groups and develop separately the principles of your unifying purpose.

4 Having done so, return to a plenary and have each group present back the version of UP that they have produced. Subsequently:

- Identify similarities and differences.
- Where there are differences, discuss what lies behind those differences.
- As a plenary, refine the principles to come to one version of UP, reflecting the conclusions of the discussion.

5 Take the time to communicate and explain UP to the wider organisation and show examples of how it is determining choices and actions.

How to execute agile strategies

8

'Action is the foundational key to all success.'

Pablo Picasso

In this chapter we do the following:

- Outline the approach to Horizon tracking.
- Describe in more detail the nature and content of Horizon gateways.
- Describe how you execute Horizon shift planning.
- Consider how to apply RADAR at a group, divisional and business unit level.

Having designed your Horizon and identified the key commitments beyond it, you must act. As the American philosopher Elvis urged – we now need a little less conversation, a little more action.

The anchor of RADAR's action is Horizon management. However, this is not a linear process. The reality of agile strategy is iterative: testing, learning and adapting; design and action are no longer discrete. The three mechanisms which drive Horizon management are:

1 Horizon tracking;
2 Horizon planning;
3 Horizon gateways.

This chapter explores the practical management of each. Before we do, however, a brief word on the concerns many have with the idea of 'agile practices'. If done poorly, these concerns are justified, as they can result in a loss of control, short-termism and poor decision making. However, much of this is the result of three issues, each of which are addressed through Horizon management:

1 **Not having the right information:** working with partial data can lead to the wrong decisions. As we saw in Chapter 5, RADAR's MEDS addresses this by aligning insight with the organisation's strategic intent and ensuring a balance across the SIS objectives (anticipation, control, improvement, communication) and timeliness (SCORE, ERAs and ARC offering lagging, leading and anticipatory measures respectively). Good data is the foundation of an organisation's RAC rating.

2 **Not seeing the bigger picture:** the classic example of this is continuously iterating the product when you should be changing the business model (see, for example, the rise of subscription models in music). Through defining UP and regularly interrogating your Horizon, the key elements 'Beyond the Horizon' and your target outcomes (via the results framework), collective organisational awareness of the bigger picture can be clearly established and maintained.

3 **Not involving the right people:** this, in part, drives the above two issues, particularly as more profound decisions are being taken increasingly quickly. Detractors of agile thinking worry that delegating decisions to lower levels of the organisation may result in poor decision making as people lack the broader appreciation of other changes in the market or organisation. However, senior executives face a mirrored issue, as, by dint of the breadth and nature of their role, they cannot have the required depth of understanding in every area. Neither is a failing but rather a consequence of the fast-moving and complex nature of their environment. RADAR makes decision making more effective and timely by bringing together the senior team and those with detailed or specialist understanding, both internal and external, into the room earlier and more frequently, helping identify 'implementation problems' before they happen, and addressing them.

Horizon tracking

Horizon tracking is the process by which you evaluate the performance and validity of your current Horizon. Its objectives are to:

1 Evaluate the current Horizon.

2 Identify if and how you should adjust or shift your Horizon.

Horizon tracking is addressed through the RADAR results framework (see Chapter 9), and formally reviewed in the Horizon gateways. The setting of the initial Horizon (see Chapter 7) with its metrics, activities and targets forms part of the design activity and comprises the following elements:

- *Horizon statements:* simple but substantive expressions that describe your Horizon.
- *SCOREcard:* targets are set as part of Horizon setting, and these are the numbers against which the performance of the Horizon will be judged.

- *ERAs:* these can be both quantitative and qualitative in nature, and therefore tracking can take different forms (e.g. percentage achieved, red/amber/green).
- *ARC:* tracking the ARC of the Horizon enables an organisation to evaluate the ongoing validity of its current Horizon. If the ARC is no longer valid, then the Horizon must shift.

The relevant measures and data associated with each of these areas form part of the organisation's MEDS (Chapter 5). As with any business intelligence platform, the challenge lies in drawing together the various types of data consistently on an ongoing basis.

Horizon planning: stick, adjust or shift

We have explored initial Horizon setting (see Chapter 7). Here, ongoing Horizon tracking leads to the pursuit of one of three Horizon planning choices.

A Horizon shift represents a fundamental change in strategic intent. If it is required, consider the following:

1 **What has changed:** be systematic and explicit in identifying what has changed across the market, customers, competition and organisation (e.g. competitive position). Which Horizon statements, SCORE, ERAs and ARC elements are most affected, and why?

2 **Stability:** reflecting Jeff Bezos' views on not changing, highlighted at the end of the previous chapter, determine which elements of your current competitive position (the 3Ps) and AIR remain valid in the face of these identified changes. For example, how could you leverage your competitive position or AIR to make the Horizon shift (e.g. existing customers or channels, existing products in new contexts or markets).

3 **Minimum change:** from this starting point, consider what would be the minimum change required to your competitive position (3Ps) and AIR in order to adapt to the new environment identified. Use the 5KQs to test your thinking.

4 **Extreme change:** in contrast to the previous point, what are the most extreme changes you would feasibly make to your competitive position and AIR to address the business environment changes. How do the benefits of these changes compare to those related to the minimum changes?

5 **Beyond the Horizon:** explore how the stability, minimum and extreme change discussions relate to what you have been tracking, testing or venturing beyond the Horizon. Do these offer obvious options for how to respond?

6 **Unifying purpose:** on the basis of the above, revisit your unifying purpose and your 5KQs to define your new Horizon statements, target SCORE, ERAs and beyond the Horizon commitments, and update your ARC tracker.

Table 8.1 Conditions for Horizon changes

Choice	Conditions
No change (stick)	This is the correct choice where the Horizon's performance is: • in line with or above SCORE targets, ERAs are on plan and the ARC has not materially changed; • behind SCORE targets and/or ERAs are behind plan, but the ARC still holds true and maintaining the same Horizon is the most appropriate choice (e.g. when a product launch is delayed).
Moderate adjustments (adjust)	The Horizon statements reflect market opportunities that are still broadly attractive, and the organisation's underlying competitive position *potential* is still sufficiently strong to address them (i.e. the focus of the Horizon is still attractive, feasible and viable). However: • some specific elements of the opportunity may have changed (e.g. a different segment needs to be prioritised, new legislation has been introduced); • the competitive position (3Ps) may need further refinement; • AIR factors need to be further adjusted to fulfil the competitive position's promise.
Horizon shift (shift)	You must Horizon shift if both of the following conditions are met: **1 The market, competition or organisation has materially changed, and with it the ARC** The most common cause is a change in market dynamics (e.g. Tunisian visitor numbers dropped by 25% in 2016 following the 2015 terrorist attacks). However, changes in the organisation can also materially affect it, as exemplified by Tesla losing three autopilot leaders in 18 months, leading to delays to its self-drive programme.[53] **2 These changes invalidate or significantly and adversely affect the current Horizon** The changes identified above are only meaningful if they result in the Horizon no longer being valid, by which I mean that the market opportunity no longer exists (e.g. mass-market typewriters) or else the organisation's competitive position has substantially weakened (e.g. Polaroid cannot compete with mobiles for instant photos). In either case, the original target outcomes (SCORE, ERAs) can no longer be met.

[53] See https://arstechnica.com/cars/2018/04/tesla-autopilot-crisis-deepens-with-loss-of-third-autopilot-boss-in-18-months [accessed 7 May 2018].

7 **Transition:** explore the operational realities of this transition to a new Horizon (e.g. people, structures, process changes, system implications, contractual constraints). Create a critical path with key actions that mark the Horizon shift. The extent to which dynamism by design has been implemented in the operating model and the beyond the Horizon commitments are aligned will determine the ease with which the organisation can Horizon shift.

Figure 8.1 The Horizon shift

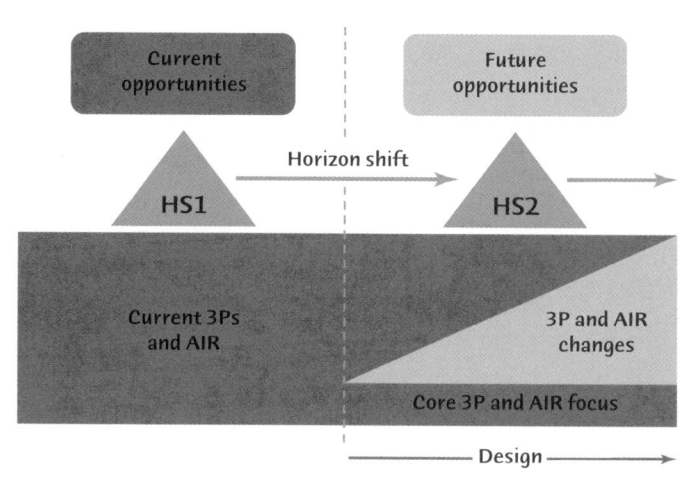

Contract killer

In the run up to the 1999 festive holidays, Toys 'R' Us was a top destination for online toy shopping. However, the limitations of its platform and infrastructure meant it failed to fulfil many of these orders in time for Christmas, earning it a $350,000 fine from the US Federal Trade Commission. In the following year, replete with a fresh injection of $60m from SoftBank, a Japanese technology conglomerate, Toys 'R' Us took a different tack and signed a ten-year deal with Amazon, through which it was contracted to be the exclusive vendor of toys and baby products for the online business. Part of this deal included redirecting all traffic from ToysRUs.com directly to Amazon.com

▶

However, cracks started to show in the arrangement and, by spring 2003, other vendors were also selling toys and baby goods through Amazon. Toys 'R' Us successfully sued Amazon, allowing it to terminate the deal in 2006 and set up its own website again (as well as receiving a settlement of $51m three years later). Nevertheless, this period had provided Amazon with an accelerated entry into toys and baby goods and had significantly delayed Toys 'R' Us' own foray into online.

Fast-forward to 2018, and the combination of three key factors have led to its demise:

- A continued shift of toy purchasing online, especially for branded toys, where range trumps even that of specialist offline stores.
- A massive debt burden created under private equity ownership.
- The associated inability to invest sufficient capital expenditure in its proposition or online offering (It only started to attempt to significantly revamp its original website in 2017, in a world where competitors had been offering click and collect to all stores and online stock checks for years).

In this case, Toys 'R' Us' 'store first' Horizon was at odds with the toy market's ongoing shift of sales online, and it was late to transform its online capability, in part hampered by its financial constraints. One wonders what a Horizon shift involving stronger private label ranges, more compelling product exclusives (particularly in STEM/STREAM toys), greater integration of online and in-store customer experience and simply making the stores more fun might have done for the business. Contrast this with the Ireland and UK toy retailer Smyths toys, which provides a genuine 'digital first' approach, and yet successfully delivers 'big-box stores' in similar locations to Toys 'R' Us.

Horizon gateways

Horizon gateways are the governing mechanism through which Horizon tracking and planning takes place. It is the beating heart of action, the forum in which to review, decide and take action on:

1. the performance and validity of the current Horizon (Horizon tracking);
2. potential areas beyond the Horizon;
3. whether, and how, to Horizon shift (Horizon planning).

The table below shows a typical agenda for a Horizon Gateway.

Table 8.2 Agenda for a typical Horizon gateway

Frequency/ Duration	Inputs	Agenda

• Monthly
 • Two hours
	DIRECTION SETTERS
	 1. Unifying purpose
	 2. Horizon statements
	 3. Performance targets (SCORE)
	 HORIZON MANAGEMENT TOOLS
	 4. Monthly SCOREcard
	 5. ERAs tracker
	 6. ARC tracker
	 7. Beyond the Horizon insight
	 MEETING ACTIONS
	 8. Action log
		1 Actions from last gateway
		 2 Horizon tracking
		    2.1. SCOREcard
		    2.2. ERAs updates
		    2.3. ARC updates
		 3 Beyond the Horizon insight
		 4 Horizon adjustments and shifts
		 5 Confirmation of MEDS changes
		 6 Summary of new actions

Attendees	Outputs
• Executive leads • Specialist representatives • External representatives	• Confirmed/revised/new Horizon • Updated results framework • Revised data requirements (one-offs and revised MEDS) • 'Beyond the Horizon' commitments

Frequency

The Horizon gateway meetings typically take place monthly. For practical reasons, they can be integrated into existing governance structure, or potentially treated as a section within a broader executive team meeting, to which the wider range of attendees are invited.

Attendees

In this book, I have regularly returned to the importance of multiple perspectives. The attendees of Horizon gateways require a detailed and practical understanding of the business and its customers, markets and competition, so that the operational realities of the topics under discussion can be surfaced. This requires the attendees list to include three groups:

- *Executive leads:* the minimum number of representatives from the executive team required to represent the key areas of the current Horizon and what lies beyond it. Note that this may not be the entire executive team (although it can be).

- *Specialist representatives:* these will vary depending on the topic areas that are most critical to the Horizon and beyond the Horizon, but could be functional (e.g. IT), stakeholder-related (e.g. wholesale) or even thematic (e.g. innovation).

- *External representatives:* engaging the networks that support your competitive position more closely is an important element of agile strategy. This group can include suppliers, strategic partners, customers or even regulators in some cases.

When considering the above three groups, there are naturally concerns that must be addressed. For example, a balance must be struck between the group being too unwieldy and having insufficient detail to take decisions in the room. Confidentiality can also be an issue – there are certainly topics to which external representatives should not be party. In addition, the fact that not every member of the executive team may attend every gateway could also create tensions. Practical solutions to these issues include:

- Bringing people in for only part of the session, or for only some sessions. This may be the case for external representatives, where confidentiality around certain themes must be preserved.

- Holding people on standby if needed, so that they can join if required at short notice.

- Circulating documentation to a wider group (e.g. executives, heads of departments) before and after the gateway meeting for review and input.

- Directly following the gateway session with a full executive team meeting to ensure that the whole leadership team is informed and consulted on the decisions.

- Creating a follow-up mechanism to iterate decisions (e.g. a weekly 30-minute call).

Remember, however, that this is not an activity to be run alongside business as usual – this *is* business as usual. The Horizon gateways are decision-making sessions, not simply recommendation-making ones.

Inputs

The gateway's inputs are drawn from three sources:

1 *Direction setters:* the three elements driving the direction of the business – unifying purpose, the Horizon statements and target SCORE.

2 *Horizon management tools:* the lagging and leading indicators of performance (SCORE and ERAs respectively), ARC tracker used to test the Horizon's validity and insight relating to any beyond the Horizon commitments.

3 *Meeting actions:* the ongoing gateway action log.

Agenda

The agenda begins with a review of the previous gateway's actions, followed by Horizon tracking – a review of the performance and validity of the current Horizon informed by the SCOREcard, ERAs and ARC (see below). Should any SCOREcard, ERA or ARC variances be identified, these will be discussed, root causes explored and actions to address agreed (see some of the framing techniques in Chapter 2).

The ARC may be further refined through discussion of the next topic 'Beyond the Horizon'. This focuses on specific longer-term market and organisational changes, trends, risks, issues and opportunities which might affect the organisation. The purpose of this is to identify:

- potential future Horizon adjustment or shift requirements;
- the need for new insight, 'Beyond the Horizon' experiments or real option investments (i.e. investments to enable, evaluate or maintain long-term options).

Based on all this, you are then ready to determine the Horizon adjustments or shifts described above, capturing any required changes to your MEDS. Finally, the new actions are agreed, and the meeting closed.

Outputs

The primary outputs of the gateway are:

- Confirmed, revised or new Horizon statements.
- Updates to the target SCORE, ERAs, ARC, competitive position and Beyond the Horizon commitments resulting from any changes to the Horizon statements.

This may also necessitate changes to your MEDS, and other updated data requirements may come from new Beyond the Horizon commitments.

Concluding on action

All three factors of the RAC rating find their expression in RADAR's action component – responding and adapting (Horizon planning) and control (Horizon tracking and gateways). What binds design and action ultimately, however, is the results framework, and that is the subject of the next chapter.

Summary

- RADAR addresses three concerns many of us have with poorly executed agile practices: not having the right information, not seeing the bigger picture, and not involving the right people.
- The anchor of RADAR's 'action' is Horizon management, and the three mechanisms through which it is achieved: Horizon tracking, planning and gateways.

▶

- Horizon tracking is the process by which you evaluate the performance and validity of your current Horizon. It does so through the three key elements of the results framework: SCORE, ERAs and ARC.
- Horizon planning requires the pursuit of one of three choices: no change (stick), moderate adjustments (adjust) and Horizon shift (shift).
- Horizon gateways are the governing mechanism through which Horizon tracking and planning takes place. It serves three roles: to understand the performance and validity of the current Horizon, to evaluate potential areas beyond the Horizon, and to determine whether, and how, to Horizon shift.

Case story: Acting UP

As is so often the case, it is only when ideas get truly tested that they show their worth. So, it was with Leisurious' ARC tracker.

Emma, Sam and the cross-functional team that had been drawn together to support the new agile strategy approach had created the tracker during the development of UP and its first Horizon. The assumptions, risks and choices/consequences had come thick and fast, and at that time it had felt like a classroom exercise – each person seeing who could come up with something new to add to it.

It did not feel like that any more. Sam could not pin down exactly when the ARC tracker turned into a living, breathing part of their day-to-day lives: perhaps when the market data had invalidated the assumption about the Portuguese market being an attractive opportunity, or when the choice to orientate the proposition towards an assumed fashion-conscious younger customer was proven unsuitable in the face of the realities of its core customer base. Whatever the reason, the ARC tracker now held a different position in the eyes of those who used it.

It is true that, through using it, the team had learned to pitch the level of its entries more appropriately. Gone was the logging of overly detailed choices that swelled the tracker to an unmanageable size, gone too were broad-brush risks that could not meaningfully be evaluated and acted upon. As the team had grown in confidence with the techniques, they had adapted to them and indeed updated them to make them their own.

How they tested the elements of the ARC had also improved with time, as they had got better at determining 'next best proxies' and statistical methods to detect inflections in the tracked numbers. Emma's personal favourite had been the predictive model of consumer confidence that Simon had developed, and the mitigating promotional and merchandising actions that the team had identified to offset them and smooth the sales line whilst maintaining target cash margins. As the year had progressed, and more data had been generated, the team had been able to adapt and refine the model further and gain ever greater confidence in its predictions and conclusions.

Not everything had gone smoothly, of course. Mike still felt some of the unifying purpose 'was just wordsmithing', although even he had to concede it had served a guiding role when the team had debated the Portuguese exit. Sam's bad pun about him 'acting UP' seemed to capture the mood – the clichés of having 'plenty to do' and 'moving in the right direction' suddenly had new overtones.

'Onwards and UPwards' muttered Sam under her breath, feeling two bad puns in a row was too much even for her. Onwards and UPwards.

In your organisation

Exercise 8: New Horizons

Circulate the research and analysis output resulting from Exercises 4 and 6, and the unifying purpose defined in Exercise 7, to the core group.
Reconvene the group to create your Horizon, following these steps:

1 Summarise the results of the research and analysis by referring to the 5KQs and how this data relates to them.

2 In the context of your unifying purpose, what conclusions do you draw as a group on where to play and how to win? Capture these on a flipchart.

3 Split the attendees into three groups, and have each group represent one of three stakeholder types: customers, employees and investors. Ask each of these groups to review the comments captured on the flipchart from that stakeholder's perspective. What changes or comments would they make?

4 Bring the groups back together and formulate the Horizon statements, taking into account the different stakeholder perspectives.

5 Review the set of statements as a whole and debate the extent to which they are:

- reinforcing and complementary (cohesive);
- compelling (appealing to different stakeholder groups);
- competitive (distinctive and meaningful in the context of the competition).

6 Finalise the collective Horizon statements on the basis of this discussion.

7 Finally, capture separately anything that sits outside this Horizon and warrants a beyond the Horizon commitment.

[PART FOUR]

Results

How to measure success

9

'Success is a science; if you have the conditions, you get the result.'
Oscar Wilde

In this chapter we do the following:

- Introduce the three functions of the RADAR results framework.
- Explore each element of SCORE.
- Explain a useful technique for defining ERAs.
- Explore the approach for defining your Horizon's ARC.
- Provide examples of a SCOREcard, ERAs and the ARC tracker.

If strategy, as we saw in the introduction, is ultimately about creating value, then results are how it keeps a tally. This chapter explores the RADAR results framework, the role of which is to.

- set targets for the Horizon, reflecting the organisation's intended impact on the world;
- evaluate the current Horizon's performance;
- determine the validity of the Horizon and the need to Horizon shift.

These roles are fulfilled through the following mechanisms.

Table 9.1 How the results framework fulfils its three functions

| | | | Role served | |
Mechanism	Description	Targets	Performance	Validation
SCORE	Read collectively, your unifying purpose, Horizon statements and considerations beyond the Horizon to define your strategic intent. SCORE provides a balanced set of measures for both setting targets for this intent and evaluating performance.	✓	✓	
ERAs	Experienced RADAR achievements (ERAs) are the milestones along the way to achieving your outcomes – the leading indicators of progress that you can touch, see, hear, smell or taste. They are created by 'backcasting' from your Horizon and target SCORE.	✓	✓	
ARC	Whilst SCORE and ERAs indicate progress, the Horizon's ARC is used to *anticipate* change. Defined and updated throughout RADAR, the ARC is used to test the current Horizon's validity. If your assumptions, risks and choices are no longer valid, then your Horizon must change.			✓

This chapter shows how the results framework, and these three elements specifically, link together the design and action elements of the RADAR approach.

Figure 9.1 The RADAR results framework

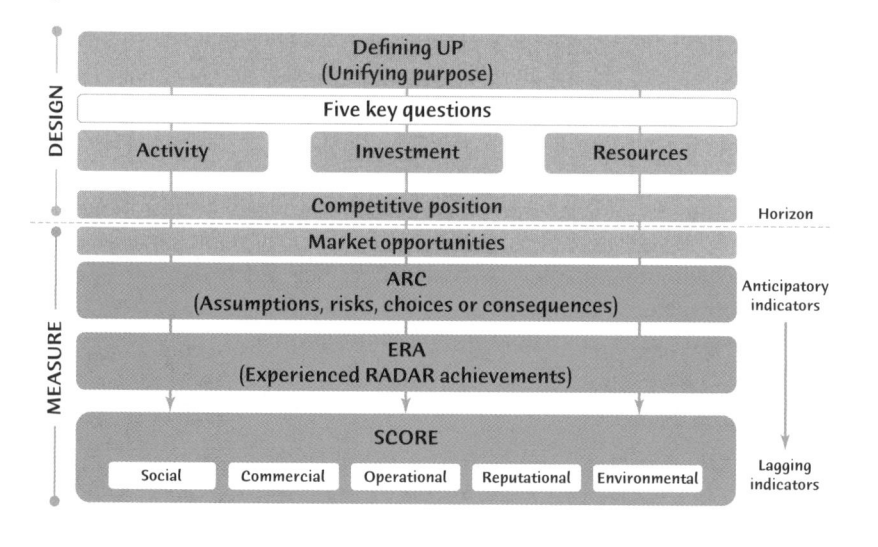

Setting your target SCORE

When leaders speak of achieving goals and delivering results, they inevitably express them through some mix of the five domains that comprise SCORE – social, commercial, operational, reputational and environmental. SCORE maps to John Elkington's classic 'triple bottom line' model[54] – profit, people and planet – which underpins many corporate social responsibility (CSR) approaches. Whilst there remains significant variance in the extent to which CSR is embraced across organisations, the tide has turned in recent years, as customers increasingly expect it. Let us briefly explore each element of SCORE in turn.

Social

The first SCORE element measures the social impact of the organisation on its stakeholders, starting within the organisation but extending out to communities and wider society. It evaluates the extent to which an organisation does the following:

Treats people fairly (equality and welfare)
Equality is a huge topic, and one that has garnered significant press coverage in recent times. In the context of organisations, it can be considered in three areas:[55]

[54] Elkington, J. (1999) *Cannibals With Forks: The triple bottom line of 21st century business*, Oxford: Capstone.
[55] Spicker, P. (2006) *Liberty, Equality, Fraternity*, Bristol: The Policy Press.

1 **Treatment:** treating people or situations without bias, prejudice or unequal special conditions.

2 **Opportunity:** enabling everyone to have access to the same opportunities and compete with the same rights and conditions.

3 **Outcomes:** this involves all types of outcome, from salaries to recruitment.

Typical performance measures in this area focus on diversity, inclusion and employee wellbeing.

Trades and operates ethically (ethical trading)[56]

Growing awareness of unethical trading, from the human rights violations of sweatshops to the controversies of zero-hour contracts, means many organisations are pushing for far greater transparency in their practices.

Serves a broader role in its community (communities)

The idea of businesses contributing to the wider public good has been around since the 1950s, with a focus on creating jobs, training staff and supporting local development. The German apprenticeship scheme is often held up as an exemplar of this, leading to lower youth unemployment.[57]

Contributes to wider society (philanthropy)

The broadest impact of an organisation is on wider society, often achieved through either financial contributions (e.g. donating a percentage of profits to charity) or non-financial ones (e.g. law firms donating pro bono legal advice).

The figure below summarises these social elements.

Figure 9.2 SCORE – social domains

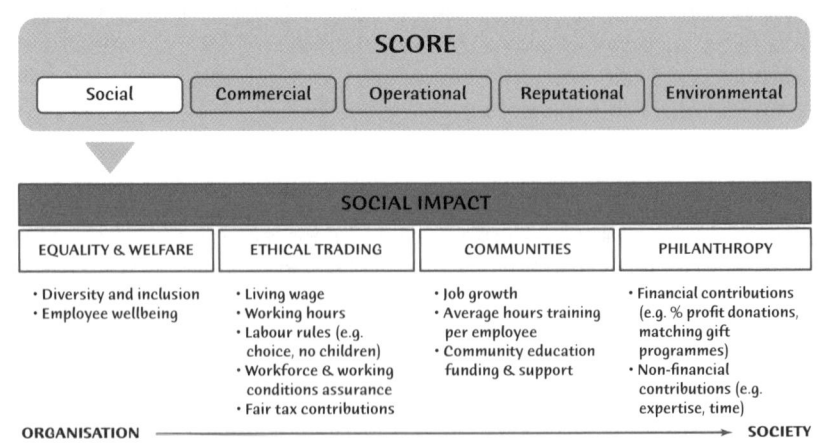

[56] For more information on ethical trading, please refer to the Ethical Trading Initiative website at https://www.ethicaltrade.org [accessed 5 August 2018].

[57] See the *Financial Times* article, Germany's apprenticeship scheme success may be hard to replicate, 21 April 2017, available at https://goo.gl/Vk93bS [accessed 5 August 2018].

Measures across these categories can range from statistical (e.g. the ratio of return to work from maternity and childcare leave) through to binary yes/no (e.g. the existence of an ethical supply chain policy). Naturally, the focus on such areas is not just about measures, but also about the practices that support them (e.g. an equality committee, a philanthropy budget through which employees can do good in society). Returning to our discussion of UP in Chapters 1 and 7, which often drives the social element of SCORE, the beliefs must be authentic and the practices considered for results in this area meaningful and sustainable.

A fair pair

For some businesses, social impact has become not just a measurable outcome but a key element of their business model. Consider the following two cases:

- Warby Parker, a North American retailer of glasses and prescription eye-glasses, operates a 'buy a pair, give a pair' scheme through which, for every pair of glasses sold, a pair is distributed to someone in need.[58] It has now reached people in over 50 countries.
- L'Oréal has regularly been held up as an exemplar of ethical trading. It was one of the first companies in France to establish a code of ethics in 2000 and to appoint a chief ethics officer in 2007.[59] It organises an annual ethics day, where employees globally can engage online with the chairman, CEO and country general manager about ethics.

Commercial

Whilst social considerations are increasingly 'mission-critical', it is commercial measures that are normally top of most people's minds when discussing targets. They broadly fall into two categories:

Commercial outcomes

This is the expression of the organisation's performance in financial (e.g. net operating profit) and market terms (e.g. market share). When measuring commercial performance:

- start at the top level to 'get the shape of performance' (e.g. group sales over time, gross margin by product category over time);
- embrace the hypothesis-driven principle (Chapter 3) to focus your analysis when drilling down (i.e. ask specific questions of your data and then answer them);

---

[58] See https://www.warbyparker.com/buy-a-pair-give-a-pair [accessed 16 May 2018].
[59] See https://www.loreal.com/media/news/2018/feb/2018-wme [accessed 16 May 2018].

- use time series data and simple visualisations to spot trends in the data;
- consider different organisational units as the basis for analysis e.g. business segments (see Chapter 4), strategic business units, divisions, stores, etc.;
- look at the data through three lenses – customer, channel, and product – and try different combinations to uncover new performance insights (e.g. combine customer and product to look at business segment performance, analyse channel by customer segment to reveal different channel dynamics);
- understand movements in volume, price and mix, and their role alongside costs in shaping margin;
- interpret the results in the context of the market intelligence you have gathered, for example evaluating the extent to which you are under- or outperforming the market. As we saw in Chapter 4, you must understand the extent to which performance is driven by market/segment attractiveness vs. competitive position.

Commercial engine performance

Commercial analysis evaluates not only commercial outcomes, but also the effectiveness and efficiency of the commercial engine which generates them. The table below outlines the typical areas on which it focuses, alongside some example measures.

Table 9.2 Commercial engine performance categories

Category	Description	Example measures
Research and development	R&D is the activity undertaken to create your next set of products and services, or to improve existing ones.	<ul><li>Return on innovation</li><li>Revenue from new products as a percentage of total revenue</li><li>Percentage mix of new-to-the-world products vs. line extensions</li></ul>
Marketing	Marketing is the management process responsible for identifying, anticipating and satisfying customer requirements profitably.[60] Marketing KPIs address online and offline aspects of the 'marketing funnel' from awareness to after-sales.	<ul><li>Brand awareness</li><li># marketing qualified leads (MQL)</li><li>Net promoter score</li><li>Marketing return on investment</li></ul>

[60] See https://www.cim.co.uk/media/4772/7ps.pdf [accessed 22 July 2018].

Table 9.2 Commercial engine performance categories (*continued*)

Category	Description	Example measures
Sales	The sales function acts as a bridge between customer needs and the organisation's products and services.	• # sales qualified leads (SQL) • Conversion rate • Customer acquisition cost • Customer lifetime value
Business development	Developing new streams of business (e.g. new partnerships, channels or markets) is the role of business development, and key to the long-term future of the organisation. Some of this is classic 'Beyond the Horizon' territory.	• Reach • Percentage of gross margin generated from channel partners signed in the past 12 months • Average new deal size • Monthly recurring revenue (MRR)

Figure 9.3 SCORE – commercial domains

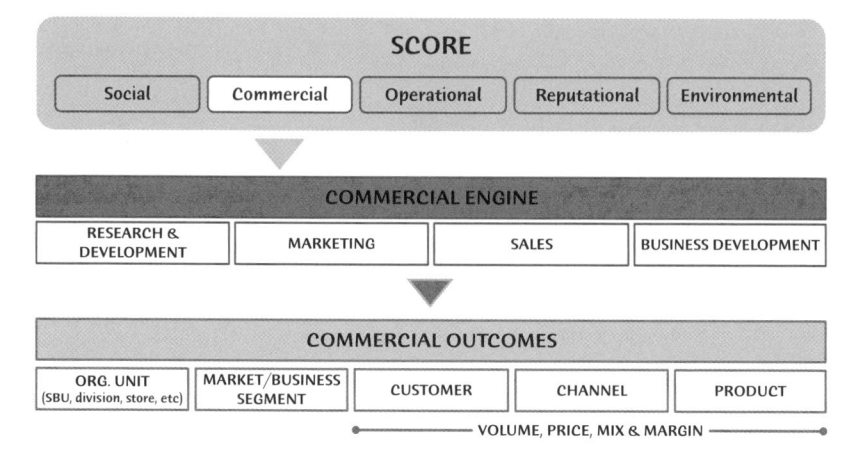

Operational

Our discussion of the 3Ps of competitive position (Chapters 4 and 7) illustrated how important operational performance is to an organisation's ability to win. These operational measures fall under six categories.

Table 9.3 Operating model performance categories

Category	Description	Example measures
Activities	Operational activity analysis typically focuses on five key areas: cost, quality, speed, dependability (i.e. getting the same result each time) and flexibility[61]	• Process capability (cpk) • % rework costs to total costs • % first-time resolution of issues
Resources	This covers both tangible assets (people, physical assets such as buildings or machines, financial assets) and intangible ones (e.g. brand, intellectual property)	• Stock availability • Overall equipment effectiveness • Occupancy rate
Data	The six criteria by which to evaluate data: completeness, consistency, uniqueness, validity, accuracy and timeliness (Chapter 5)	• % of new accounts set up with incomplete data • Average database availability time • Report production cycle time
Suppliers	When evaluating suppliers, consider the ART of supplier management: activities, relationship and transformative capabilities (i.e. their ability to support you in anticipating and responding to the changing demands of the market and new supply chain opportunities)	• Service level agreement compliance • Ease of doing business rating • Average time to issue resolution
Structure	This covers a broad range of topics including efficiency (e.g. productivity), leadership, recruitment, retention and employee engagement. Evaluation will require both quantitative and qualitative measures	• Leadership effectiveness index • Spans of control • Average time to fill vacancies
Governance	Topics such as compliance, health and safety and risk management are key elements of managing an operating model's performance	• Compliance audit rating • % policies and processes up to date • # reported incidents and near misses

[61] See Chapter 2 of Slack, N., Brandon-Jones, A. and Johnston, R. (2013) *Operations Management*, 7th edn, Harlow: Pearson Education Limited.

As with the commercial measures, to analyse operational performance we must understand it not just internally but also relative to customers' key purchase criteria and the competition (as we saw in the evaluation of AIR cover), meeting minimum requirements in non-critical areas and outperforming in critical ones. The figure below summarises the operational performance domains.

Figure 9.4 SCORE – operational domains

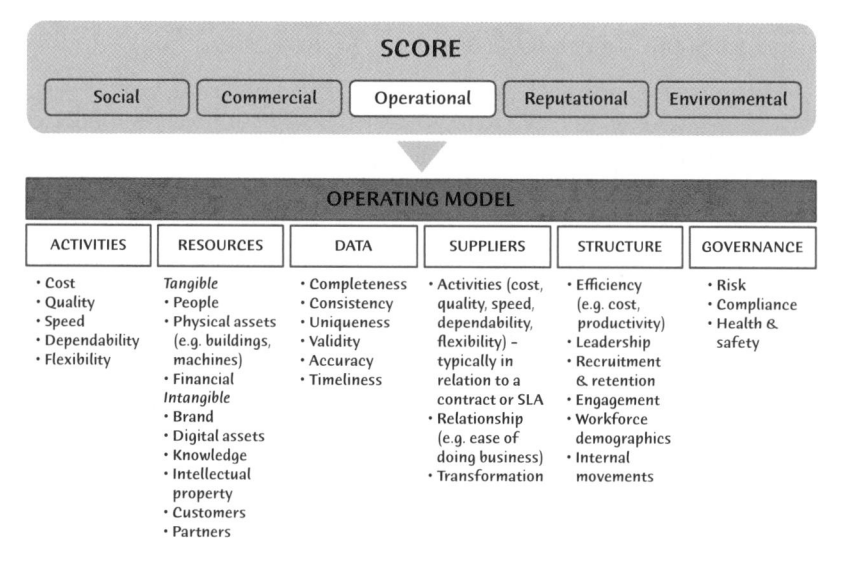

Scanning the Horizon

As part of its Horizon, a hospital sought to address a radiology bottleneck preventing the swift diagnosis and treatment of patients. Operational measures it considered included:

- *Activities:* # scans per day, # patients waiting six weeks or longer for a diagnostic test.
- *Resources:* % scanner uptime, radiologist availability.
- *Data:* average time to process radiology results.
- *Suppliers:* incident response time, mean time to repair scanner.
- *Structure:* average time to fill radiology-related vacancies.
- *Governance:* # serious untoward incidents.

Reputational

In an increasingly networked business environment, where reviews and opinion are freely expressed and easily accessible, actively managing your organisation's reputation has grown in importance – you must listen, but also involve, engage and inform. Moreover, this is not just about how customers perceive you but also employees, suppliers and other key stakeholders such as investors.

Key areas to manage, and therefore measure, include awareness, engagement, sentiment, satisfaction and relationship quality. The tools available to do so are becoming increasingly effective – from real-time CRM systems through to social media management and listening tools.

Figure 9.5 SCORE – reputational domains

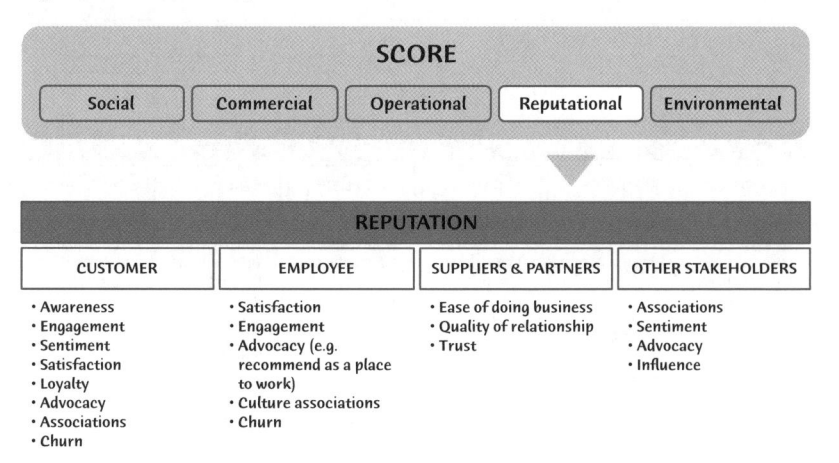

Environmental

For many organisations, environmental responsibility is increasingly becoming a requirement rather than a choice, particularly for those serving a millennial and Gen Z audience. Expectations, technology and entities including governments, regulators and charities are driving an ever-widening range of actions to reduce, reuse, recycle and replace. Environmental metrics typically sit under four categories:

- *Emissions and pollution:* reducing landfill waste, improving air quality and finding alternatives to harmful substances are all examples of how business can reduce its impact on the environment.

- *Resources:* being more efficient, and less wasteful, in the use of water, energy and land preserves a limited resource for future generations.

- *Conservation:* environmental preservation is not just about using less, but also building more. Sustainability is the watchword, from replanting trees to fostering good farming practices.

- *Safety and regulation:* preserving our planet requires robust safety practices and compliance. Just look at the environmental devastation caused by BP's Gulf of Mexico oil spill in 2010, which resulted in a $18.7bn fine for the company.

Figure 9.6 SCORE – environmental domains

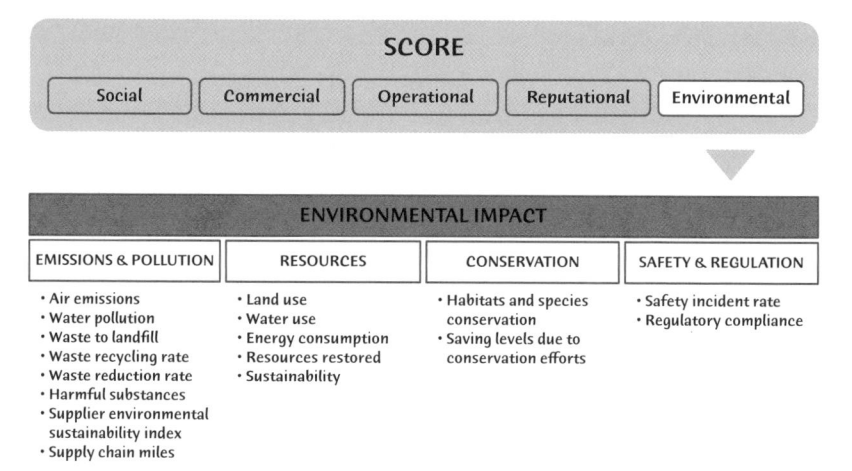

Mars – the red planet goes green[62]

Mars is a leading player in confectionery, food, drinks and pet care, with sales of about £35bn annually. In September 2017 it announced it would be investing $1bn in tackling urgent global threats including climate change, poverty in supply chains and scarcity of resources. As well as setting specific targets (e.g. reducing greenhouse gas emissions across its value chain by 67 per cent by 2050), it has partnered with Field to Market – an alliance of more than 120 organisations working to improve agricultural sustainability – to ensure a sustainable future for its key ingredients such as cocoa and peanuts.

Its CEO Grant F. Reid maintains the investment is a win–win – he believes the business can do well by doing good: 'We're doing this because it's the right thing to do, but also because it's good business. Creating mutual benefits for the people in our supply chain and mitigating our impact on the environment are sound business choices.'

The practicalities of creating a SCOREcard

So, what does a SCOREcard actually look like? Figure 9.7 shows an example extract from the value hotel chain introduced in Chapter 7.

[62] See https://www.foodbev.com/news/mars-announces-1bn-plan-tackle-urgent-global-issues/ [accessed 16 May 2018].

Figure 9.7 Extract from a hotel SCOREcard

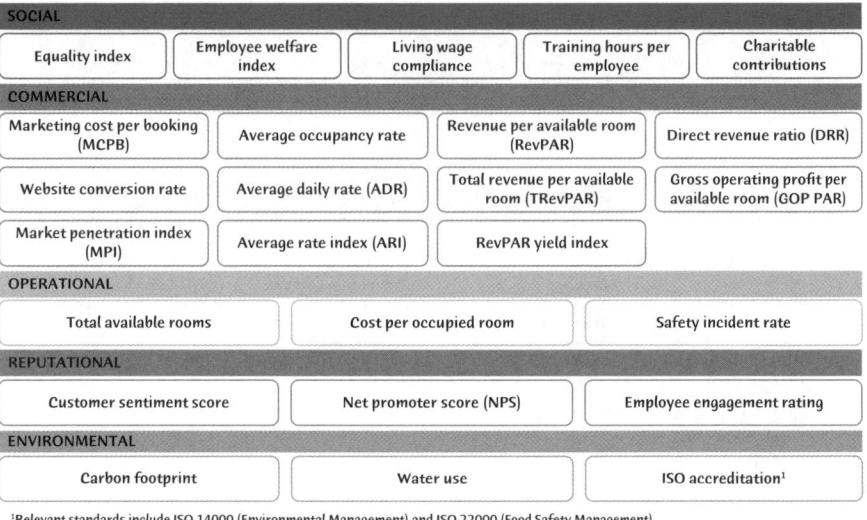

SOCIAL				
Equality index	Employee welfare index	Living wage compliance	Training hours per employee	Charitable contributions

COMMERCIAL			
Marketing cost per booking (MCPB)	Average occupancy rate	Revenue per available room (RevPAR)	Direct revenue ratio (DRR)
Website conversion rate	Average daily rate (ADR)	Total revenue per available room (TRevPAR)	Gross operating profit per available room (GOP PAR)
Market penetration index (MPI)	Average rate index (ARI)	RevPAR yield index	

OPERATIONAL		
Total available rooms	Cost per occupied room	Safety incident rate

REPUTATIONAL		
Customer sentiment score	Net promoter score (NPS)	Employee engagement rating

ENVIRONMENTAL		
Carbon footprint	Water use	ISO accreditation[1]

[1]Relevant standards include ISO 14000 (Environmental Management) and ISO 22000 (Food Safety Management)

Determining which SCORE measures to use

The SCOREcard is a key element of your MEDS and the SIS that manages it (Chapter 5). Given all the aspects of SCORE you *could* measure, which *should* you measure? There are four determining factors:

1 *Strategic intent*:

- *Horizon:* the Horizon statements are the starting point. For each one, think across the SCORE elements and determine which aspects are most relevant.

- *Unifying purpose:* not all measures and targets on the SCOREcard are specific to one Horizon. Some measures, particularly those relating to traditional corporate social responsibility areas (social, reputational, environmental), will be perennials in the organisation, determined by its unifying purpose, regulatory commitments or simply a sense of social responsibility.

- *Beyond the Horizon:* there may be some considerations beyond the Horizon which inform the SCORE measurements. In the hotel example above, changes to improve its RAC rating might be tracked through digging deeper into the contribution of responsiveness to NPS and sentiment.

2 *ARC:* the ARC tracker captures both market and organisational factors and some (e.g. supplier performance risks) may be measured through SCORE. We discuss ARC in more detail below.

3 *SIS objectives:* the four objectives covered in Chapter 5 (anticipation, control, improvement, communication) will inform what is covered on the SCOREcard.

4 *Practicality:* some areas are simply too difficult for an organisation to measure, for example, because data collection would be prohibitively expensive. In nearly all cases, a 'next best proxy' can be used (See Chapter 4).

Caught between a Rockar and a Hyundai place[63]

Rockar had one goal when it started to work with Hyundai in 2014: to revolutionise car buying. It made some bold changes to the traditional car dealership model by doing the following:

- Adopting a digital-first approach that integrated in-store, online and mobile platforms.
- Opening stores in shopping centres rather than on the edge of town to capture footfall – nearly 1m people visited one of its two UK shopping centre stores in their first four years of existence.
- Replacing salesmen with 'angels': product experts there to support, not sell. These staff members do not have sales targets or earn commission, and do not come from a motoring background. Instead, they are recruited for retail attitude and trained for four weeks to learn about engine sizes, trim options and finance packages.
- Putting customers in control – they decide whether to engage with staff or simply use the array of screens available in the store unaided to browse, exchange and purchase. A customer can go from entering the store to buying a car in three minutes, and can even test drive a car, collected from the shopping centre car park, unaccompanied.

Such ambitions require a very different SCOREcard to that seen in a normal car dealership – with typical commercial figures set alongside more customer-focused reputational and operational measures such as brand awareness, net promoter score, customer effort score and percentage of first-time buyers.

In a twist to this tale, Hyundai dissolved its partnership with Rockar in April 2018. For Rockar, this means evaluating the validity of its current Horizon. Three months after the Hyundai relationship ended, an adjustment to its Horizon has seen Rockar strike a three-way partnership alongside Ford and Next to start selling Ford cars in Next's store at Manchester's Arndale Shopping Centre. As more retail sales move online, could targeting retailers and landlords to fill excess UK retail space with a car offering form part of Rockar's new Horizon?

---

[63] See https://www.autocar.co.uk/car-news/new-cars/hyundai-split-online-car-seller-rockar-and-expand-its-own-service and http://cardealermagazine.co.uk/publish/hyundai-creates-digitaldealership-rockar/84904 [accessed 29 June 2018].

Setting targets

Setting the right target levels for the selected SCORE measures can be challenging: set them too low and the organisation may not fulfil its potential; set them too high and staff can become demotivated and fatalistic. Factors that can help guide the setting of targets include:

- *Baselining and existing data:* if you are already capturing relevant data, then use it. If you don't have it, could you start collecting it? Consider the minimum number of data points required to be statistically significant, and any cyclicality that can skew performance over the year, month, week or even daypart.

- *Market norms or minimum requirements:* these can be set by regulation (e.g. emission rates), customer expectations (e.g. no animal testing) or competitors (e.g. free returns for online orders).

- *Multiple perspectives:* exploring what is possible (e.g. through consultation with different organisational functions, suppliers and experts) can support the setting of targets that are both stretching and achievable.

- *Modelling:* sometimes, a simple model of the implications of a target outcome can help illustrate its achievability. For example, if you plan to increase sales by 30 per cent over two years, what does that mean for areas such as market share, manufacturing productivity and capacity, sales leads growth and awareness to purchase conversion? Are these implications sensible? This exercise will also help a team understand where the constraints and levers lie.

- *Aspiration:* targets must be achievable, but also challenging. Aspiration can create this 'stretch' and inspire solutions (for example, surgeon Devi Prasad Shetty aspired to deliver heart surgery in India that cost under $1,000 and did so whilst delivering better outcomes than those achieved in the US, where it costs c. $90,000).[64]

Evaluating performance

SCORE on the door

Having defined measures, set targets and integrated them into your MEDS, you are ready to evaluate performance. This is done through the Horizon gateways (Chapter 8), and includes regular updates to the SCOREcard, which can range from daily to quarterly depending on the measures involved. Current data analytics and visualisation tools enable drill-downs and interrogation of the data, provided the data has been structured accordingly. However, do not let the desire to build a more complex data set delay the creation of something

---

[64] See https://eu.usatoday.com/story/opinion/2017/01/29/health-care-surgery-india-americadisruption-column/97056938/ [accessed 23 September 2018].

more basic but usable in the short term. As with other areas of agile strategy, getting something useful out there earlier and iterating its development is the way to go.

Define your ERA

Whilst the SCOREcard is useful for understanding outcomes, the next level of the results framework – ERAs – considers 'leading' indicators, changes or improvements that can be 'experienced' (i.e. seen, heard, felt – physically or emotionally, tasted or smelt). These could take the form of interim performance improvements or milestones in the development of the solution and are an observable outward expression of the Horizon you have developed, visible before the SCORE measures are.

To define ERAs, I borrow a long-serving technique of futurists and policy planners: backcasting.[65] Applied to long-term complex issues and technological changes, backcasting flips the traditional approach of forecasting by focusing on how desirable futures can be obtained, rather than what futures are likely to happen. For RADAR, backcasting works by taking the Horizon statements and associated target SCOREs and working back from their endpoints. Returning to the example of the hospital's radiology improvements, see below a simplified example of the ERAs that might deliver one Horizon statement.

Figure 9.8 ERA example for hospital radiology service improvement

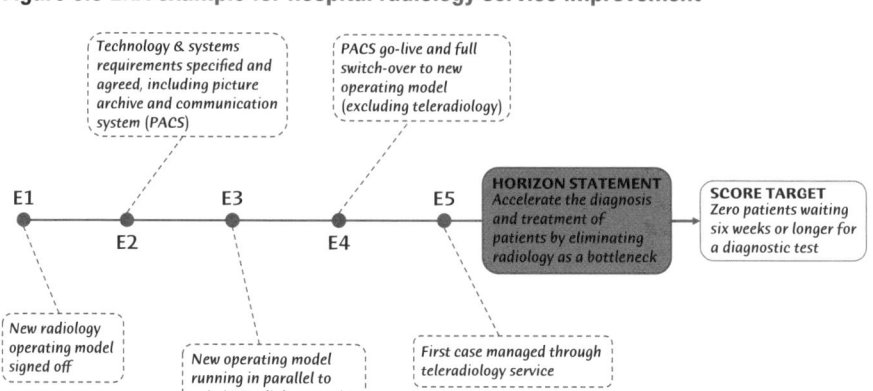

The act of backcasting will also result in additions to the ARC tracker, as further assumptions, risks and choices/consequences will be identified when defining ERAs (for example, one assumption might be that 20 per cent of all cases will be managed through teleradiology by the end of the first year).

[65] The term was first introduced in Robinson, J. (1982). Energy backcasting: A proposed method of policy analysis, *Energy Policy*, 10(4), pp 337–44. Robinson credits the idea to Amory Lovins.

Validating your Horizon: the ARC of anticipation

The final tier of the results framework is the ARC. This is your early warning system, the anticipatory measures that test the validity and viability of your Horizon. For example, returning to the hospital example once more, one underlying assumption is that hospital-based radiology processing capacity is a constraint and that remote teleradiology services will alleviate it. To test this, one might introduce revised reason codes for patient treatment delays, and group and report on those that would be addressed through a picture archiving and communication system (PACS), used to share digital scans, and teleradiology, to understand whether these adaptations will truly give the operational throughput improvement sought.

Figure 9.9 Example of Horizon ARC metrics

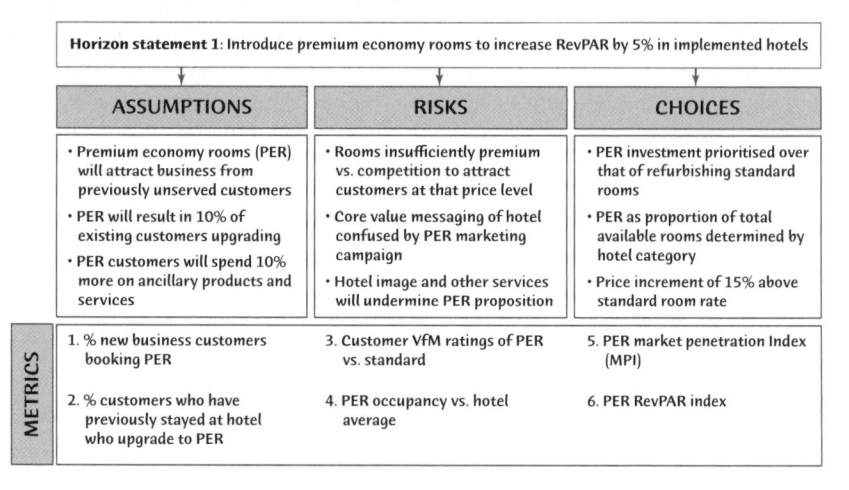

ARC runs through every aspect of RADAR, like letters running through seaside rock. No meaningful discussion of the organisation's external environment and strategic intent can happen without reviewing or updating the ARC tracker in its wake. Consider one of the value hotel chain Horizon statements we discussed in Chapter 7, and how it translates to the ARC tracker and feeds the MEDS.

The previous table is an extract from example ARC logs, each of which reference the associated measures shown in the KPI definitions sheet below (part of the MEDS documentation in the organisation).

In each learn/gateway meeting, the validity of the ARC tracker elements is re-examined. The conditions that determine whether you continue as planned, make moderate adjustments or Horizon shift were discussed in Chapter 8.

Table 9.4 Example of ARC logs

ASSUMPTIONS

Ref.[1]	Description	MEDS ref	Linked to:[2]
A1	Premium economy rooms (PER) will attract business customers previously unserved by the company	M1	HS1
A2	PER will result in 10% of existing customers upgrading to PER	M2	HS1
A3	PER customers will spend 10% more on ancillary products and services	M6	HS1

RISKS

Ref.[1]	Description	Likelihood[3]	Impact[4]	Mitigating actions	MEDS ref	Linked to:[2]
R1	Rooms insufficiently premium vs. competition to attract customers at that price level	2	4	• Co-create with customer groups • Capture feedback to refine PER proposition before roll-out	M3, M4	HS1
R2	Core value messaging of hotel confused by PER marketing campaign	2	2	• Emphasise core value messaging in PER marketing campaign	M3	HS1
R3	Hotel image and other services will undermine PER proposition	3	3	• Tier hotel service offer to reflect PER option	M4, M5	HS1

CHOICES/CONSEQUENCES

Ref.[1]	Description	Associated MEDS Ref	Linked to:[2]
C1	PER investment prioritised over that of refurbishing standard rooms	M3, M4	HS1
C2	PER as proportion of total available rooms set at 20% in parts of the estate categorised as 'City Prime', 15% in 'Secondary City' and 10% in 'Leisure Prime'	M4, M5	HS1
C3	Price increment of 15% above standard room rate	M3, M5	HS1

[1] Starts with A for Assumption, R for Risk and C for Choice or Consequence
[2] HSX = Horizon statement reference,
BTH = Beyond the Horizon, UP = Unifying purpose, O = Other
[3] Ratings are 1 (Very unlikely) to 5 (Very likely)
[4] Ratings are 1 (Low), 2 (Medium) or 3 (High)

Table 9.5 Example of Horizon ARC metrics

Ref.	Name	Purpose/description	Formula(e)	Source(s)	Frequency[1]	Target	Linked to:[2]
M1	% new business customers booking PER	Measures relative attractiveness of PER to the hotel booking PER ÷ total new business customers	# business customers new to the hotel booking PER ÷ total new business customers	Booking system	W	75%	HS1
M2	% customers who have previously stayed at TL who upgrade to PER	Measures relative attractiveness of PER to standard rooms for existing customers	# customers who have stayed at hotel in past 2 years who book PER ÷ total # customers who have stayed at hotel in past 2 years who book any room	Booking system	W	20%	HS1
M3	Customer VfM ratings of PER vs. standard	Determine PER value for money relative to the standard room offering	PER Customer VfM rating ÷ standard customer VfM rating	Survey	Q	≥4 (out of 5)	HS1
M4	PER occupancy vs. hotel average	Determine relative performance of PER	PER % occupancy ÷ hotel % occupancy	Booking system	W	>1	HS1
M5	PER market penetration index (MPI)	Evaluate competitiveness of PER offering in the local market	PER % occupancy ÷ occupancy % of competitors	Market data provider, booking system	W	>1	HS1
M6	PER RevPAR index	Evaluate relative total uplift from PER proposition	PER RevPAR ÷ Non-PER	Booking system	W	≥1.1	HS1

[1] D = Daily, W = Weekly, M = Monthly, Q = Quarterly H = Half-yearly, A = Annually
[2] HSX = Horizon statement reference, BTH = Beyond the Horizon, UP = Unifying purpose, O = Other

A final thought on results

Poorly conceived agile approaches can feel like repeatedly arriving at the last stop on a trainline – forever being asked to 'all change please'. But as we saw in our discussion of control within RAC ratings (in the introduction and Chapter 4), Jeff Bezos' view on not changing (Chapter 7) and the role of minimum changes and stability in Horizon management (Chapter 8), this is not the case.

A unifying purpose provides directional stability as the organisation responds to its changing commercial circumstances, and this is reflected in those measures and targets that do not change. Shifting endlessly towards new goals would be disorientating given the barriers and frictions that exist within large-scale organisations (see the next chapter). Therefore, using the RADAR results framework requires a delicate balance between stability and progress, consistency and change. It is a challenge that The Body Shop knows well.

Body measurements

The Body Shop continues to act in accordance with its founder Anita Roddick's idea that 'business can be a force for good'[66] and its 'enrich not exploit' commitment. This commitment comprises 14 targets, ranging from environmental measures such as protecting 10,000 hectares of forest and habitat, through to a social commitment to help 40,000 economically vulnerable people to access work around the world.[67]

Note that many of these measures are associated with its unifying purpose – which includes that 'enrich not exploit' commitment – and form a fundamental part of the positioning element of its competitive position. As a business, its Horizon will necessitate many other commercial, operational and reputational measures. From an ARC perspective, it also assumes, for example, that such environmental choices will be valued by consumers (again, something that can be measured, potentially backed up by a programme of education and influence to ensure consumers value it more). In the dynamic and highly competitive world of health and beauty, The Body Shop must navigate a path that is both new and exciting and consistent with its brand promise and heritage.

---

[66] See https://www.thebodyshop.com/en-gb/about-us [accessed 20 May 2018].
[67] See https://www.thebodyshop.com/en-gb/about-us/our-commitment [accessed 20 May 2018].

Summary

- The RADAR results framework serves three Horizon-related functions: setting targets, evaluating performance, and determining ongoing validity and the need to Horizon shift.
- These functions are fulfilled through three mechanisms: SCORE, ERAs and ARC.
- SCORE – comprising social, commercial, operational, reputational and environmental components – provides a balanced set of measures for both setting targets and evaluating performance.
- Four factors determine which measures make it onto your SCOREcard: strategic intent, ARC, SIS objectives and practicality (e.g. the availability of data).
- When setting targets for the SCOREcard measures, consider the following: baselining and existing data, market norms or minimum requirements, multiple perspectives, and modelling the impact of target levels on the broader organisation.
- ERAs are leading indicators, changes or improvements that can be 'experienced'. Backcasting from Horizon statements and target SCOREs can be used to derive them.
- The ARC is your early warning system, the 'anticipatory' measures that test the validity and viability of your Horizon. If the ARC is no longer valid, then the Horizon must change.
- When applying the RADAR results framework, you must strike a delicate balance between stability and progress, consistency and change. Your unifying purpose provides directional stability, and this is reflected in those measures and targets that do not change.

Case story: No half measures

George, Leisurious' finance director, smiled as he looked across the table at the other members of the team. He had always been a commercially minded finance director, as happy striking deals as he was modelling out the cash flows that came from them. The data-driven approach of agile strategy certainly appealed, whilst nonetheless being a little outside the norm for him. But as they debated the target SCOREs for their Horizon statements, he felt he was back in his heartland.

Emma was at her animated best, talking through their unifying purpose and the importance of innovation and customer satisfaction to the DNA of Leisurious. They would have to be reflected in the SCOREcard measures, as would their very public commitment to clothing recycling and reducing landfill. In the commercial sphere, traditional Horizon targets for sales and operating profit sat alongside those for core business segment penetration and awareness conversion. Operationally, the blended margin targets for the business were translated into buying and distribution efficiency targets set for the current Horizon.

The ERAs discussion had also been educative for the participants. More than just a systematic exercise in project planning, it had drawn attention to several areas of higher risk, and opportunities to reduce that risk through pre-emptive action and real options. Thus, a decision had been made to parallel run supply chains in advance of the switchover to Turkish manufacturing of its top selling lines, enabling greater responsiveness to market demand.

Looking at their definition of the Horizon now, with its clear Horizon statements, target SCOREs, ERAs and ARC, the team felt they had a good handle on where the company was going. That was not to say that the route to every number was clear at this point, but the achievability of the targets was accepted in the context of the baselining and benchmarking that had been done. The Horizon was set; now came the challenge of moving the organisation onwards towards it.

In your organisation

Exercise 9: Settle a SCORE

Taking the Horizon statements developed in Exercise 8, convene as a group and do the following:

1 Work your way through each Horizon statement, capturing for each one:
   ● The most appropriate SCORE measures and targets (for subsequent validation).
   ● Proposed ERAs (using backcasting).
   ● Any assumptions, risks and choices/consequences for the ARC tracker.
2 Work though the areas identified beyond the Horizon. Are there any that have implications for SCORE, either existing or new?
3 For each SCORE measure identified, determine the best route to establishing a target (baselining, benchmarking, expert opinion, modelling). Create a set of actions to complete after the meeting to establish the required target levels.
4 Based on all the above, note any required changes to the existing MEDS.
5 Arrange a time to reconvene with the SCOREcard and targets completed.

10

How to hurdle the barriers to success

'**Plans are of little importance, but planning is essential.**'
Winston Churchill

In this chapter we do the following:

- Focus on eight areas which must be managed when introducing agile strategy practices into an organisation:
  - Culture
  - Working practices
  - Organisational structures and incentives
  - Governance
  - Systems and technologies
  - Leadership
  - Communication
  - Change fatigue.

Having spent the last nine chapters talking through the concepts, tools and techniques that inform RADAR, I finish here with some practical implementation considerations across eight key areas.

Culture

Does culture eat strategy for breakfast? If it does, then strategy must bite back. To counter potential cultural barriers, the leadership team must foster the following characteristics of an agile culture.

Table 10.1 Characteristics of an agile culture

Characteristic	Description
Alignment	A strong culture is united and aligned around its strategic intent, expressed in RADAR through its unifying purpose, Horizon, key considerations beyond the Horizon and target outcomes. Many of the other areas discussed in this chapter – from leadership through to communication – play an important role in creating this alignment.
Accountability and empowerment	Empowering staff to make customer-focused decisions in the moment is a key enabler of organisational agility. This requires managers to provide constructive feedback in a way that does not affect an individual's confidence in making decisions in the future, even if previous mistakes were made.
Collaboration and openness	An agile culture encourages collaboration and openness. We see this in RADAR's engagement of a broader range of participants in strategy development (e.g. drawn from different levels and from outside the organisation) and in its transparency and sharing of data. As Ed Catmull, Pixar's President, puts it: 'A hallmark of a healthy creative culture is that its people feel free to share ideas, opinions, and criticisms. Lack of candour, if unchecked, ultimately leads to dysfunctional environments.'[68]
Learning-focused and data-driven	A focus on using data to learn from success and failure, and using that learning to improve the next iteration, is the hallmark of an agile culture.
Organisational incentives	Incentives, financial and otherwise, are cultural reinforcers (or destructors). They need to encourage the right behaviours in areas such as data sharing, collaboration, continuous improvement and an unswerving focus on the customer. In practice, this can often mean shifting the emphasis from individual to collective rewards and using superordinate goals that require people to work together to achieve a desired outcome.
Resilience	Things go wrong, and remaining resilient and confident in the face of such failures, whilst learning from them, is an important aspect of agility. Resilience can be learned, and it must be encouraged and developed through coaching and other means.

[68] Catmull, E. and Wallace, A. (2014) *Creativity Inc.: Overcoming the unseen forces that stand in the way of true inspiration*, London: Bantam Press.

Working practices and legacy obligations

When discussing the concept of agile, for many the first thing that springs to mind are the working practices embodied in the agile manifesto:[69] regularly revised requirements, short-term deliverables and close working between specialists (e.g. business, technology). By translating these into a broader business context, RADAR creates strategic intent that adjusts and shifts more quickly than with traditional methods. This has its challenges:

- *It can be interpreted as indecisive management:* this can be avoided through clear communication, strong leadership and training. Staff must understand in advance that such shifts are purposeful and intended.

- *If poorly managed, it can result in a lack of control:* the RAC rating needs that final 'C' of control to avoid the trap of hyperactive change. Having the right data and people in the Horizon gateways is key to ensuring that Horizon adjustments or shifts are coordinated and controlled.

- *Legacy obligations can be at odds with the new ways of working:* an established business cannot simply leave its existing obligations to customers, suppliers or channel partners behind. Whether contractual or simply embedded in long-term relationships, working collaboratively with suppliers and partners to transition to more dynamic working practices, reflecting the dynamism by design mentality, should be a priority. In some cases, you may even run parallel processes and systems in the short term, if it is commercially advantageous to do so.

Common to all three of the bullets above is the need to develop a strong stakeholder appreciation for both what is being done, and why it is being done that way.

Organisational structures and incentives

There can be a wide gulf between the sclerotic bureaucracies of traditional large organisations and the agile structures championed by well-publicised approaches such as Scrum and the ING model.[70] Common themes within the latter include:

- Integration of practices and ideas through cross-functional, multi-disciplinary teams.
- Co-location and team structures that minimise handovers.
- Empowerment and fewer controls.
- Customer-oriented structures (rather than product- or function-oriented ones).

[69] See http://agilemanifesto.org/iso/en/principles.html [accessed 12 May 2018].
[70] See https://www.mckinsey.com/industries/financial-services/our-insights/ings-agile-transformation [accessed 22 June 2018].

Simply overlaying new team structures on to the existing organisation rarely works. I have witnessed plenty of 'transplant rejection', where discrete innovation, customer or digital teams have been implanted into a traditional organisational structure. To succeed, new structures must be supported by a range of 'integrating mechanisms', which mirror the other topics of this chapter:

- *Culture:* we mentioned above how the right culture can support the openness, learning and alignment required to integrate new structures effectively.

- *Working practices:* policies, processes and procedures that actively support multi-disciplinary, cross-functional approaches can reinforce structural changes.

- *Technology and systems:* anyone who has tried to implement collaborative working across multiple locations without the technology and systems to support it will know how painful that can be. Conversely, just telling teams to use Slack without deploying any of the other integrating mechanisms discussed here will also fall on stony ground.

- *Knowledge and data:* creating a common understanding and MEDS is a pre-requisite for supporting successful new structures, focusing attention on objective realities rather than political positions. Multi-skilling, or at least training people to have 'workable literacy' across multiple disciplines, also fosters better collaborative working and understanding.

- *Governance and performance management:* we cover this below, but it is a fundamental lever for smoothing the transition from old to new structures.

Alfred Chandler maintained that 'structure follows strategy',[71] and this may be true, but it is equally important that 'structure must not inhibit strategy'. To ensure that this does not happen, the integrating mechanisms listed above can support more flexible structures.

Governance and performance management: it always ends in tiers

To drive accountability, responsibility and therefore results through the organisation, there must be alignment in how the Horizon is understood and managed across all areas and levels of the business. But what is the right organisational level at which to apply RADAR? In a focused business, running a single instance of RADAR would work well. However, consider Sainsbury's, which includes groceries, homeware, clothing, banking, insurance, and then Argos, a general

---

[71] Chandler, A.D. Jr (1962) *Strategy and Structure: Chapters in the history of the American industrial enterprise*, Cambridge, MA: MIT Press.

merchandise retailer, within its portfolio. In such a case, the Horizon questions and the associated governance need to apply across several tiers (group, business unit and even potentially divisional):

- 'Where do we play?' has different meanings at each organisational level. Each business unit's total addressable market or TAM (Chapter 4) will be, by definition, a subset of the group's.

- Similarly, 'How do we win?' has different resonances at each organisational level. Classic 'corporate parenting advantages',[72] such as driving improved linkages between business units, exist at group level. In the case of Sainsbury's, it has expanded Argos by rolling out a store-in-store concept in selected grocery stores. Answering the question 'How do we win?' for Argos itself would involve a broader set of actions relating to the 3Ps of its competitive position.

In such cases, two or more instances of RADAR may need to be applied across the group. The figure below illustrates how multiple instances of RADAR interact under such circumstances.

Figure 10.1 How to align multiple instances of RADAR within a group

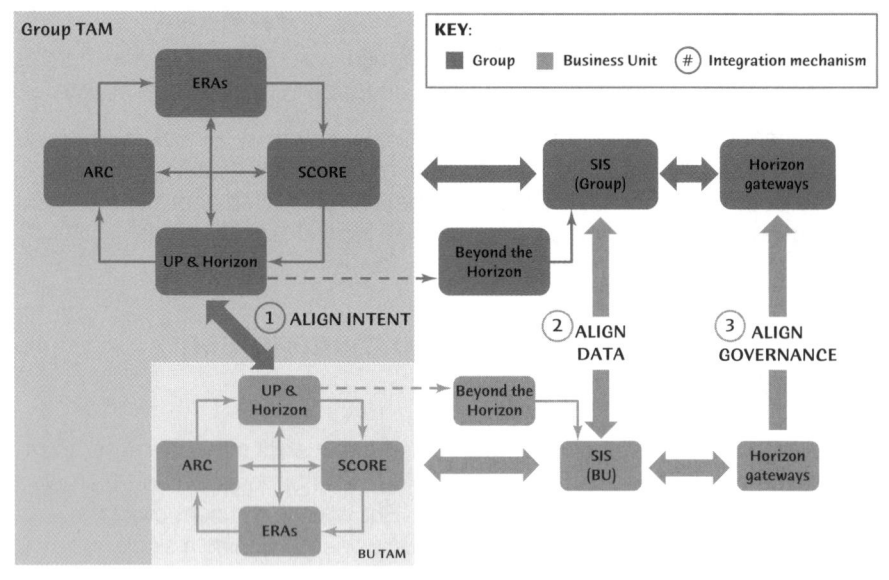

---

[72] Campbell, A., Goold, M and Alexander, M. (1995) Corporate strategy: The quest for parenting advantage, *Harvard Business Review*, Mar/Apr, 73(2), pp 120–32.

Alignment between the group and BUs or divisions is achieved through three mechanisms:

1 *Strategic intent:* defined through UP, the Horizon, beyond the Horizon commitments and target outcomes (SCORE and ERAs), intent must be aligned between the group and BU. This can work both ways, for example, where distinctive resources or capabilities in the BU allows the group to move in a new direction.

2 *Data:* the control element of an organisation's RAC rating requires the MEDS, and SIS which manages it, to be aligned between group and the BUs.

3 *Governance:* group and BU representation at their respective Horizon gateways enables the most direct form of coordination and ensures that strategic intent remains aligned if either group or the BU makes Horizon adjustments or shifts.

Systems and technologies

As with our discussion of legacy organisational structures and working practices, the reality of transitioning to agile strategy is that old and new worlds will need to co-exist, at least in the short to medium term. In the case of systems and technology, certain principles and practices can help make this more manageable, such as:

- *DevOps:* there has been significant growth in the adoption of a 'DevOps' approach, which unifies software development and operations to increase development speed whilst maintaining reliability.

- *Automation:* this underpins the DevOps approach and is a building block of continuous delivery,[73] enabling the rapid execution of key areas, such as functional, integration and performance testing, and accelerating the delivery of new software releases.

- *Interfaces:* where possible, organisations should look to decouple architecture, and use APIs, microservices and other interfaces to enable infrastructure, applications and data to interact. This provides greater architectural flexibility, reducing development time.

Such approaches can further improve the responsiveness and adaptability element of the organisation's RAC rating, Furthermore, as technologies and systems become ever more flexible, the opportunities to integrate and expand functionality and data will grow (see the discussion of data vaults and lakes

---

[73] Humble, J. and Farley, D. (2010) *Continuous Delivery: Reliable software releases through build, test, and deployment automation*, Boston, MA: Pearson.

in Chapter 5). Whilst this remains a challenging area, underinvestment is increasingly not an option – see the string of financial IT system failures at TSB, Visa and Tesco Bank in one year alone[74] as a warning of where it leads.

Leadership

Good leadership – whether that originates from one person or a leadership team – is a critical element in an organisation's successful transition to agile strategy. Firstly, you need the right people in leadership roles, reinforcing the agile culture characteristics outlined above. Secondly, they must lead in the right way. Steve Radcliffe's FED leadership model[75] focuses on three elements, each of which has an important role to play:

- *Future:* painting a clear picture of what agile strategy means, and demonstrating a commitment to it, is the starting point for its successful adoption.
- *Engage:* engaging the wider organisation through meaningful and honest interactions, rather than 'broadcasting' and forcing it upon people, is also critical. Consistency is vital – there are too many cases where there has been a major gap between what leaders have said and how they have reacted in the moment (the rhetoric and reality of 'embracing failure' being the classic example).
- *Deliver:* having engaged the organisation around this vision for the future, the final stage is ensuring that it happens. As one of the 4Ds of strategic agility, the practical impetus of delivery is entirely in keeping with the goals of RADAR.

Communication

An agile culture communicates to the right people, inside and outside the organisation, at the right times (e.g. context, frequency) and in the right way (e.g. content, manner, tone, interactivity). The organisation must ensure that the MEDS is defined correctly, supported by the right systems to deliver it and accessible to those who need it both inside and outside the organisation. It must also ensure that the human side of communication and interaction (e.g. meetings, collaboration) is fostered and developed appropriately.

As we saw earlier, clear, regular and relevant communication is fundamental to developing the right culture, bringing about and succeeding with new working practices and governing at pace.

[74] See https://www.telegraph.co.uk/business/2018/06/05/tesco-bank-latest-hit-failures-customers-unable-log/[accessed 8 June 2018].
[75] Radcliffe, S. (2012) *Leadership: Plain and simple*, Harlow: Pearson Education Limited.

Change fatigue and passive resistance

Do not underestimate the role that change fatigue and passive resistance can play in constraining an organisation's agility. As we all operate in increasingly fast-paced environments, the layering on of further change can result in resistance or simply ignoring it in the hope it goes away.

To overcome this, here are some suggestions:

- Staff must understand why the change is important.
- If it has failed previously, they must understand why this time will be different.
- The imperative for change must be clear.
- Staff must feel engaged and vested in the opportunities that changes can bring.
- They must have confidence in the leadership's ability to realise them.
- You must communicate often and meaningfully.
- Early successes should be widely shared.

All eight of the above areas require consideration and sustained development when adopting RADAR and agile strategy practices. The challenge, and the opportunity, is to create a system that starts to feed itself as confidence and success grows.

Summary

- There are eight aspects of large-scale organisations which must be developed when introducing an agile approach to strategy development: culture, working practices, organisational structures and incentives, governance, systems, leadership, communication and change fatigue.
- To foster an agile culture, focus on alignment, accountability and empowerment, openness, learning and data, incentives and resilience.
- Gaining acceptance of agile working practices requires strong leadership, governance and communication. Working collaboratively with suppliers to instil the dynamism by design mindset and running parallel processes and systems are long- and short-term measures to support the transition to new practices.
- A range of integrating mechanisms can be used to support new agile organisational structures. These include culture, working practices, technology and systems, knowledge and data, and governance.
- Multiple instances of RADAR may be deployed in diversified groups or businesses, integrated through the governance and management of strategic intent, data and representation in Horizon Gateways.

▶

- Sufficient investment in systems and technology is key to the success of agile strategy. The embracing of the increasingly established practices of DevOps, automation and decoupled architecture can further improve the responsiveness and adaptability element of the organisation's RAC rating.
- Good leadership, whether that originates from one person or a leadership team, is a critical element in an organisation's successful transition to agile strategy. Steve Radcliffe's FED leadership model – future, engage, deliver – frames the RADAR leadership contribution well.
- An agile culture communicates to the right people, at the right times (e.g. context, frequency) and in the right way (e.g. content, manner, tone, interactivity).
- Staff must feel engaged and vested in the opportunities that changes can bring and must have confidence in the leadership and organisation's ability to realise them.

Case story: Shabby ChIC

Emma and Sam collapsed into their two seats at the corner table of The Red Lion, their favourite after-work pub. It had been just over a year since that morning coffee had set in motion Project ChIC, and a lot had changed since then.

Emma: What a week!

Sam: What a year! We can certainly be proud of what we have achieved. The numbers are looking good, and you can feel the excitement and belief across the company.

Emma: I agree – getting the whole team engaged in our strategy has made a real difference. We are making better choices and have a more motivated team. It has not been without its challenges, though – some of the early changes gave new meaning to the term 'shabby chic'!

Sam: Ha ha. We did get a little carried away early on. In retrospect, a little more time at the beginning engaging people and getting them on board would have helped. However, the internal comms we launched early on, and have continued, has certainly helped. In fact, it was the more senior staff that found it toughest. My junior team seemed to thrive in the new environment, but some of the directors, and Mike in particular, needed some hand-holding.

Emma:	Yes. He is a really reliable operations director, but he does need encouragement sometimes to see the bigger picture.
Sam:	Now that he has got it, though, he is RADAR's biggest champion. He has certainly fulfilled his role as operations leader – that team are engaged and hungry to hit the numbers.
Emma:	And Simon has done a good job of making those numbers accessible. It is a little patched together currently, but he believes he can reduce the work required to manage our MEDS to around half of the current level over the next 12 months.
Sam:	That data has helped us make some tough choices. I am not sure I would have been confident about pulling out of Portugal had the Horizon focus, and data supporting it, not shown us some of the bigger opportunities we were forfeiting in its stead.
Emma:	That was the big learning for me. Sometimes, we can get so carried along by what we are currently doing that strategic decisions become consequences of where we are, rather than where we need to be. Defining UP really drove that home for me – reminding me why we are doing all this in the first place, and guiding what we shouldn't be doing, as well as what we should.
Sam:	Half a gin and tonic and suddenly you are a philosopher!
Emma:	Ha ha. I think it is as much tiredness as it is the gin – it has been a long week. We had a positive steering group session again this week on the beyond the Horizon lead-time reduction initiative. As we discussed in our last gateway, it is taking us further than I originally envisaged. It will enable us to adjust the Horizon and provide the launch of monthly capsule collections, which alongside the other changes we are making should really drive brand engagement and footfall in store.
Sam:	It has got me really excited. I have been working with the marketing team this week on finalising the campaign cycles and tying it in to the celebrity and fashion leaders we have signed up for the 20th anniversary push.
Emma:	No rest for the wicked.
Sam:	No rest, but I do think we deserve more gin.

Sam headed to the bar and Emma took a moment to reflect. A philosopher indeed. . .

In your organisation

Exercise 10: Breaking down barriers

Allow the RADAR process to bed in for the first three months, and then adjourn a special meeting with the Horizon gateway attendees to discuss the following questions:

1 Where have the biggest barriers to agility been experienced across the eight domains of:

- Culture
- Working practices
- Organisational structures
- Governance
- Systems
- Leadership
- Communication
- Change fatigue?

2 What steps can you take as an organisation and a team to remove or reduce these barriers?

3 What have been the unexpected consequences of this new way of working?

4 What would you do differently if you were starting again?

Take the collective responses from these questions and determine a clear set of actions to address them.

Epilogue: How to continue the conversation

'Life is not accumulation, it is about contribution.'

Stephen Covey

In this chapter we do the following:

- Get on with implementing RADAR.
- Commit to sharing our experiences and continuing the discussion on www.AgileStrategyHub.com

I started this book with a confession, and I end it with one too: I do not consider this to be the final word on agile strategy. As the tools and practices gain a wider audience and are applied across a wide range of different market and organisational settings, no doubt we will learn, adapt and go further with the RADAR approach. What matters is that we start the journey.

If you have not done so, now is the time to share what you have read with others and form a core group to baseline your organisation, define UP, set your Horizon, determine the key considerations beyond it, define your target SCORE and ERAs, build your SIS and instigate Horizon management. It does not need to be perfect, but it does need to be considered and planned. The buy-in and the mechanisms need to be in place to learn and adapt as you go, as do the plans to address the potential barriers raised in the previous chapter.

In keeping with the spirit of this book, RADAR itself must iterate and change – your questions, reflections and experiences can make a key contribution, so please share them on www.AgileStrategyHub.com, where you can get in contact with me and access further RADAR materials.

I look forward to hearing from you.

Index